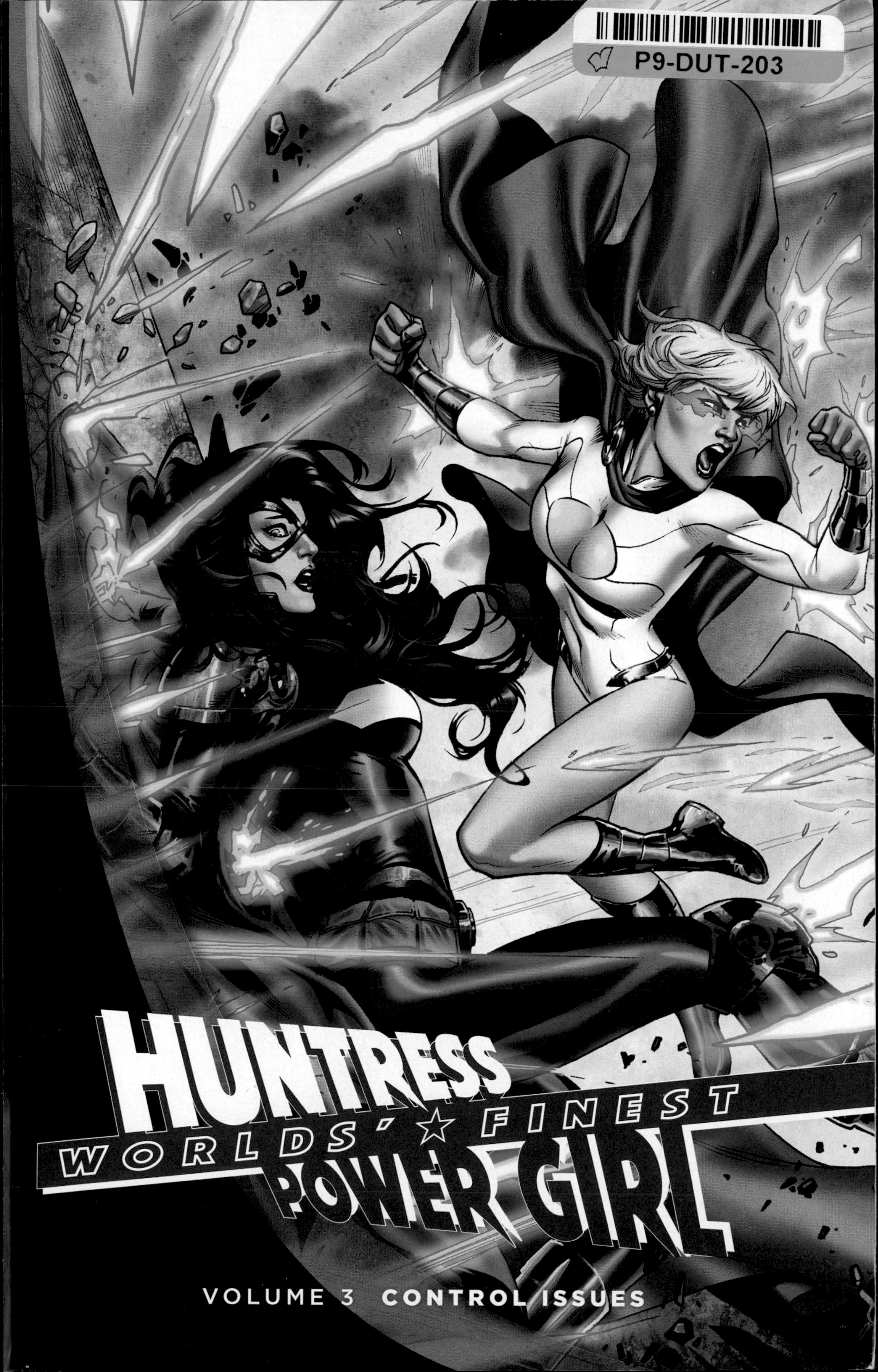
HUNTRESS
WORLDS' ★ FINEST
POWER GIRL
VOLUME 3 CONTROL ISSUES

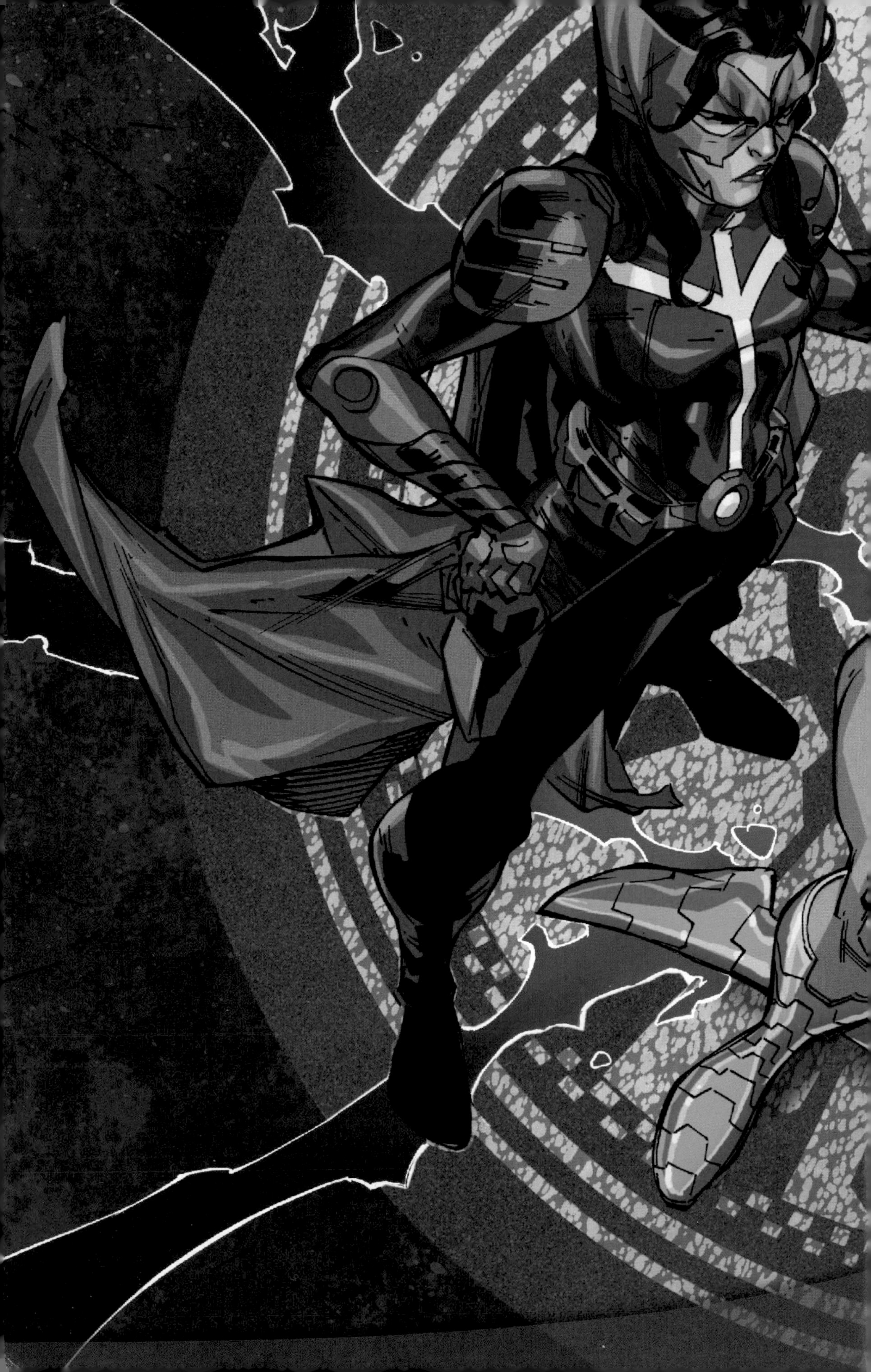

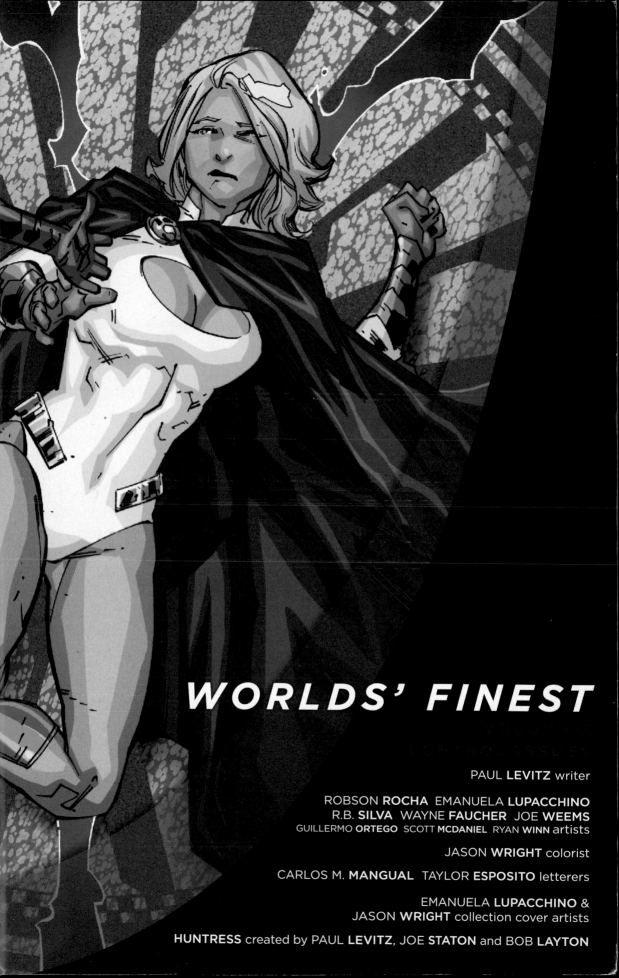

WORLDS' FINEST

PAUL **LEVITZ** writer

ROBSON **ROCHA** EMANUELA **LUPACCHINO**
R.B. **SILVA** WAYNE **FAUCHER** JOE **WEEMS**
GUILLERMO **ORTEGO** SCOTT **MCDANIEL** RYAN **WINN** artists

JASON **WRIGHT** colorist

CARLOS M. **MANGUAL** TAYLOR **ESPOSITO** letterers

EMANUELA **LUPACCHINO** &
JASON **WRIGHT** collection cover artists

HUNTRESS created by PAUL **LEVITZ**, JOE **STATON** and BOB **LAYTON**

MIKE COTTON Editor – Original Series ANTHONY MARQUES Assistant Editor – Original Series
RACHEL PINNELAS Editor ROBBIN BROSTERMAN Design Director – Books ROBBIE BIEDERMAN Publication Design

BOB HARRAS Senior VP – Editor-in-Chief, DC Comics

DIANE NELSON President DAN DIDIO and JIM LEE Co-Publishers
GEOFF JOHNS Chief Creative Officer JOHN ROOD Executive VP – Sales, Marketing and Business Development
AMY GENKINS Senior VP – Business and Legal Affairs NAIRI GARDINER Senior VP – Finance
JEFF BOISON VP – Publishing Planning MARK CHIARELLO VP – Art Direction and Design
JOHN CUNNINGHAM VP – Marketing TERRI CUNNINGHAM VP – Editorial Administration
ALISON GILL Senior VP – Manufacturing and Operations HANK KANALZ Senior VP – Vertigo and Integrated Publishing
JAY KOGAN VP – Business and Legal Affairs, Publishing JACK MAHAN VP – Business Affairs, Talent
NICK NAPOLITANO VP – Manufacturing Administration SUE POHJA VP – Book Sales
COURTNEY SIMMONS Senior VP – Publicity BOB WAYNE Senior VP – Sales

WORLDS' FINEST VOLUME 3: CONTROL ISSUES

Published by DC Comics. Copyright © 2014 DC Comics. All Rights Reserved.

Originally published in single magazine form in WORLDS' FINEST 13-18. Copyright © 2013, 2014 DC Comics. All Rights Reserved.
All characters, their distinctive likenesses and related elements featured in this publication are trademarks of DC Comics.
The stories, characters and incidents featured in this publication are entirely fictional.
DC Comics does not read or accept unsolicited ideas, stories or artwork.

DC Comics, 1700 Broadway, New York, NY 10019
A Warner Bros. Entertainment Company.
Printed by RR Donnelley, Salem, VA, USA. 5/9/14. First Printing.
ISBN: 978-1-4012-4616-7

Library of Congress Cataloging-in-Publication Data

Levitz, Paul, author.
Worlds' Finest. Vol. 3, Control Issues / Paul Levitz ; illustrated by Kevin Maguire.
pages cm. — (The New 52!)
ISBN 978-1-4012-4616-7 (paperback)
1. Graphic novels. I. Maguire, Kevin, illustrator. II. Title. III. Title: Control Issues.
PN6728.W7L53 2014
741.5'973—dc23
2014008610

SUSTAINABLE FORESTRY INITIATIVE Certified Chain of Custody
20% Certified Forest Content,
80% Certified Sourcing
www.sfiprogram.org
SFI-01042
APPLIES TO TEXT STOCK ONLY

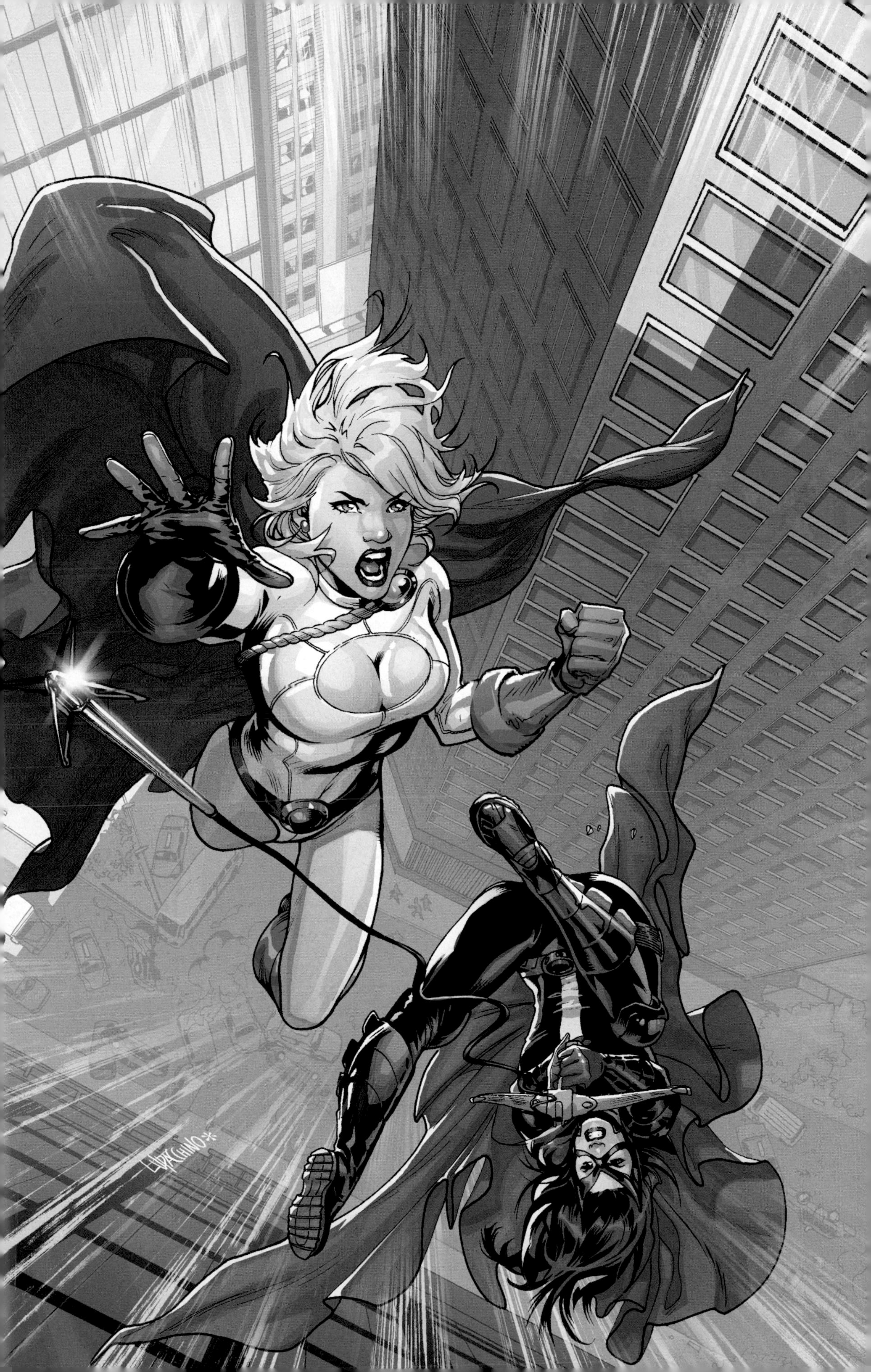
LUPACCHINO

HIDE AND SEEK

ROBSON ROCHA penciller **WAYNE FAUCHER** inker cover art by **EMANUELA LUPACCHINO** with **HI-FI**

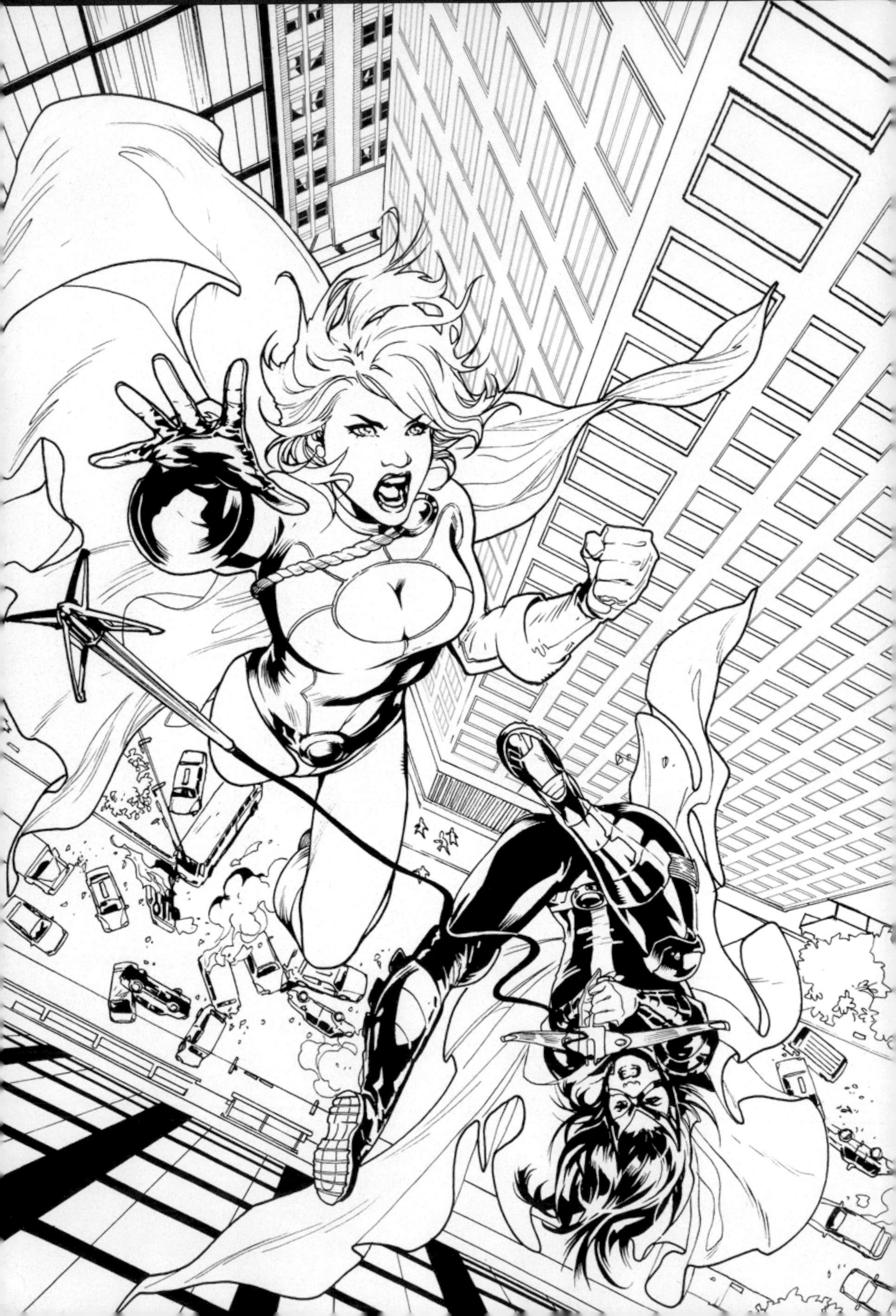

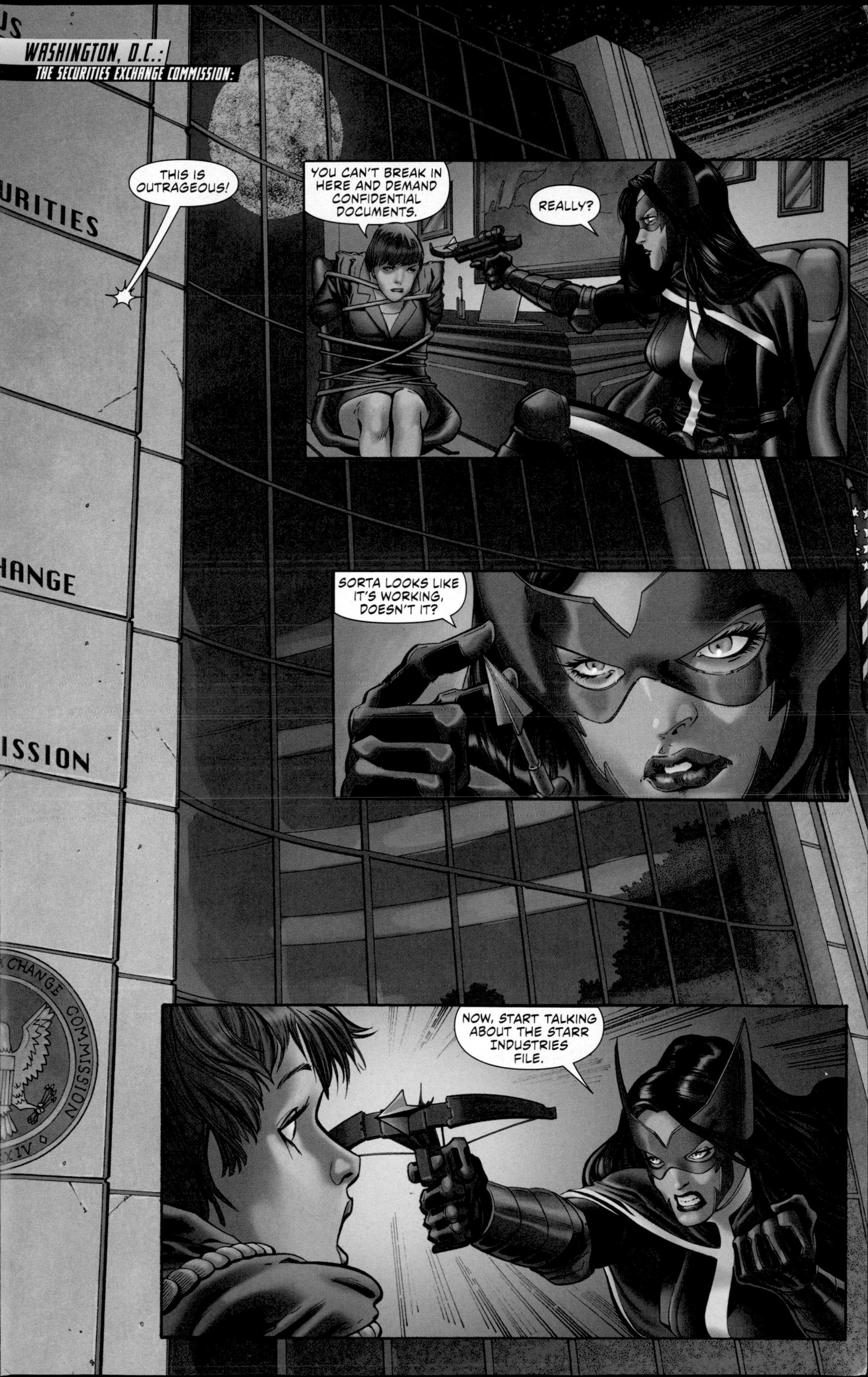
WASHINGTON, D.C.:
THE SECURITIES EXCHANGE COMMISSION:
THIS IS OUTRAGEOUS!
YOU CAN'T BREAK IN HERE AND DEMAND CONFIDENTIAL DOCUMENTS.
REALLY?
SORTA LOOKS LIKE IT'S WORKING, DOESN'T IT?
NOW, START TALKING ABOUT THE STARR INDUSTRIES FILE.
URITIES
HANGE
ISSION

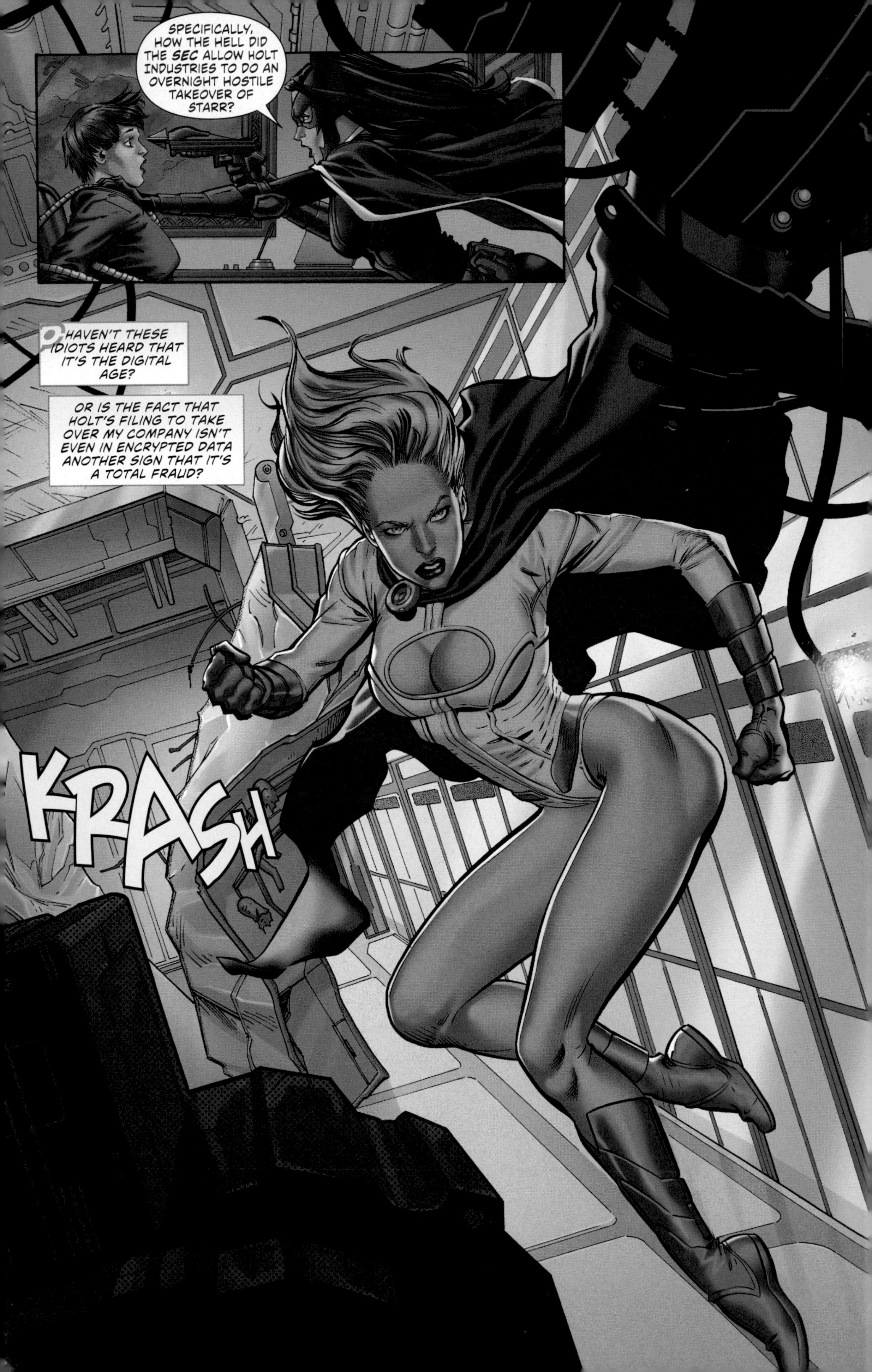
SPECIFICALLY, HOW THE HELL DID THE SEC ALLOW HOLT INDUSTRIES TO DO AN OVERNIGHT HOSTILE TAKEOVER OF STARR?
HAVEN'T THESE IDIOTS HEARD THAT IT'S THE DIGITAL AGE?
OR IS THE FACT THAT HOLT'S FILING TO TAKE OVER MY COMPANY ISN'T EVEN IN ENCRYPTED DATA ANOTHER SIGN THAT IT'S A TOTAL FRAUD?
KRASH

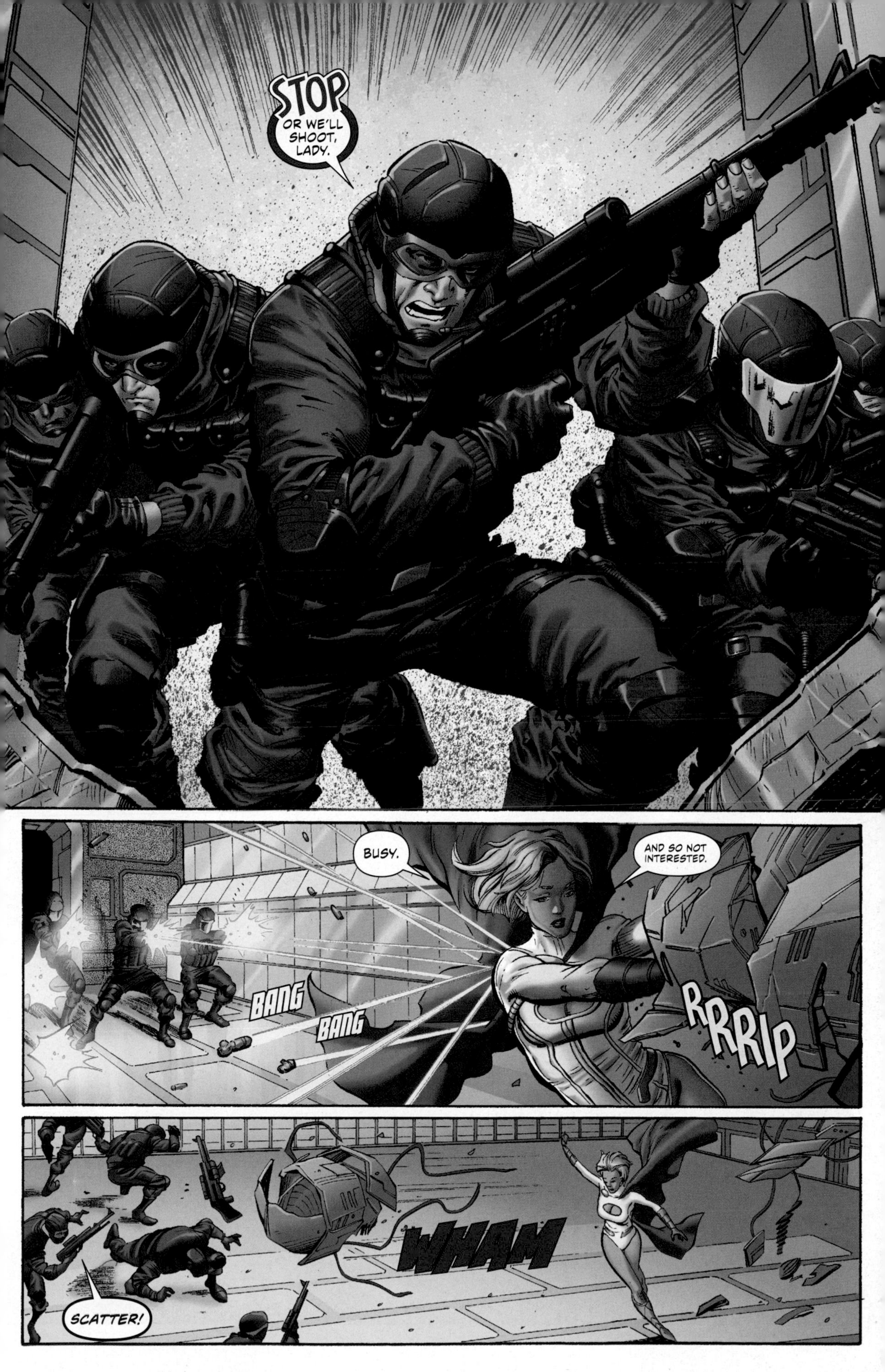
STOP OR WE'LL SHOOT, LADY.
BUSY.
AND SO NOT INTERESTED.
BANG
BANG
RRRIP
WHAM
SCATTER!

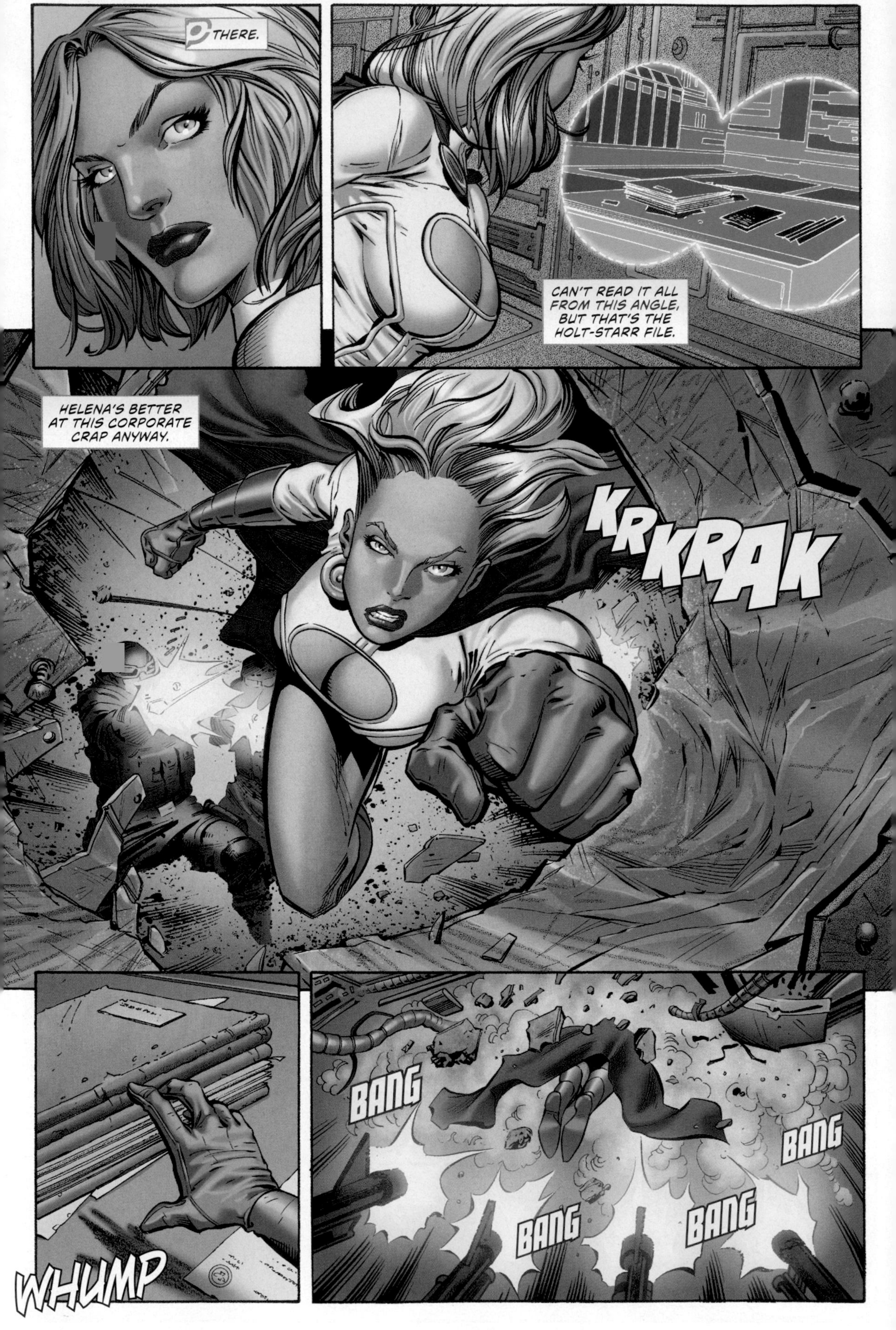
THERE.
CAN'T READ IT ALL FROM THIS ANGLE, BUT THAT'S THE HOLT-STARR FILE.
HELENA'S BETTER AT THIS CORPORATE CRAP ANYWAY.
KRKRAK
WHUMP
BANG
BANG
BANG
BANG

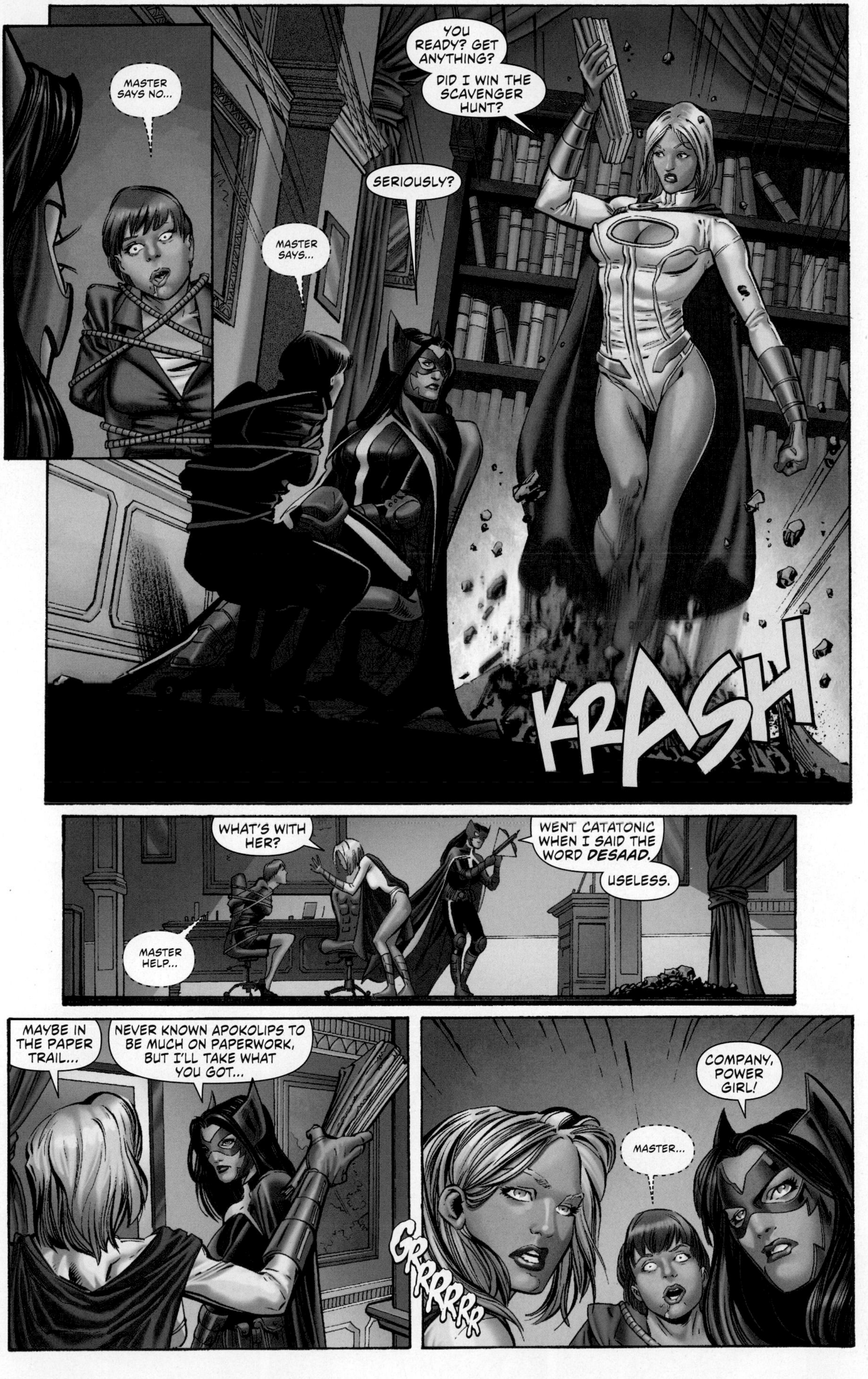

MASTER SAYS NO...
YOU READY? GET ANYTHING?
DID I WIN THE SCAVENGER HUNT?
SERIOUSLY?
MASTER SAYS...
KRASH
WHAT'S WITH HER?
WENT CATATONIC WHEN I SAID THE WORD DESAAD.
USELESS.
MASTER HELP...
MAYBE IN THE PAPER TRAIL...
NEVER KNOWN APOKOLIPS TO BE MUCH ON PAPERWORK, BUT I'LL TAKE WHAT YOU GOT...
GRRRRRR
COMPANY, POWER GIRL!
MASTER...

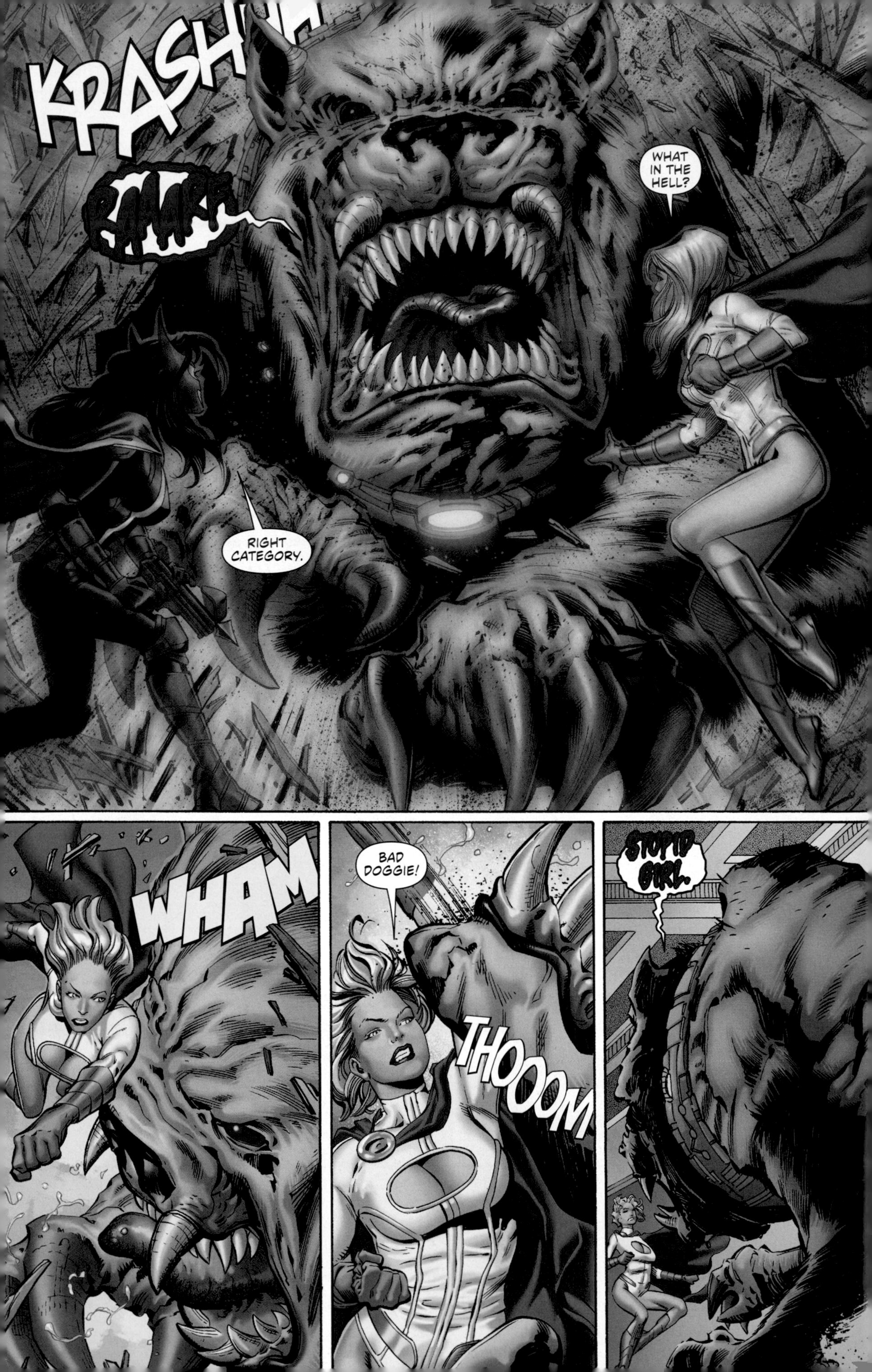
KRASH
WHAT IN THE HELL?
RIGHT CATEGORY.
WHAM
BAD DOGGIE!
THOOOM
STUPID GIRL.

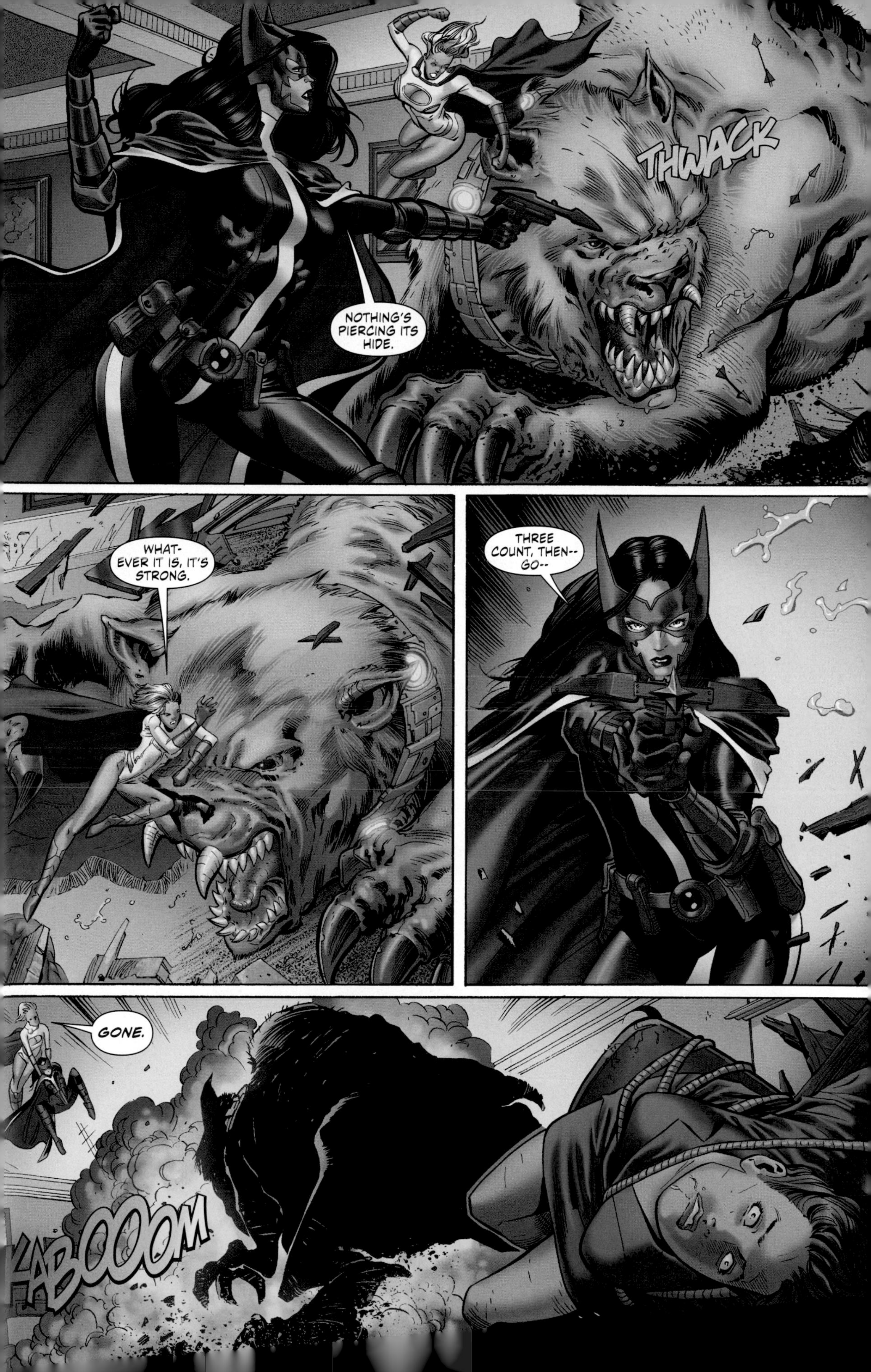
THWACK
NOTHING'S PIERCING ITS HIDE.
WHAT-EVER IT IS, IT'S STRONG.
THREE COUNT, THEN--GO--
GONE.
KABOOOM

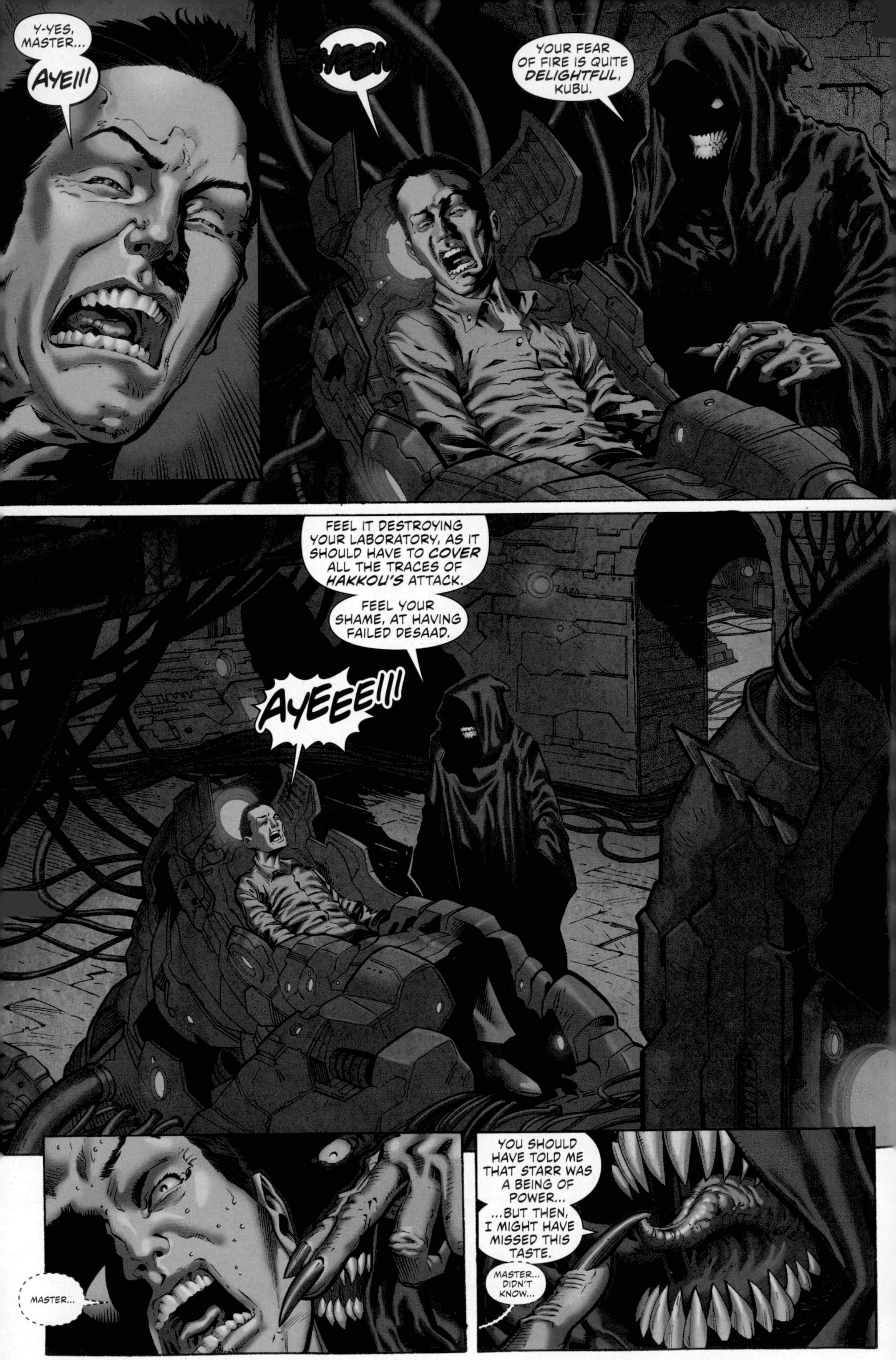

Y-YES, MASTER...
AYE!!!
HEEE!!
YOUR FEAR OF FIRE IS QUITE DELIGHTFUL, KUBU.
FEEL IT DESTROYING YOUR LABORATORY, AS IT SHOULD HAVE TO COVER ALL THE TRACES OF HAKKOU'S ATTACK.
FEEL YOUR SHAME, AT HAVING FAILED DESAAD.
AYEEE!!!
MASTER...
YOU SHOULD HAVE TOLD ME THAT STARR WAS A BEING OF POWER...
...BUT THEN, I MIGHT HAVE MISSED THIS TASTE.
MASTER... DIDN'T KNOW...

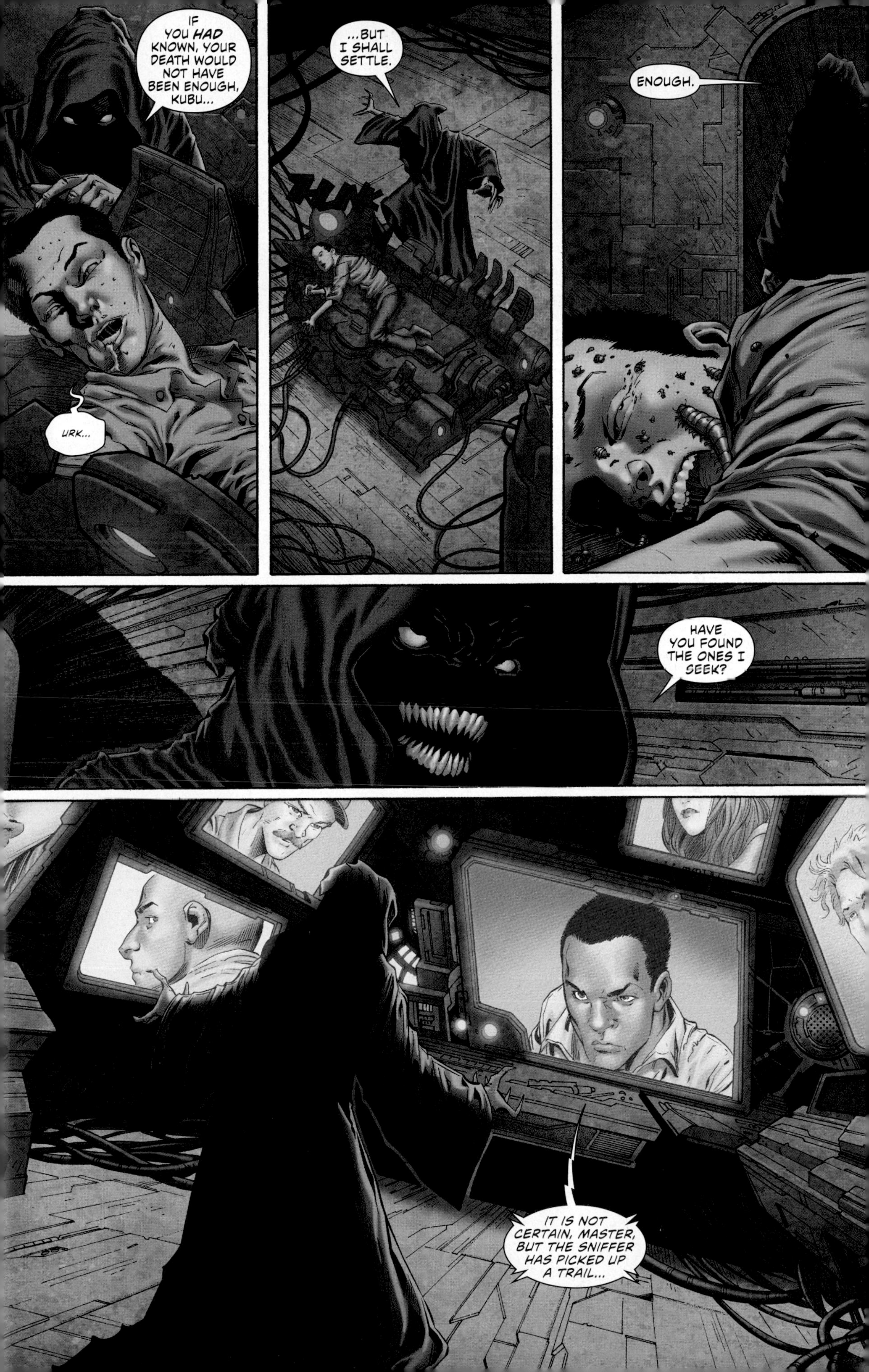
IF YOU HAD KNOWN, YOUR DEATH WOULD NOT HAVE BEEN ENOUGH, KUBU...
URK...
...BUT I SHALL SETTLE.
ENOUGH.
HAVE YOU FOUND THE ONES I SEEK?
IT IS NOT CERTAIN, MASTER, BUT THE SNIFFER HAS PICKED UP A TRAIL...

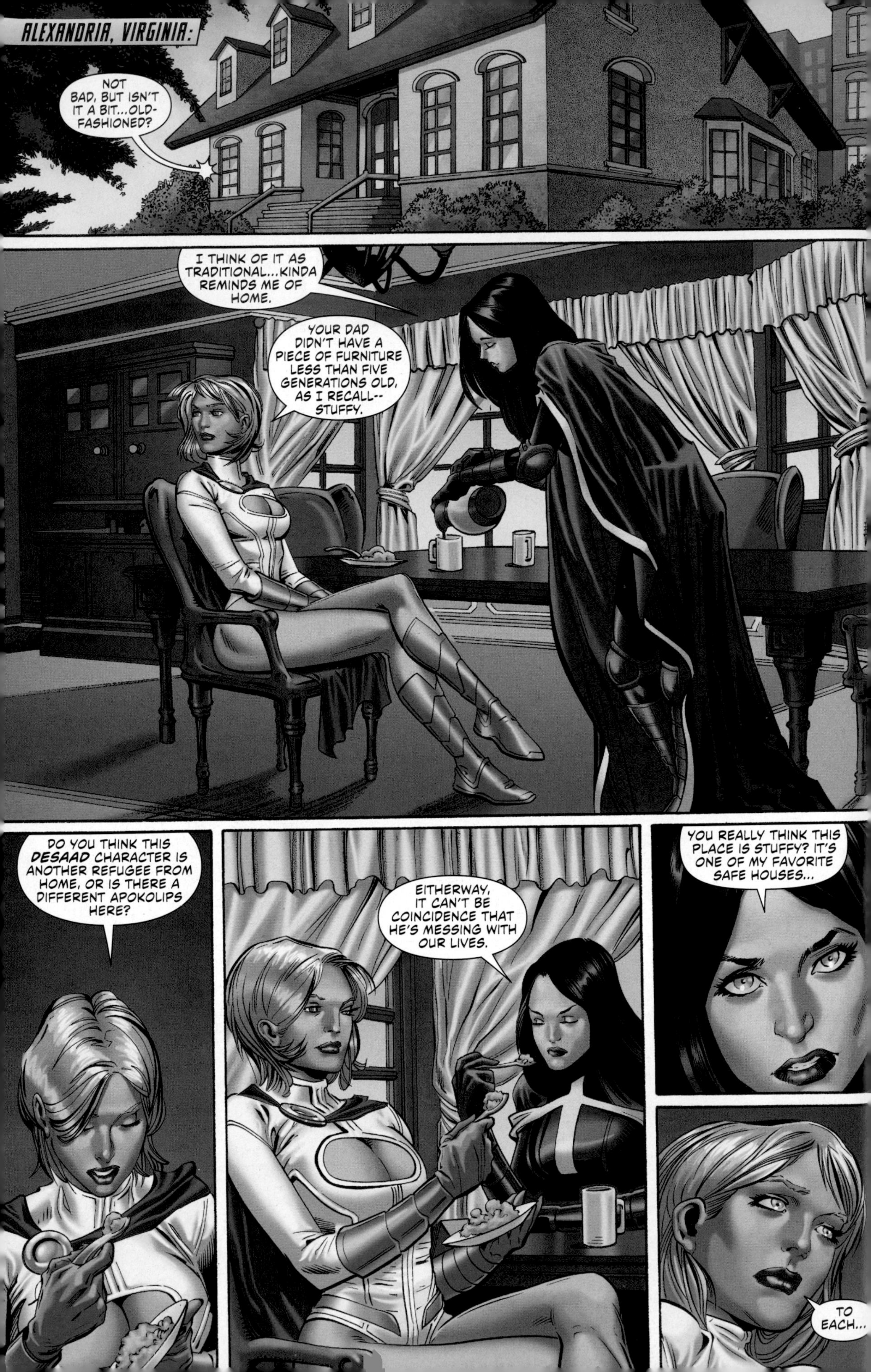
ALEXANDRIA, VIRGINIA:
NOT BAD, BUT ISN'T IT A BIT...OLD-FASHIONED?
I THINK OF IT AS TRADITIONAL...KINDA REMINDS ME OF HOME.
YOUR DAD DIDN'T HAVE A PIECE OF FURNITURE LESS THAN FIVE GENERATIONS OLD, AS I RECALL--STUFFY.
DO YOU THINK THIS DESAAD CHARACTER IS ANOTHER REFUGEE FROM HOME, OR IS THERE A DIFFERENT APOKOLIPS HERE?
EITHERWAY, IT CAN'T BE COINCIDENCE THAT HE'S MESSING WITH OUR LIVES.
YOU REALLY THINK THIS PLACE IS STUFFY? IT'S ONE OF MY FAVORITE SAFE HOUSES...
TO EACH...

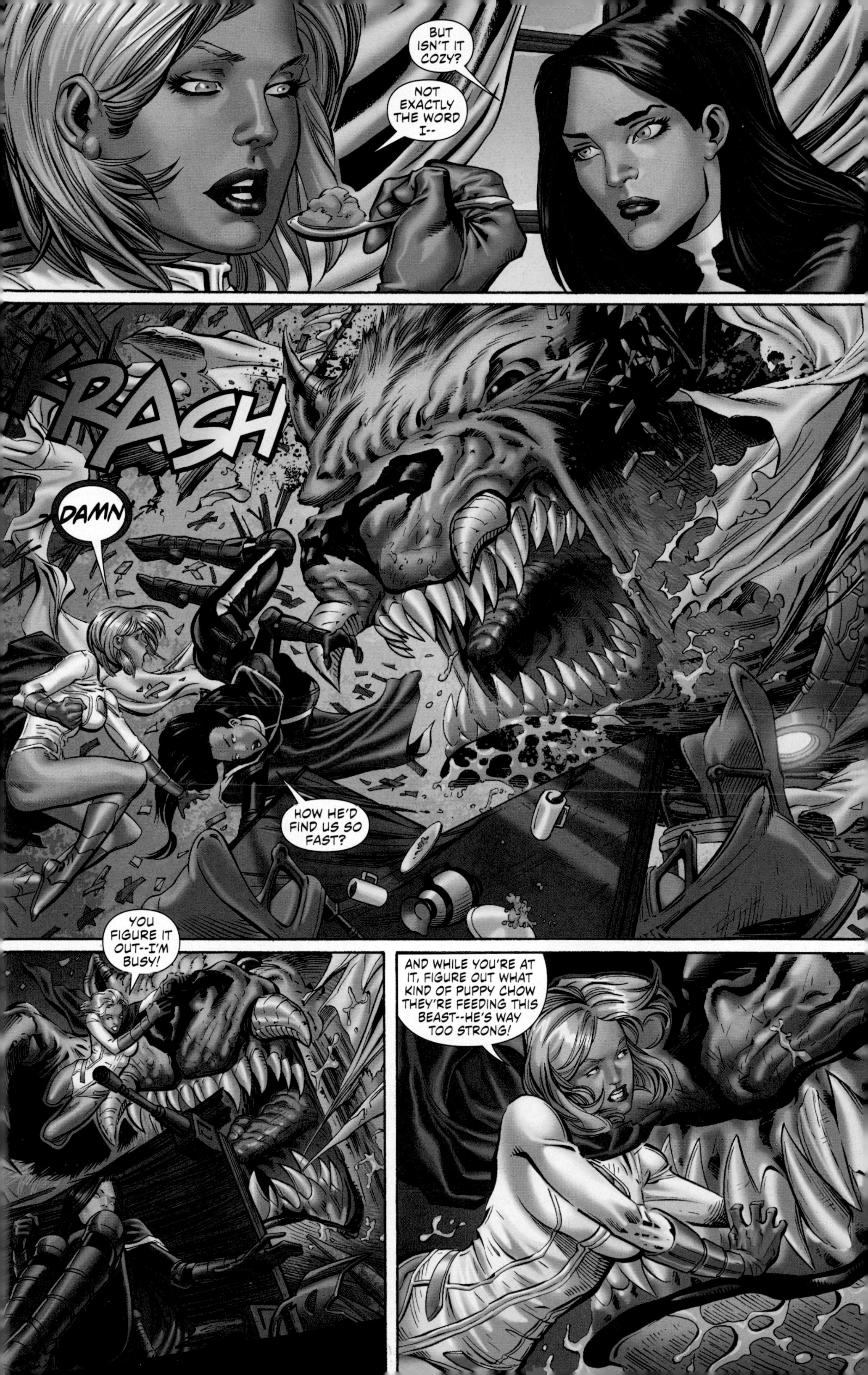
BUT ISN'T IT COZY?
NOT EXACTLY THE WORD I--
KRASH
DAMN
HOW HE'D FIND US SO FAST?
YOU FIGURE IT OUT--I'M BUSY!
AND WHILE YOU'RE AT IT, FIGURE OUT WHAT KIND OF PUPPY CHOW THEY'RE FEEDING THIS BEAST--HE'S WAY TOO STRONG!

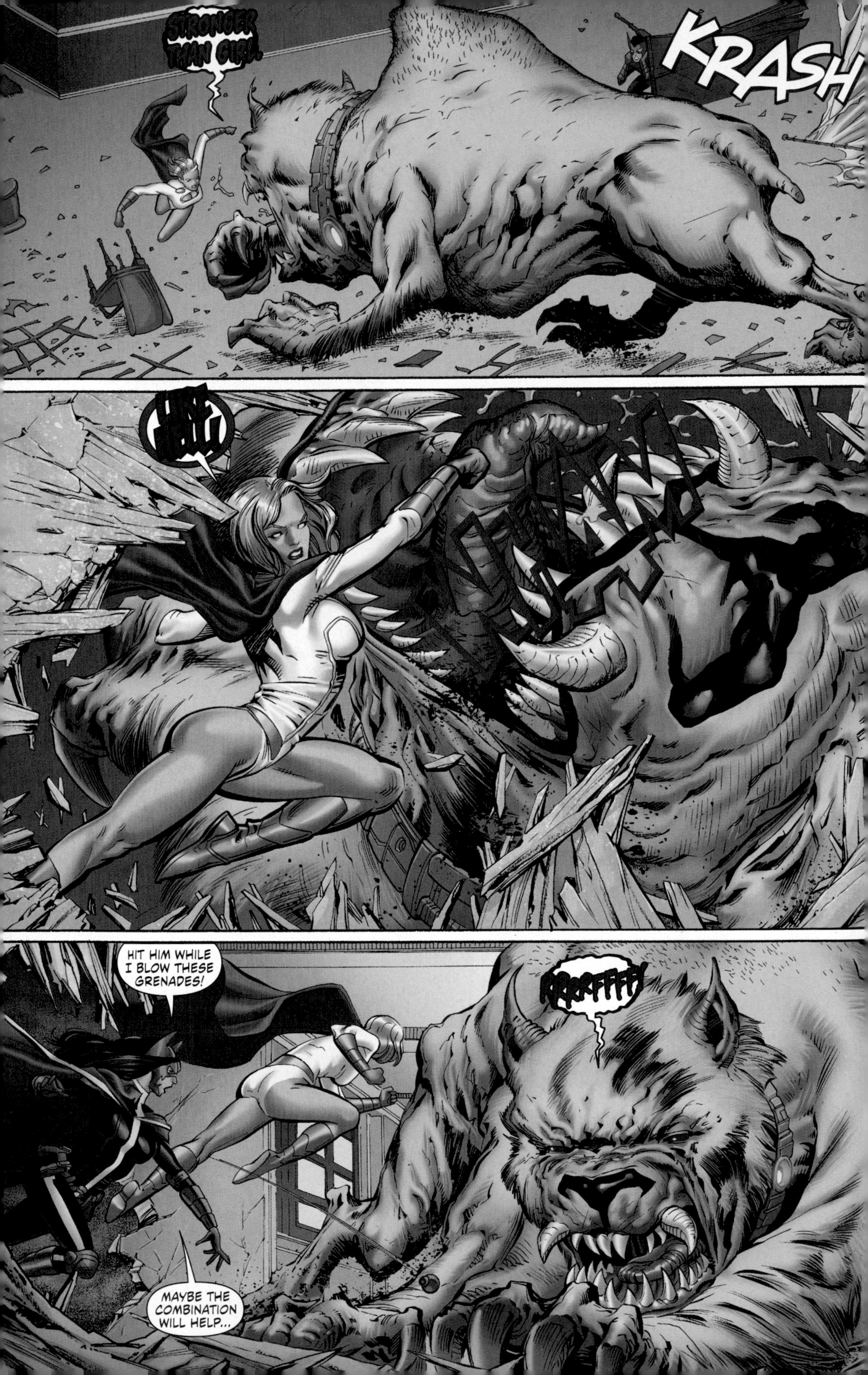
STRONGER THAN GIRL.
KRASH
HIT HIM WHILE I BLOW THESE GRENADES!
MAYBE THE COMBINATION WILL HELP...

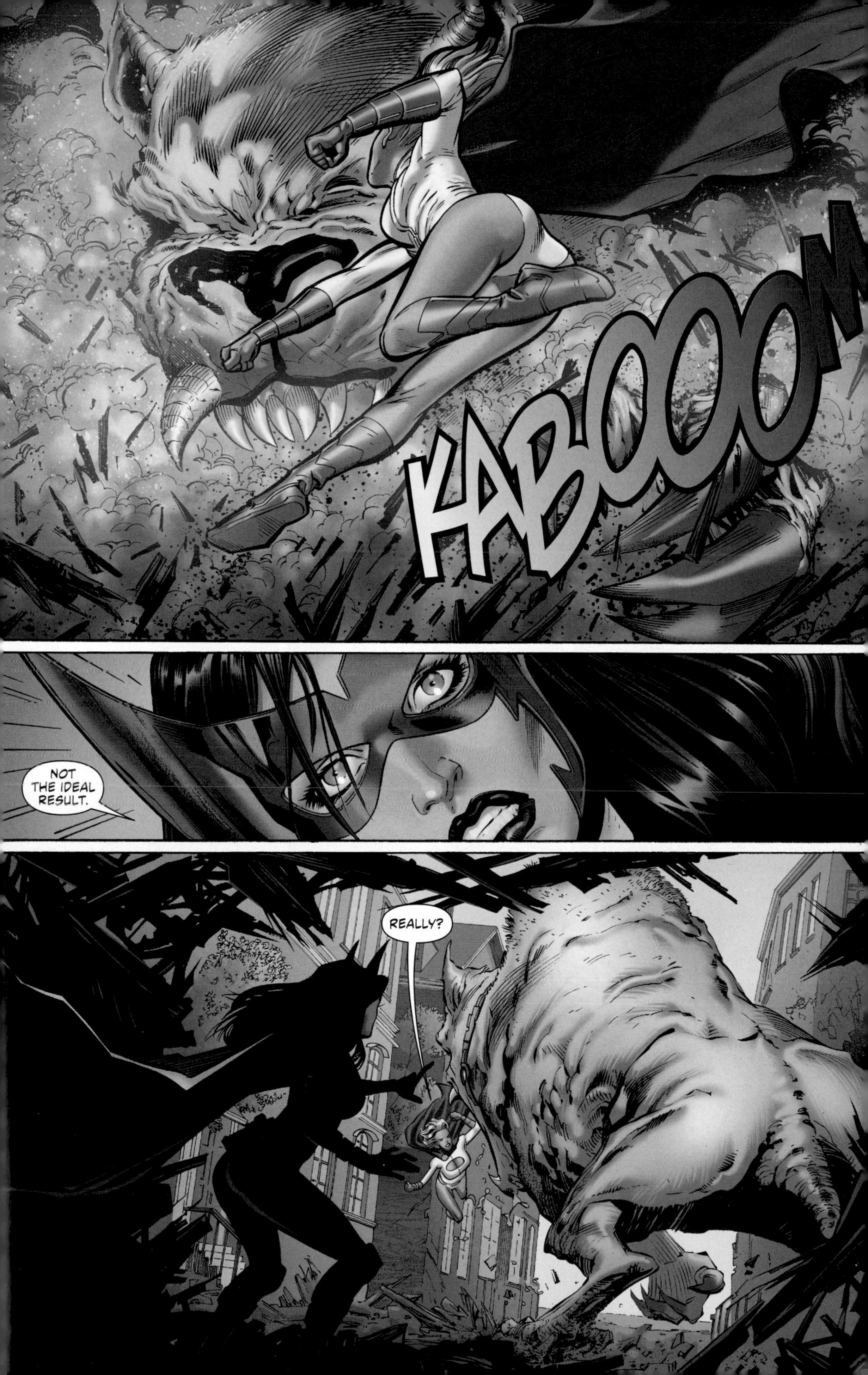
KABOOOM
NOT THE IDEAL RESULT.
REALLY?

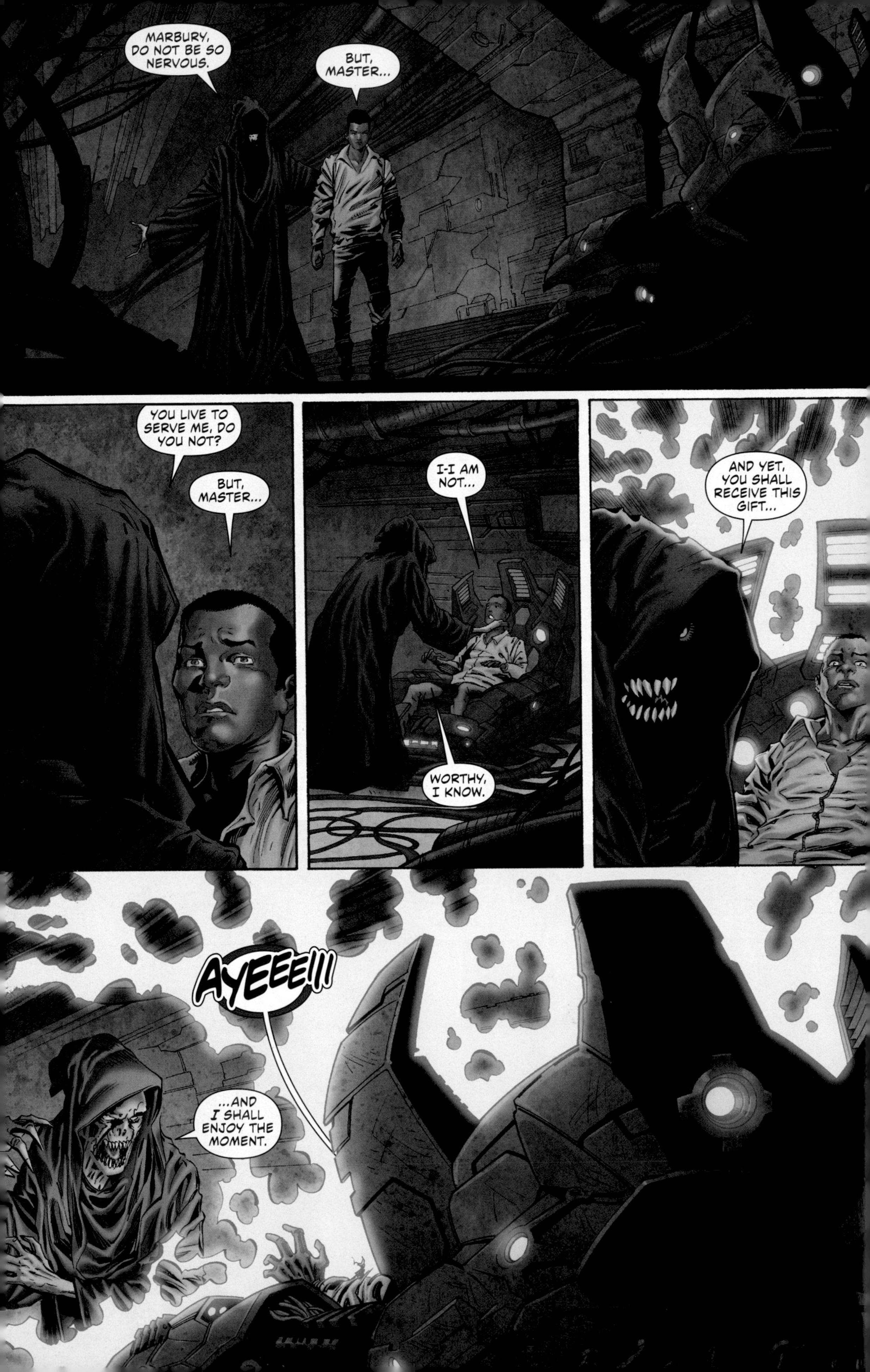
MARBURY, DO NOT BE SO NERVOUS.
BUT, MASTER...
YOU LIVE TO SERVE ME, DO YOU NOT?
BUT, MASTER...
I-I AM NOT...
WORTHY, I KNOW.
AND YET, YOU SHALL RECEIVE THIS GIFT...
AYEEE!!!
...AND I SHALL ENJOY THE MOMENT.

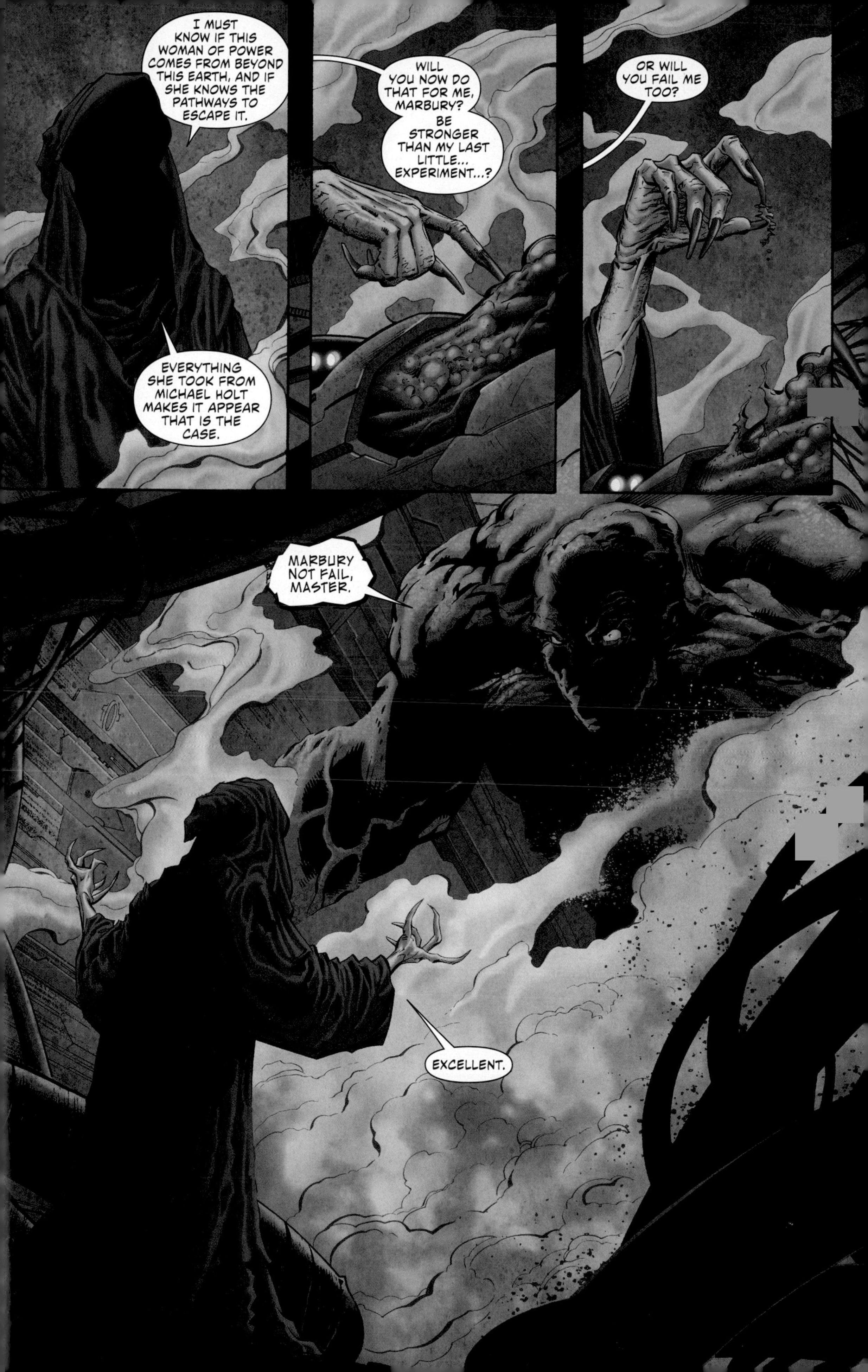
I MUST KNOW IF THIS WOMAN OF POWER COMES FROM BEYOND THIS EARTH, AND IF SHE KNOWS THE PATHWAYS TO ESCAPE IT.
EVERYTHING SHE TOOK FROM MICHAEL HOLT MAKES IT APPEAR THAT IS THE CASE.
WILL YOU NOW DO THAT FOR ME, MARBURY?
BE STRONGER THAN MY LAST LITTLE... EXPERIMENT...?
OR WILL YOU FAIL ME TOO?
MARBURY NOT FAIL, MASTER.
EXCELLENT.

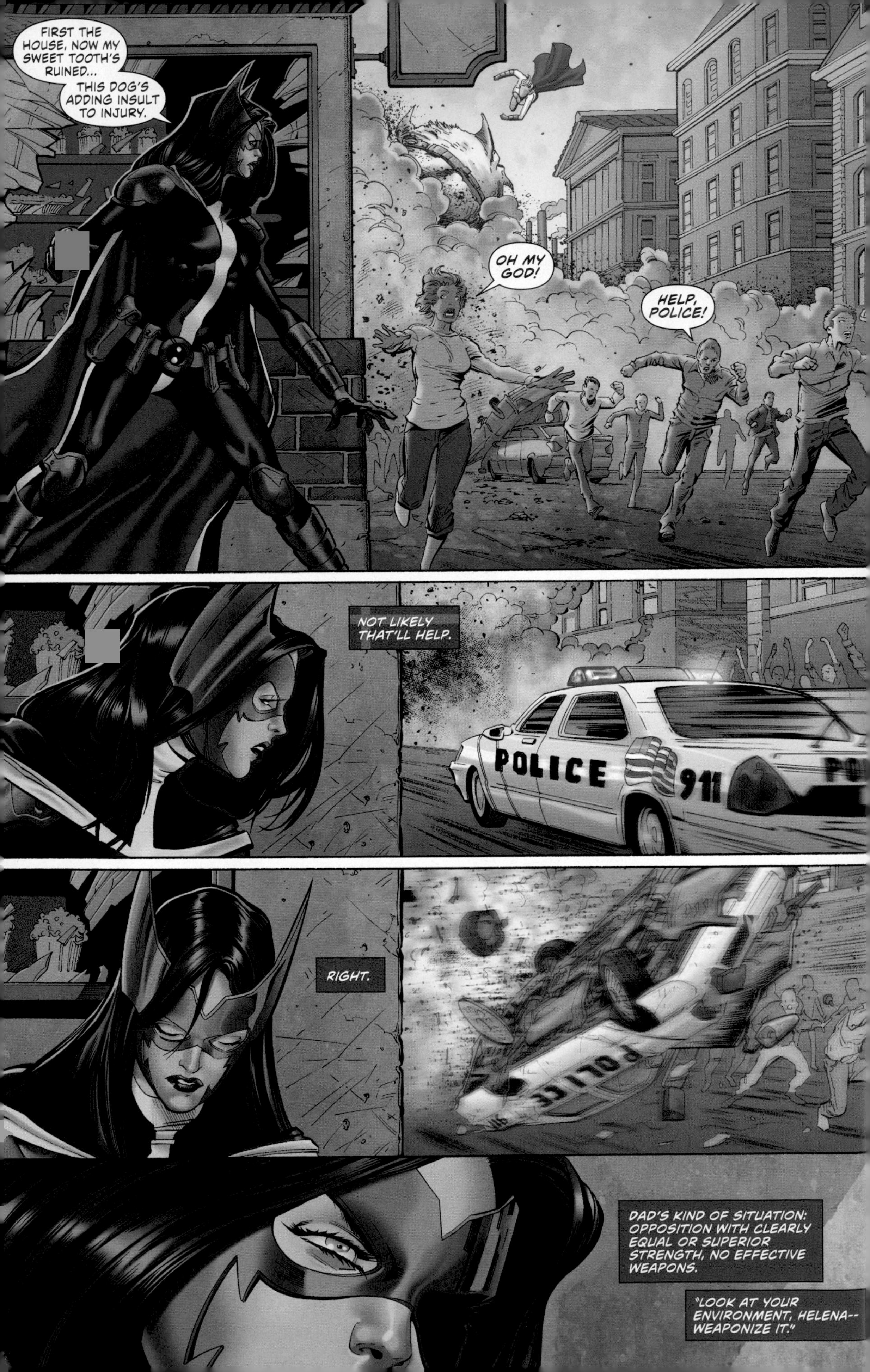
FIRST THE HOUSE, NOW MY SWEET TOOTH'S RUINED...
THIS DOG'S ADDING INSULT TO INJURY.
OH MY GOD!
HELP, POLICE!
NOT LIKELY THAT'LL HELP.
POLICE
911
RIGHT.
DAD'S KIND OF SITUATION: OPPOSITION WITH CLEARLY EQUAL OR SUPERIOR STRENGTH, NO EFFECTIVE WEAPONS.
"LOOK AT YOUR ENVIRONMENT, HELENA-- WEAPONIZE IT."

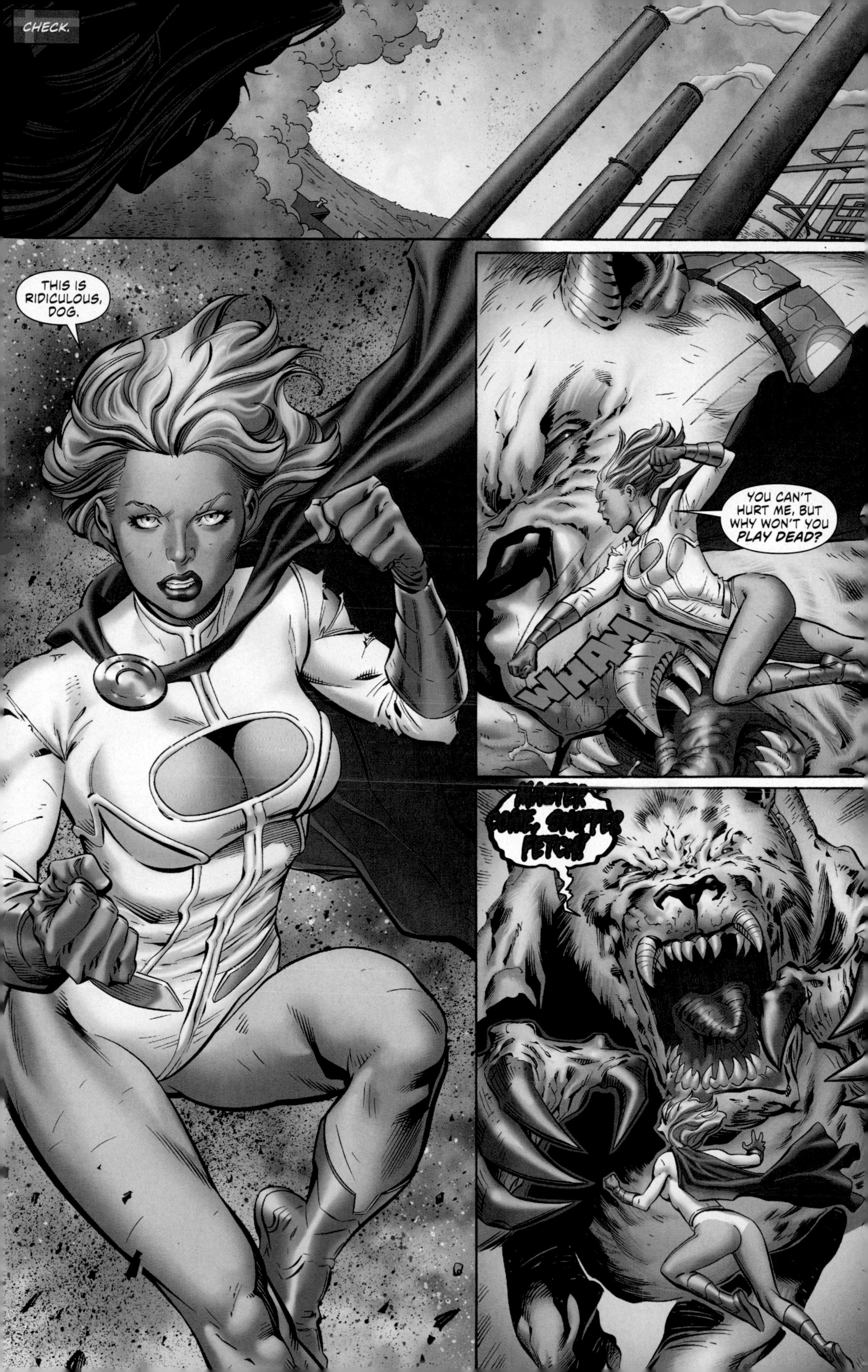
CHECK.
THIS IS RIDICULOUS, DOG.
YOU CAN'T HURT ME, BUT WHY WON'T YOU PLAY DEAD?
WHAM
MASTER GONE, SNIFFER FETCH!

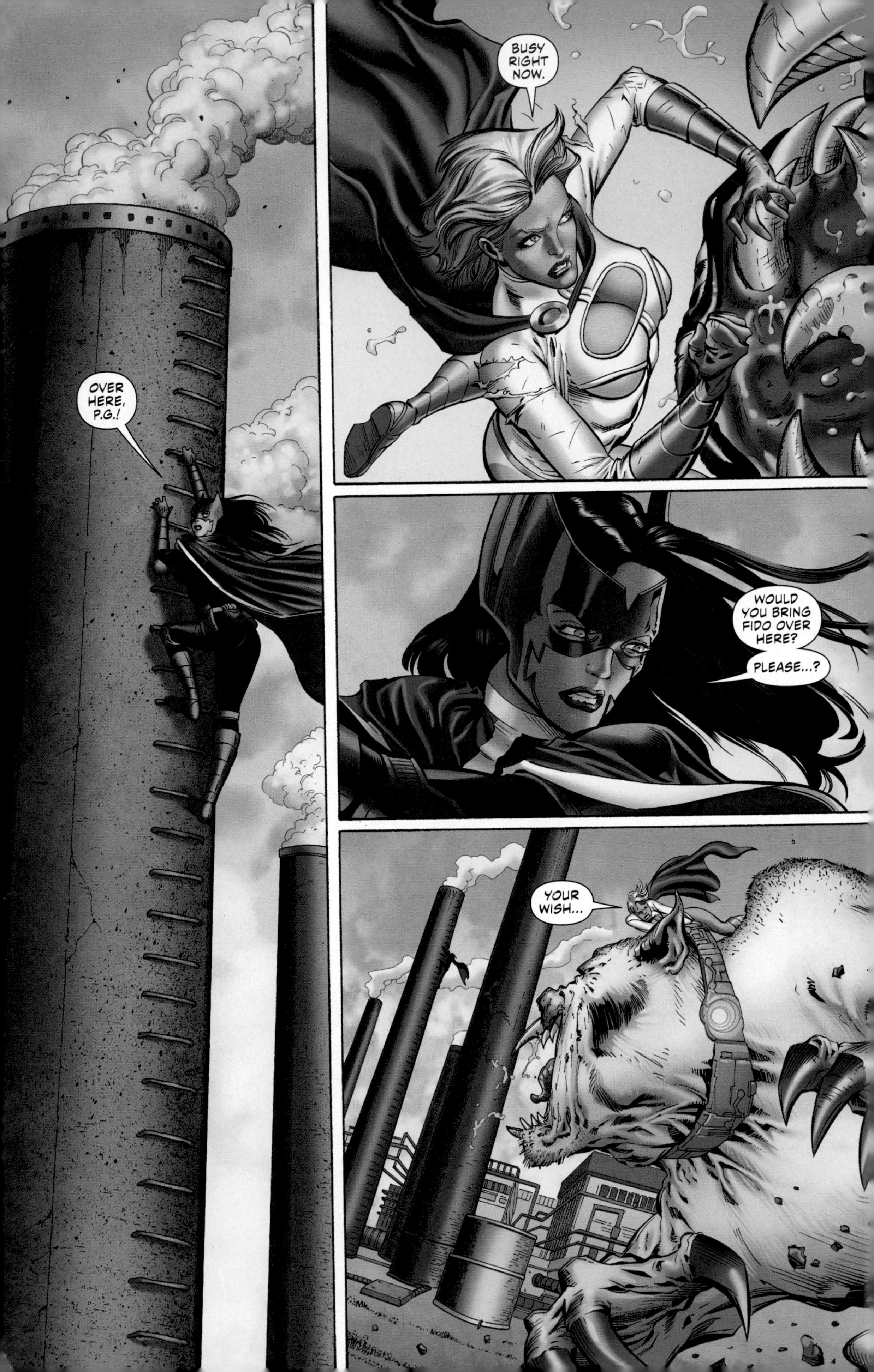
OVER HERE, P.G.!
BUSY RIGHT NOW.
WOULD YOU BRING FIDO OVER HERE?
PLEASE...?
YOUR WISH...

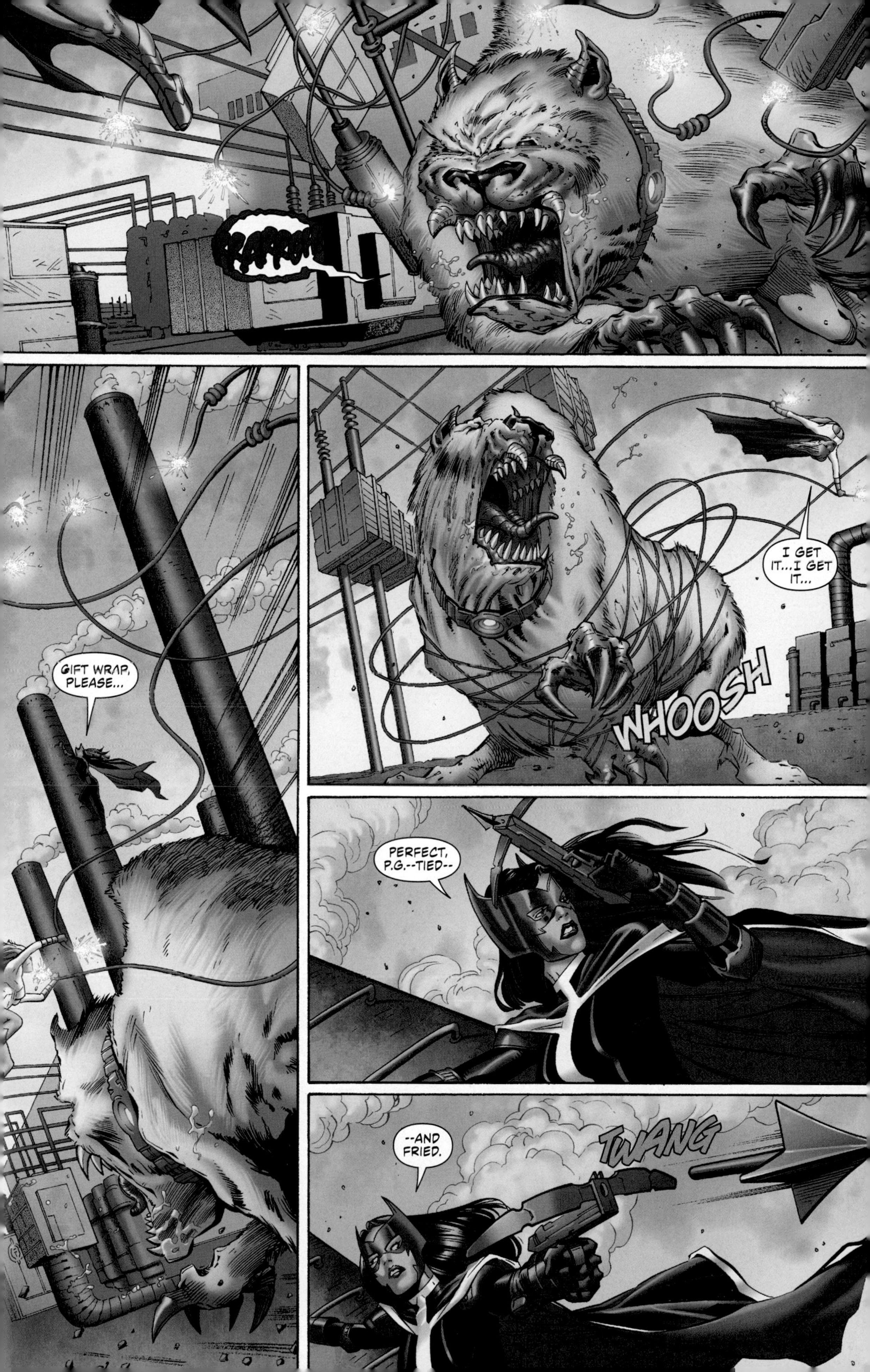
GIFT WRAP, PLEASE...
I GET IT...I GET IT...
WHOOSH
PERFECT, P.G.--TIED--
--AND FRIED.
TWANG

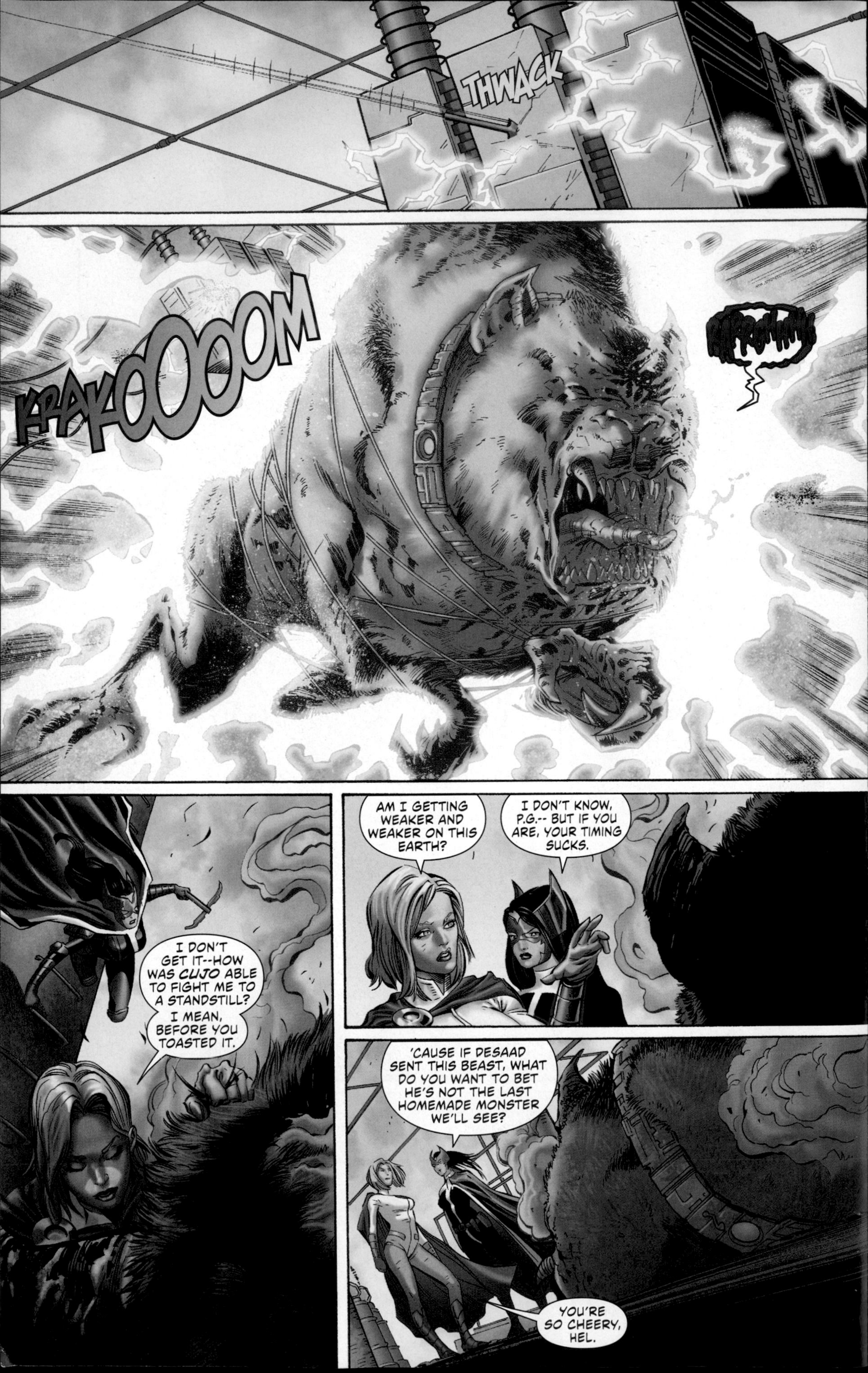
THWACK
KRAKOOOOOM
I DON'T GET IT--HOW WAS CUJO ABLE TO FIGHT ME TO A STANDSTILL?
I MEAN, BEFORE YOU TOASTED IT.
AM I GETTING WEAKER AND WEAKER ON THIS EARTH?
I DON'T KNOW, P.G.-- BUT IF YOU ARE, YOUR TIMING SUCKS.
'CAUSE IF DESAAD SENT THIS BEAST, WHAT DO YOU WANT TO BET HE'S NOT THE LAST HOMEMADE MONSTER WE'LL SEE?
YOU'RE SO CHEERY, HEL.

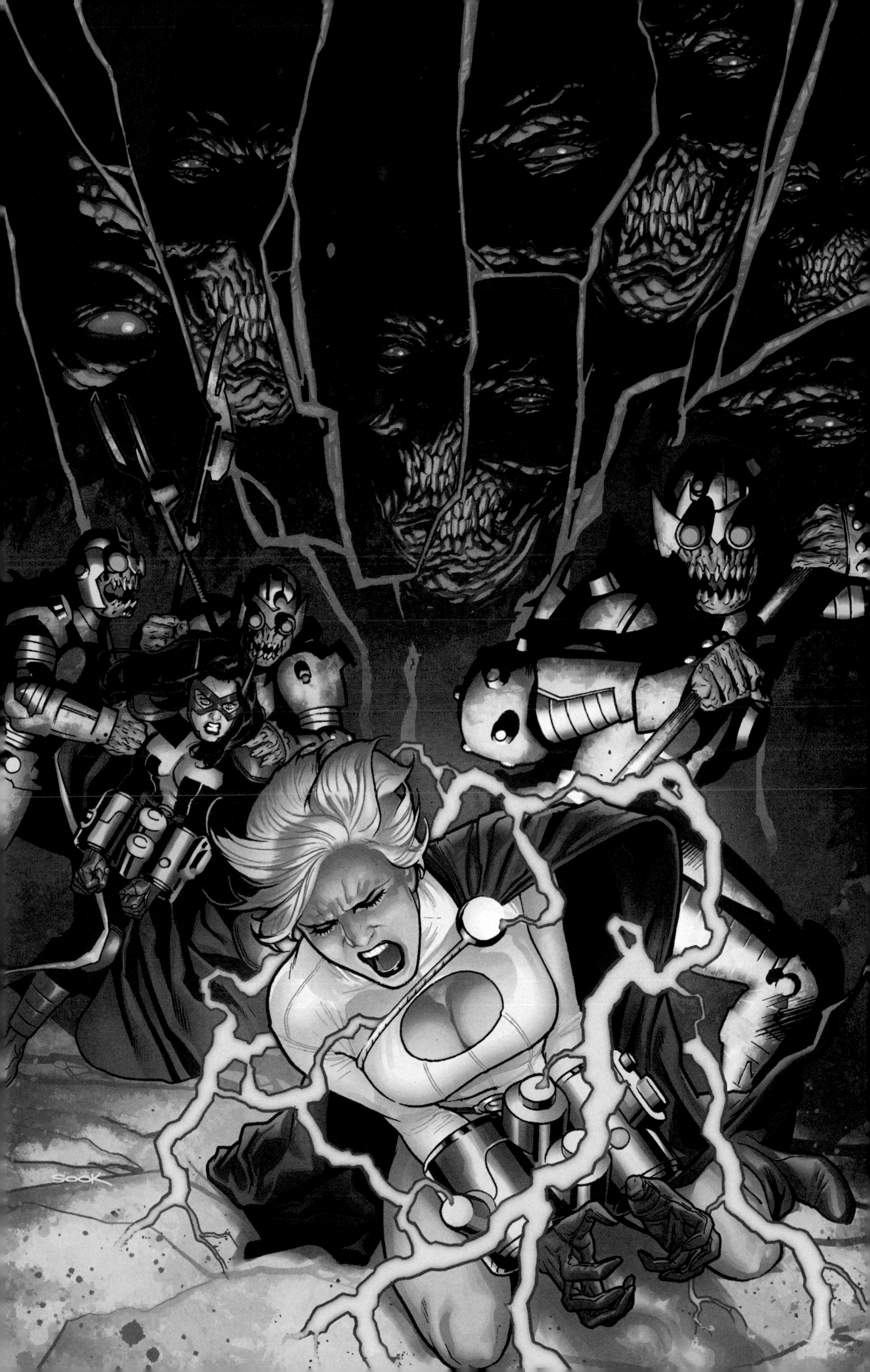
SOOK

LOSSES

ROBSON ROCHA penciller WAYNE FAUCHER inker cover art by RYAN SOOK

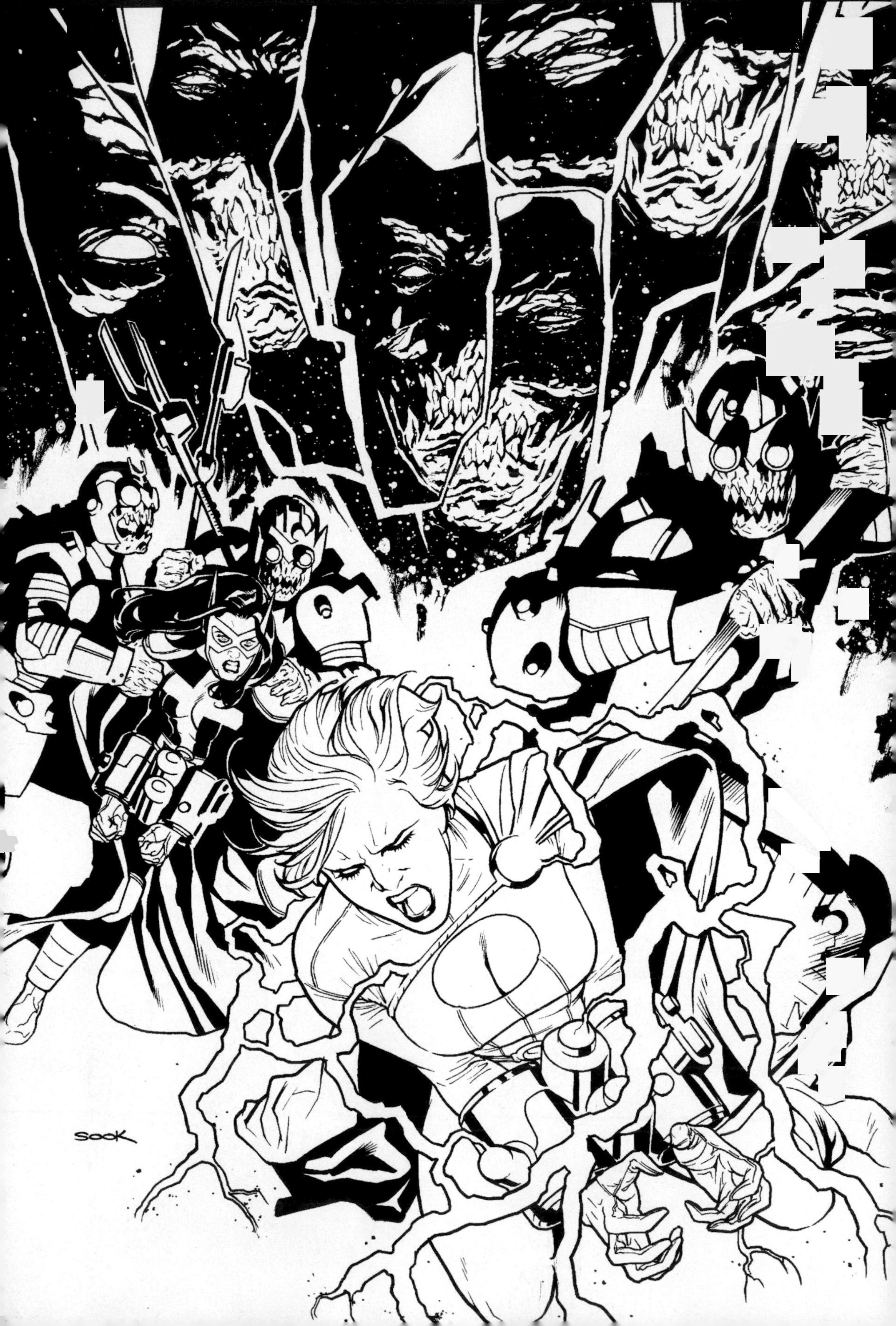
SOOK

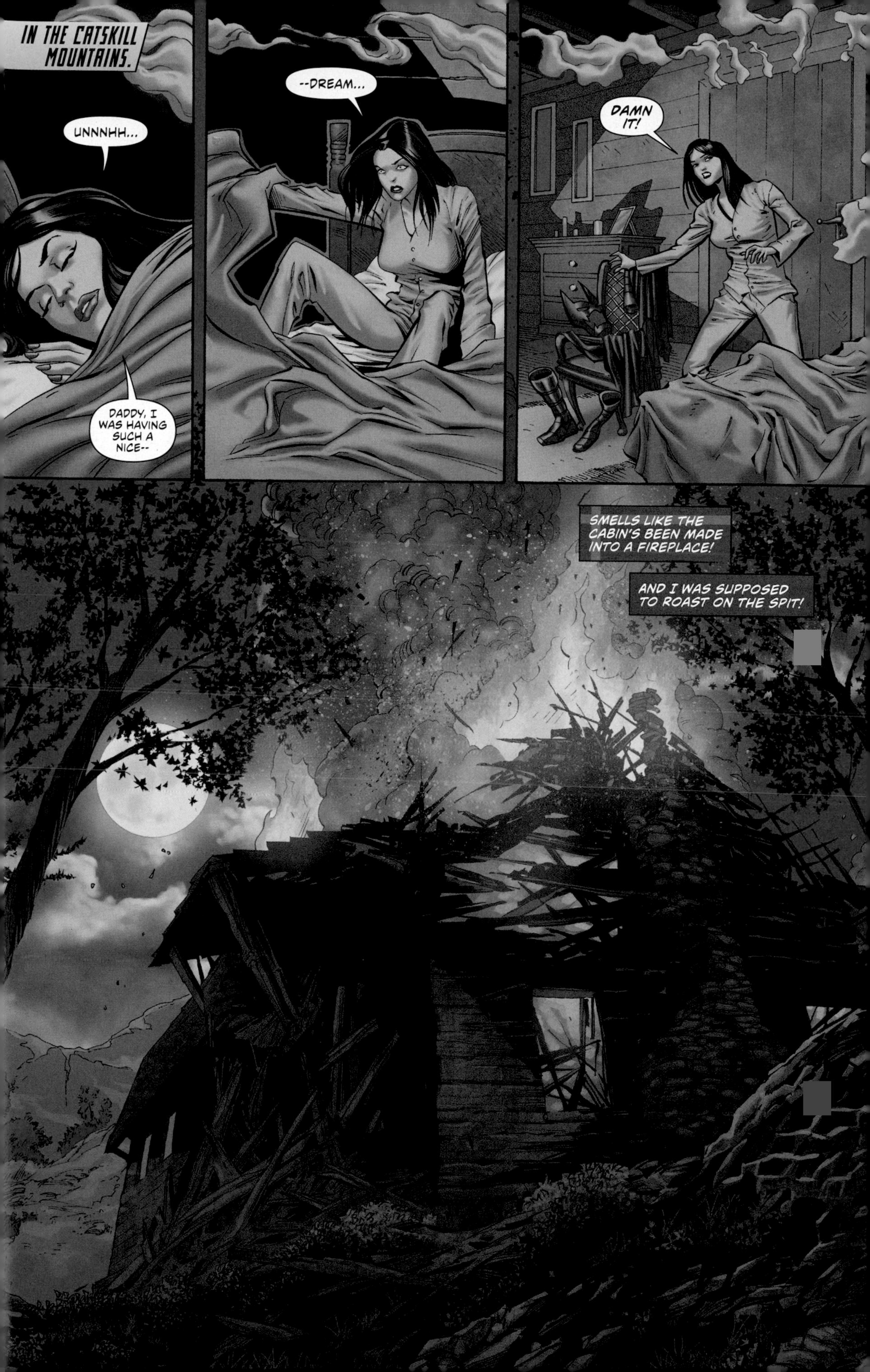
IN THE CATSKILL MOUNTAINS.
UNNNHH...
DADDY, I WAS HAVING SUCH A NICE--
--DREAM...
DAMN IT!
SMELLS LIKE THE CABIN'S BEEN MADE INTO A FIREPLACE!
AND I WAS SUPPOSED TO ROAST ON THE SPIT!

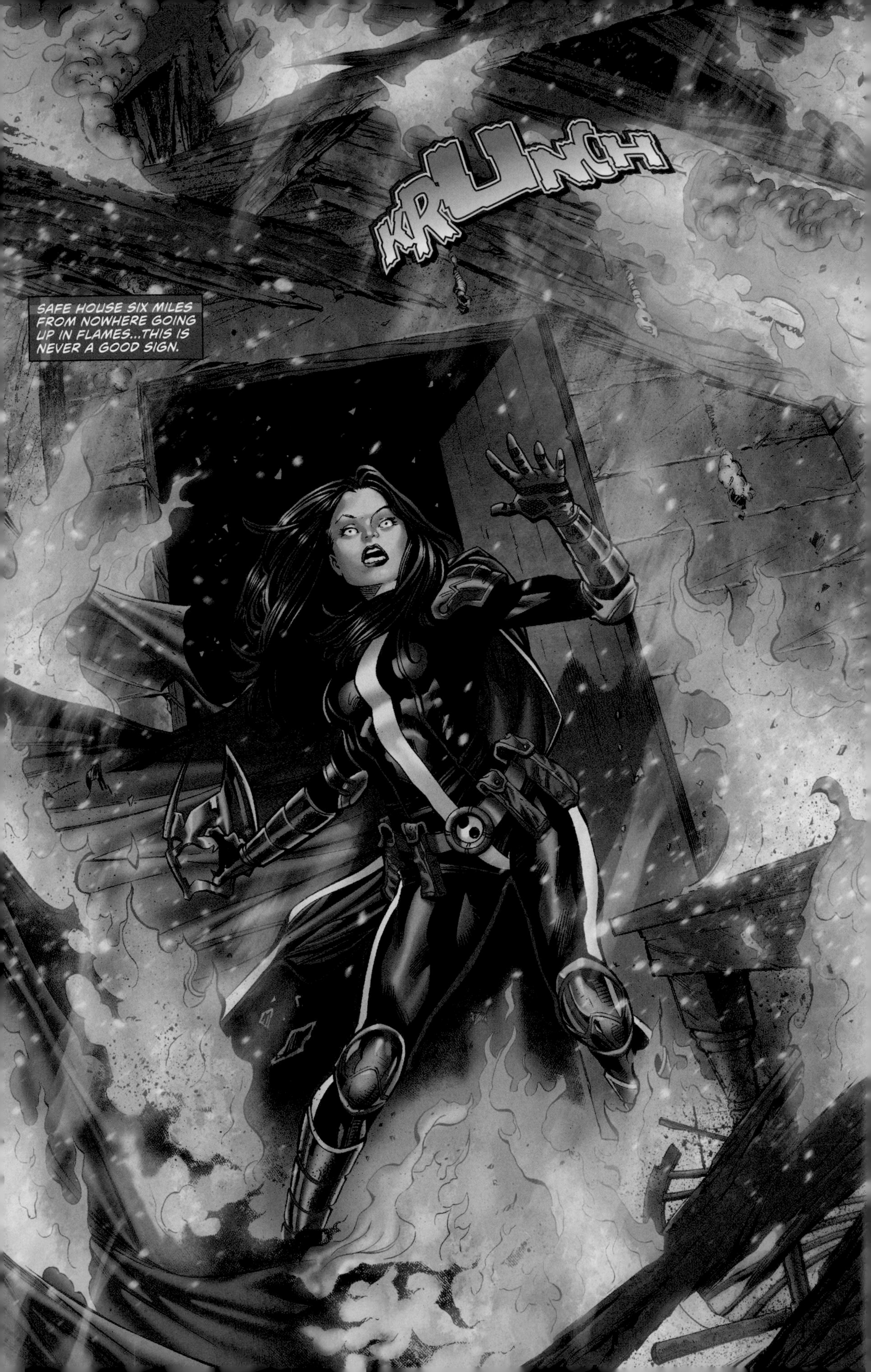
KRUNCH
SAFE HOUSE SIX MILES FROM NOWHERE GOING UP IN FLAMES...THIS IS NEVER A GOOD SIGN.

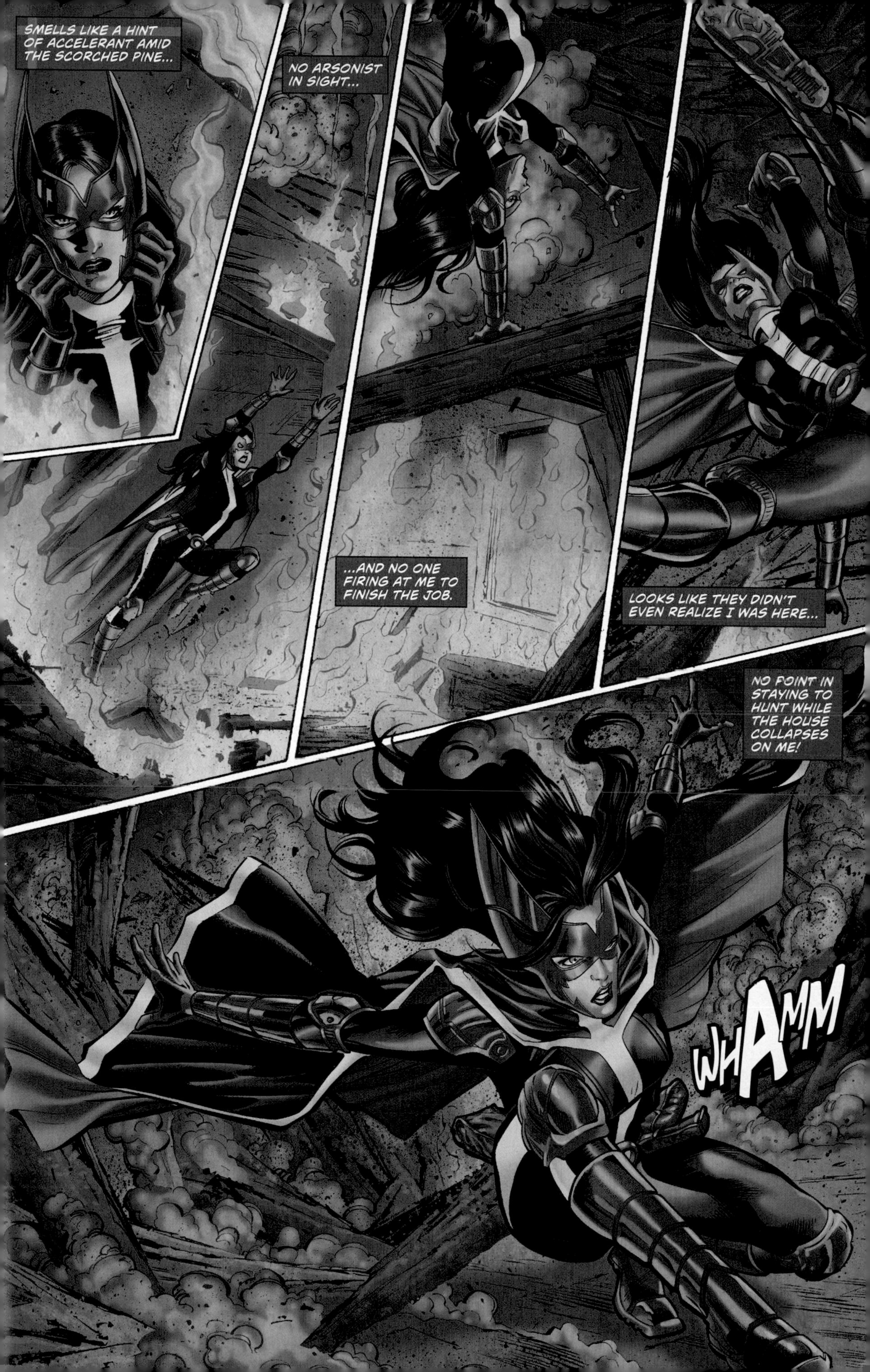
SMELLS LIKE A HINT OF ACCELERANT AMID THE SCORCHED PINE...
NO ARSONIST IN SIGHT...
...AND NO ONE FIRING AT ME TO FINISH THE JOB.
LOOKS LIKE THEY DIDN'T EVEN REALIZE I WAS HERE...
NO POINT IN STAYING TO HUNT WHILE THE HOUSE COLLAPSES ON ME!
WHAMM

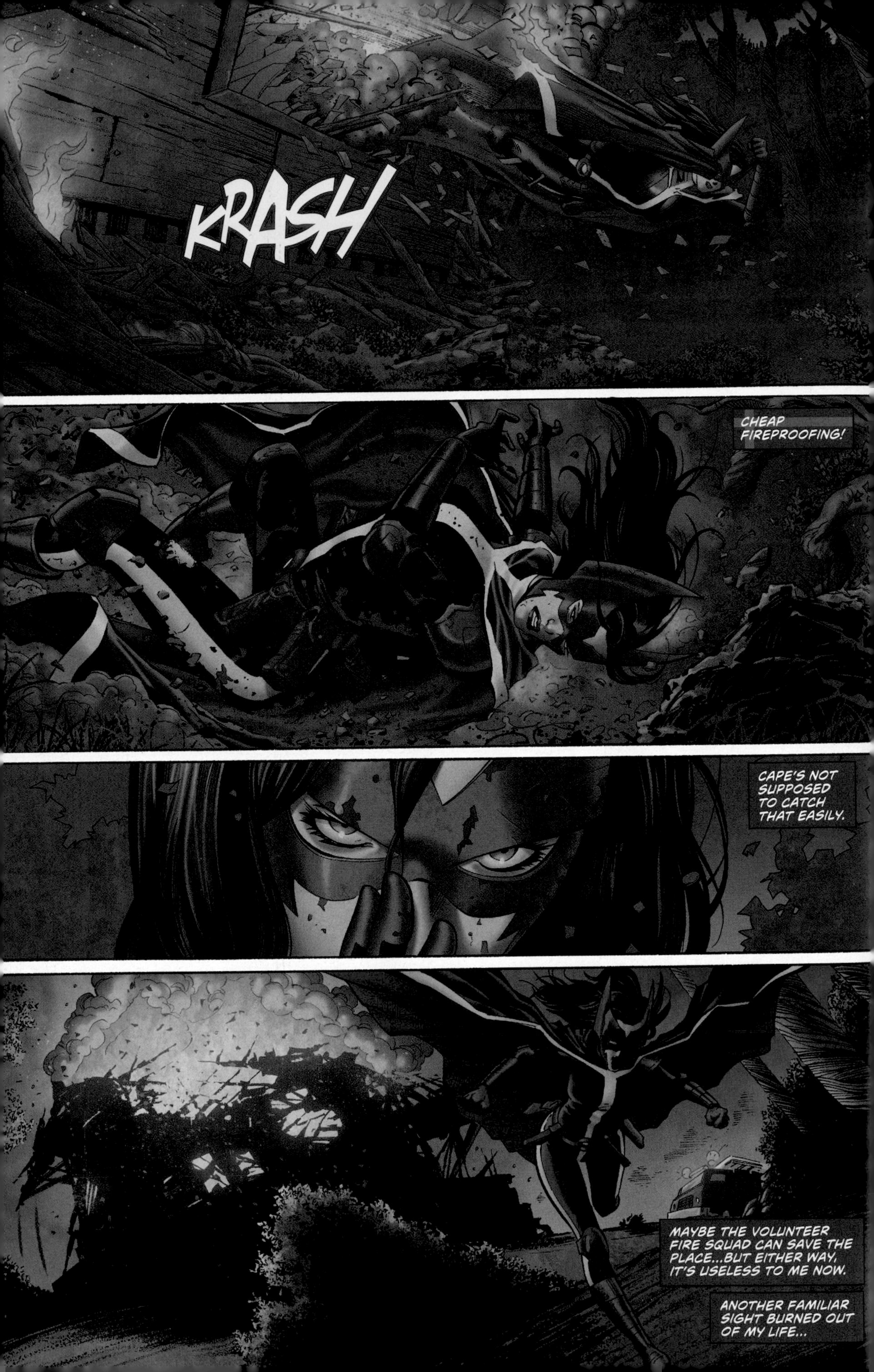
KRASH
CHEAP FIREPROOFING!
CAPE'S NOT SUPPOSED TO CATCH THAT EASILY.
MAYBE THE VOLUNTEER FIRE SQUAD CAN SAVE THE PLACE...BUT EITHER WAY, IT'S USELESS TO ME NOW.
ANOTHER FAMILIAR SIGHT BURNED OUT OF MY LIFE...

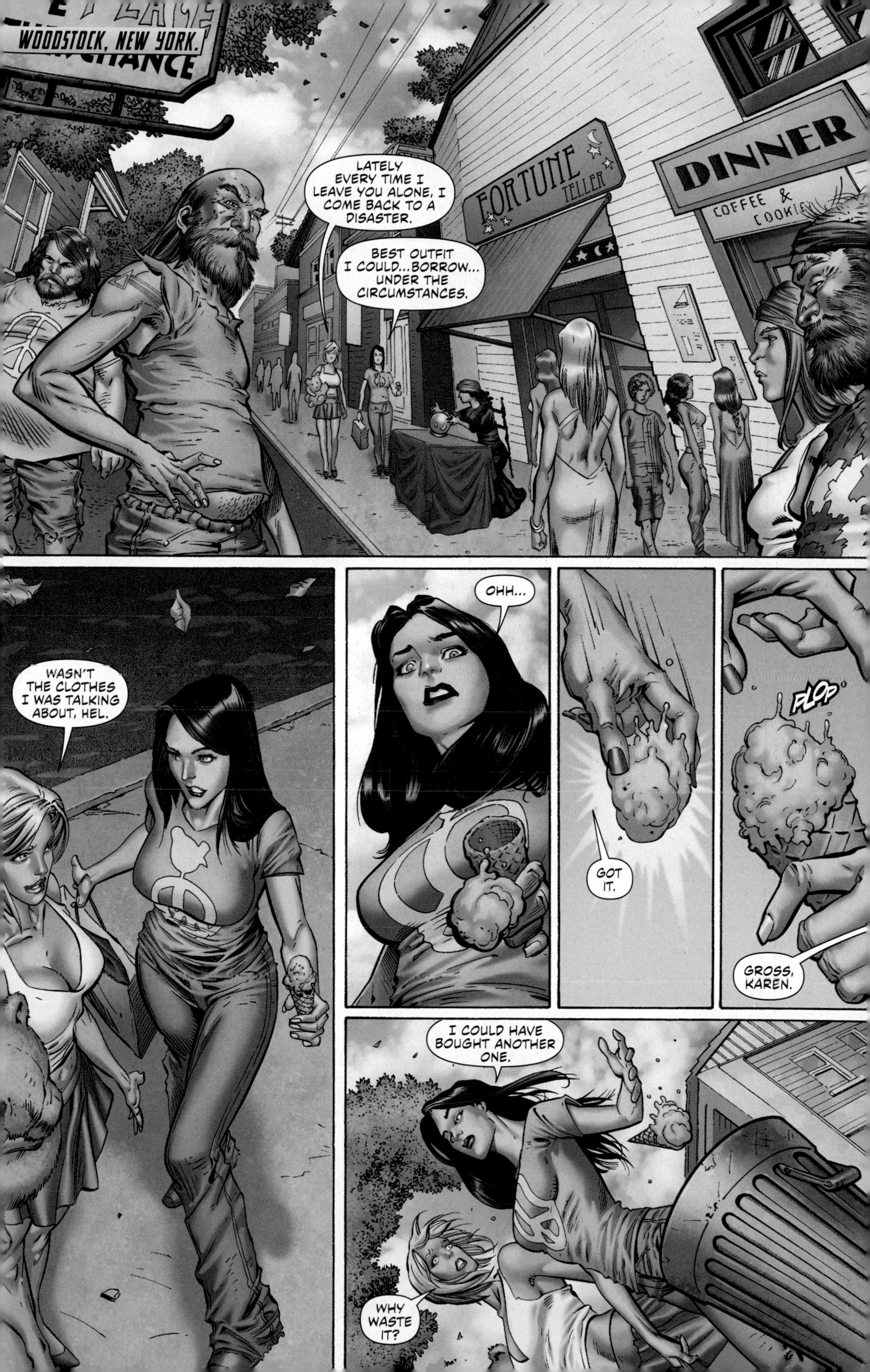
WOODSTOCK, NEW YORK.
CHANCE
FORTUNE TELLER
DINNER
COFFEE & COOKIE
LATELY EVERY TIME I LEAVE YOU ALONE, I COME BACK TO A DISASTER.
BEST OUTFIT I COULD...BORROW... UNDER THE CIRCUMSTANCES.
WASN'T THE CLOTHES I WAS TALKING ABOUT, HEL.
OHH...
GOT IT.
PLOP
GROSS, KAREN.
I COULD HAVE BOUGHT ANOTHER ONE.
WHY WASTE IT?

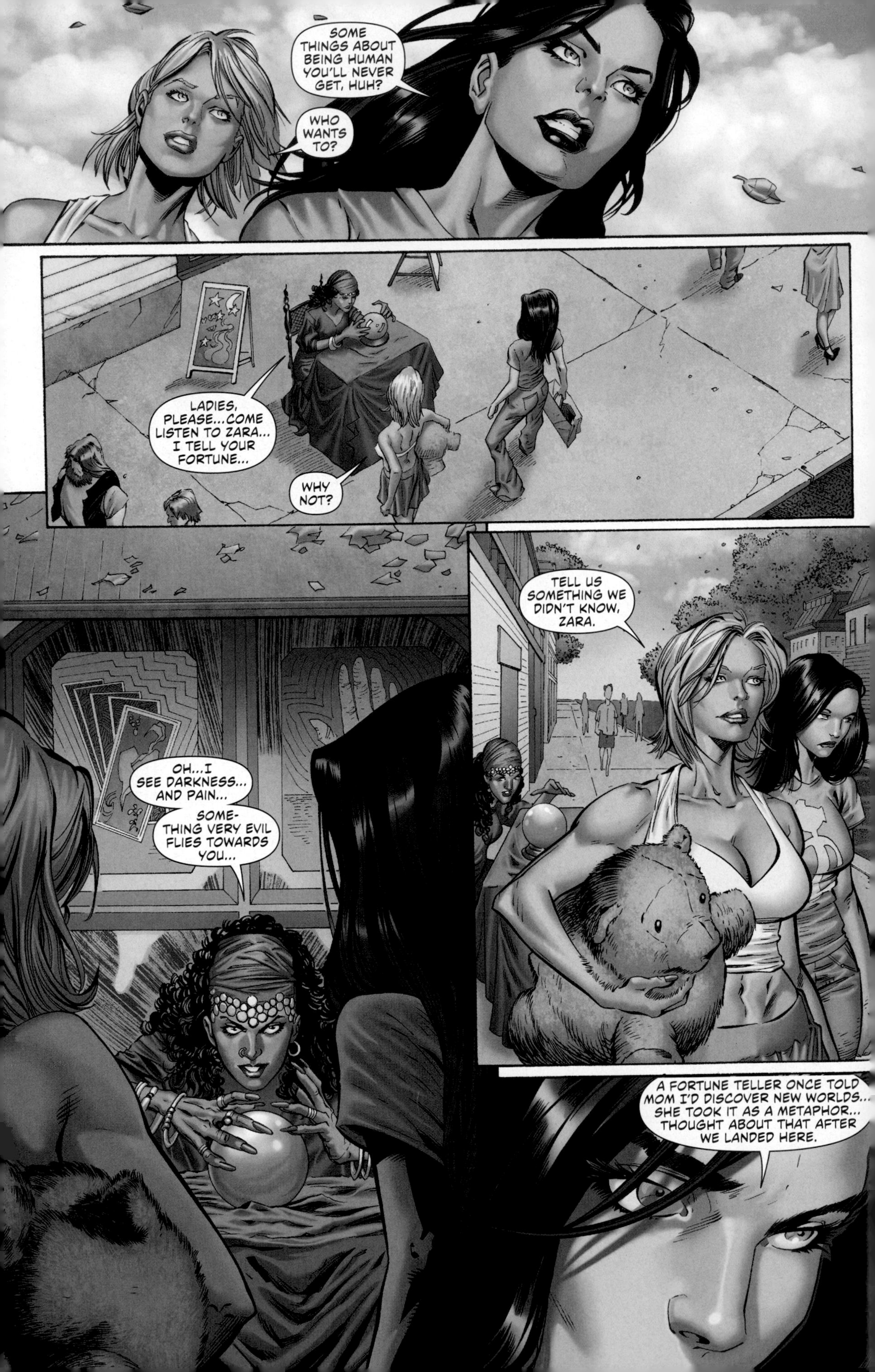
SOME THINGS ABOUT BEING HUMAN YOU'LL NEVER GET, HUH?
WHO WANTS TO?
LADIES, PLEASE...COME LISTEN TO ZARA... I TELL YOUR FORTUNE...
WHY NOT?
OH...I SEE DARKNESS... AND PAIN...
SOME-THING VERY EVIL FLIES TOWARDS YOU...
TELL US SOMETHING WE DIDN'T KNOW, ZARA.
A FORTUNE TELLER ONCE TOLD MOM I'D DISCOVER NEW WORLDS... SHE TOOK IT AS A METAPHOR... THOUGHT ABOUT THAT AFTER WE LANDED HERE.

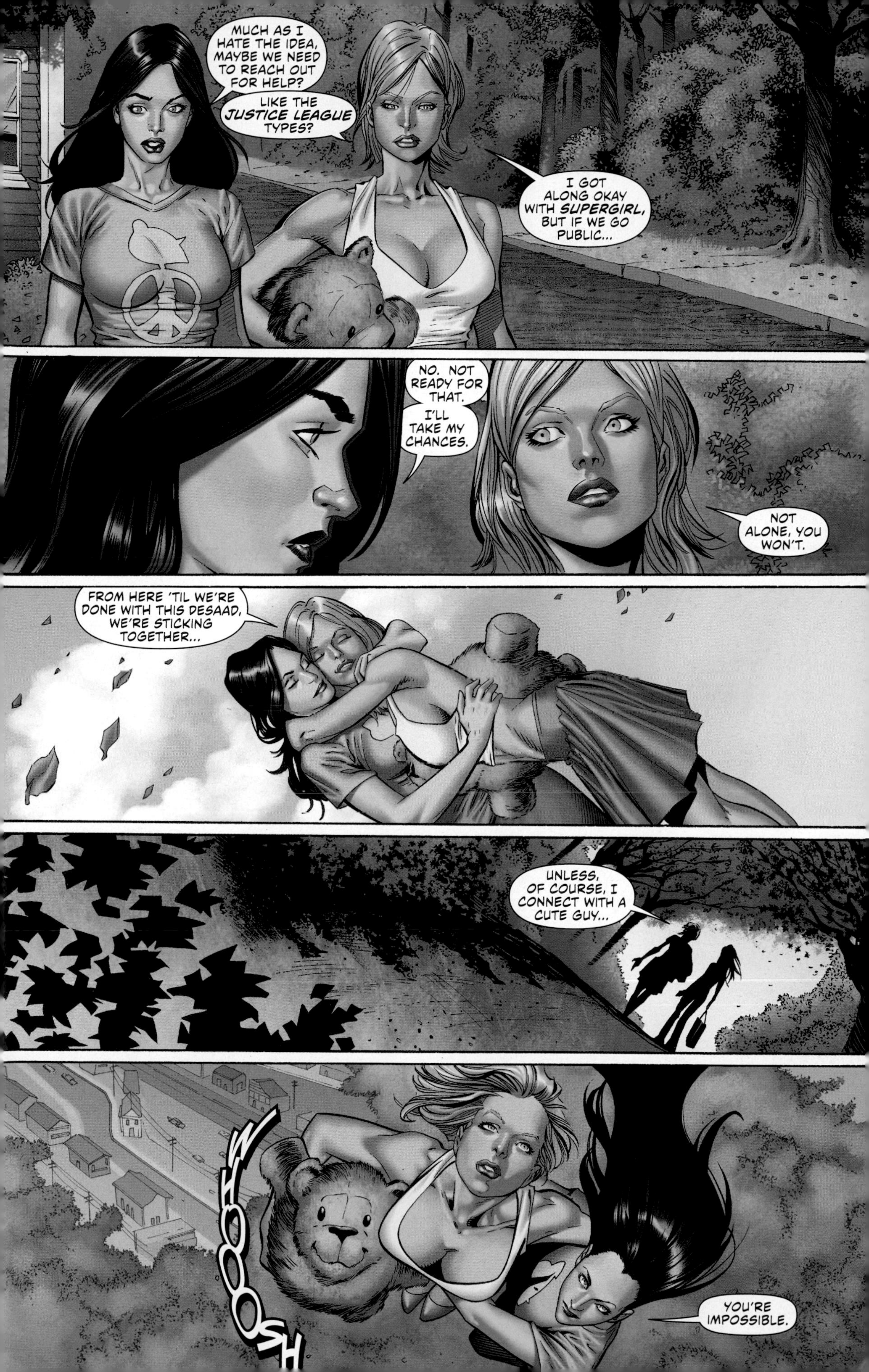

MUCH AS I HATE THE IDEA, MAYBE WE NEED TO REACH OUT FOR HELP?
LIKE THE JUSTICE LEAGUE TYPES?
I GOT ALONG OKAY WITH SUPERGIRL, BUT IF WE GO PUBLIC...
NO. NOT READY FOR THAT.
I'LL TAKE MY CHANCES.
NOT ALONE, YOU WON'T.
FROM HERE 'TIL WE'RE DONE WITH THIS DESAAD, WE'RE STICKING TOGETHER...
UNLESS, OF COURSE, I CONNECT WITH A CUTE GUY...
WHOOOOSH
YOU'RE IMPOSSIBLE.

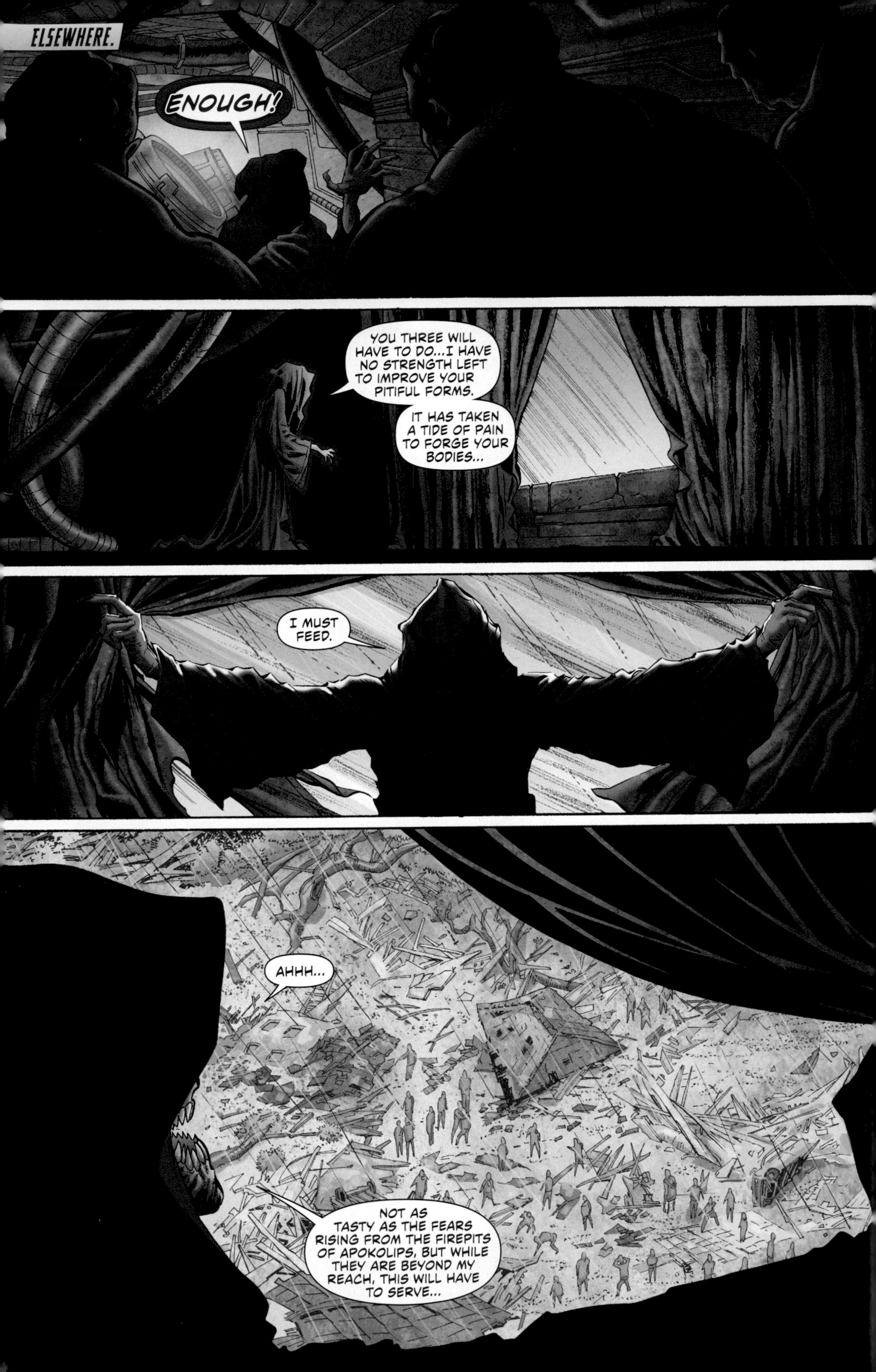
ELSEWHERE.
ENOUGH!
YOU THREE WILL HAVE TO DO...I HAVE NO STRENGTH LEFT TO IMPROVE YOUR PITIFUL FORMS.
IT HAS TAKEN A TIDE OF PAIN TO FORGE YOUR BODIES...
I MUST FEED.
AHHH...
NOT AS TASTY AS THE FEARS RISING FROM THE FIREPITS OF APOKOLIPS, BUT WHILE THEY ARE BEYOND MY REACH, THIS WILL HAVE TO SERVE...

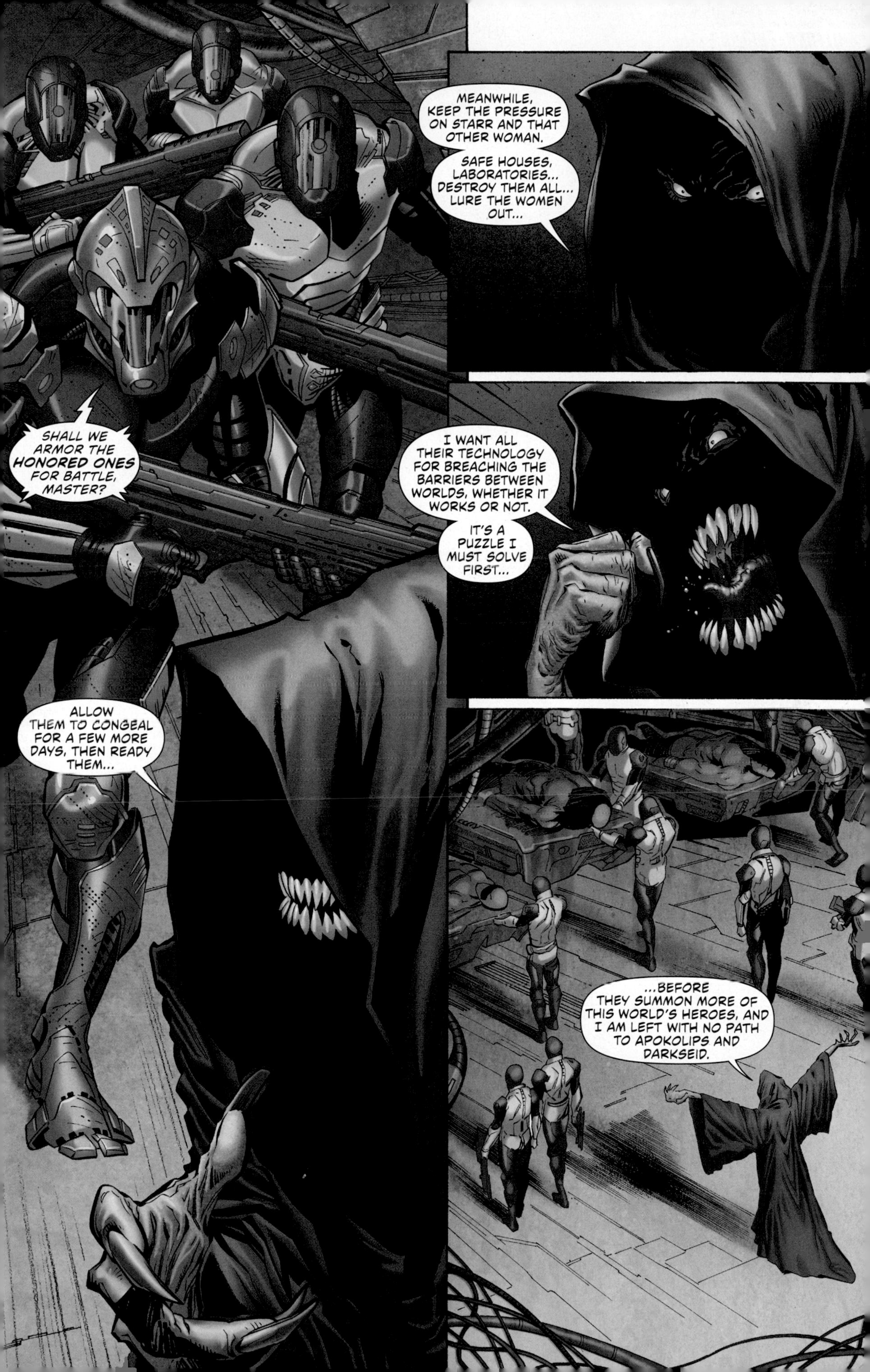
MEANWHILE, KEEP THE PRESSURE ON STARR AND THAT OTHER WOMAN.
SAFE HOUSES, LABORATORIES... DESTROY THEM ALL... LURE THE WOMEN OUT...
SHALL WE ARMOR THE **HONORED ONES** FOR BATTLE, MASTER?
I WANT ALL THEIR TECHNOLOGY FOR BREACHING THE BARRIERS BETWEEN WORLDS, WHETHER IT WORKS OR NOT.
IT'S A PUZZLE I MUST SOLVE FIRST...
ALLOW THEM TO CONGEAL FOR A FEW MORE DAYS, THEN READY THEM...
...BEFORE THEY SUMMON MORE OF THIS WORLD'S HEROES, AND I AM LEFT WITH NO PATH TO APOKOLIPS AND DARKSEID.

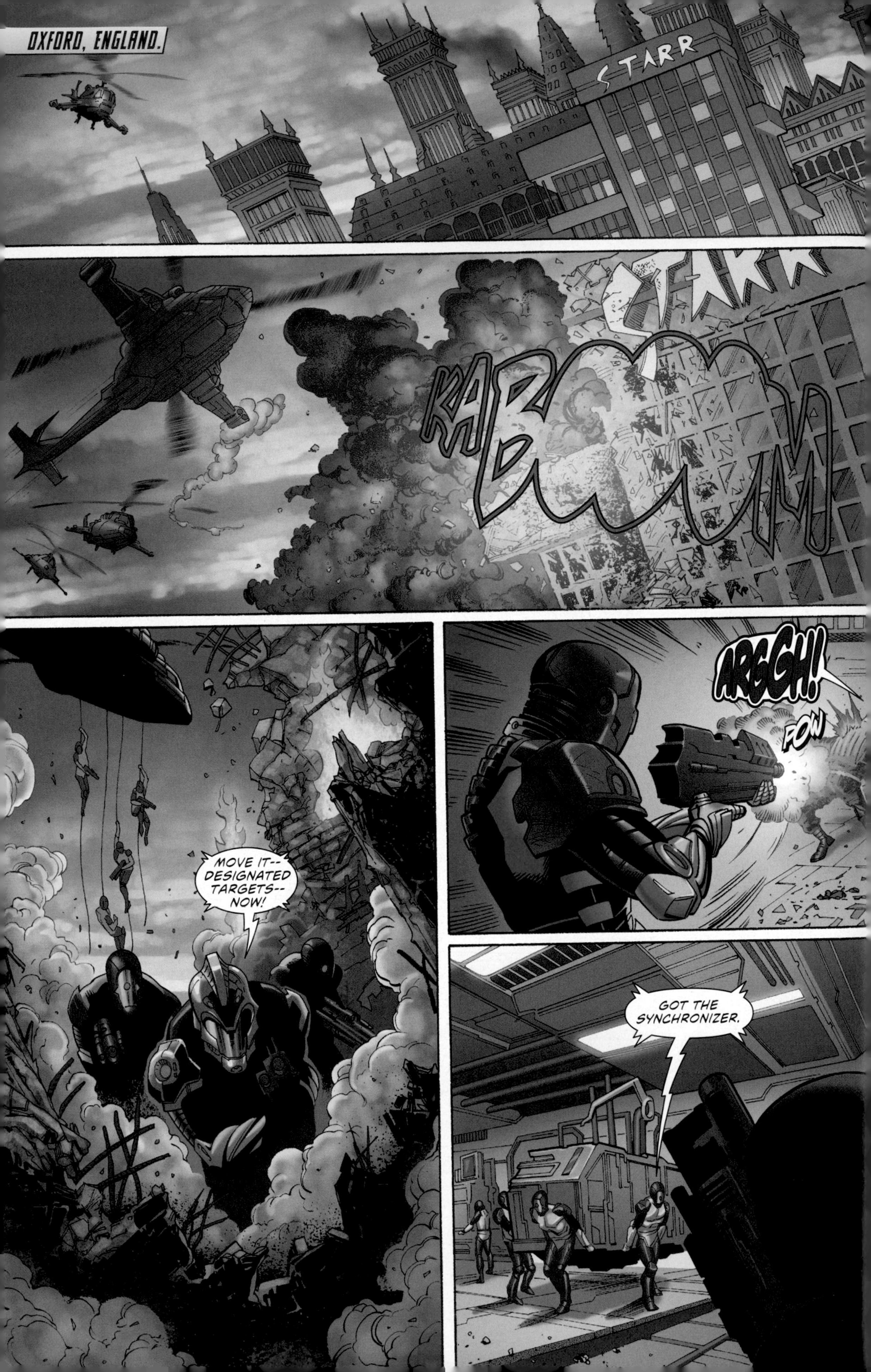
OXFORD, ENGLAND.
STARR
KA-BOOM
MOVE IT-- DESIGNATED TARGETS-- NOW!
ARGGH!
POW
GOT THE SYNCHRONIZER.

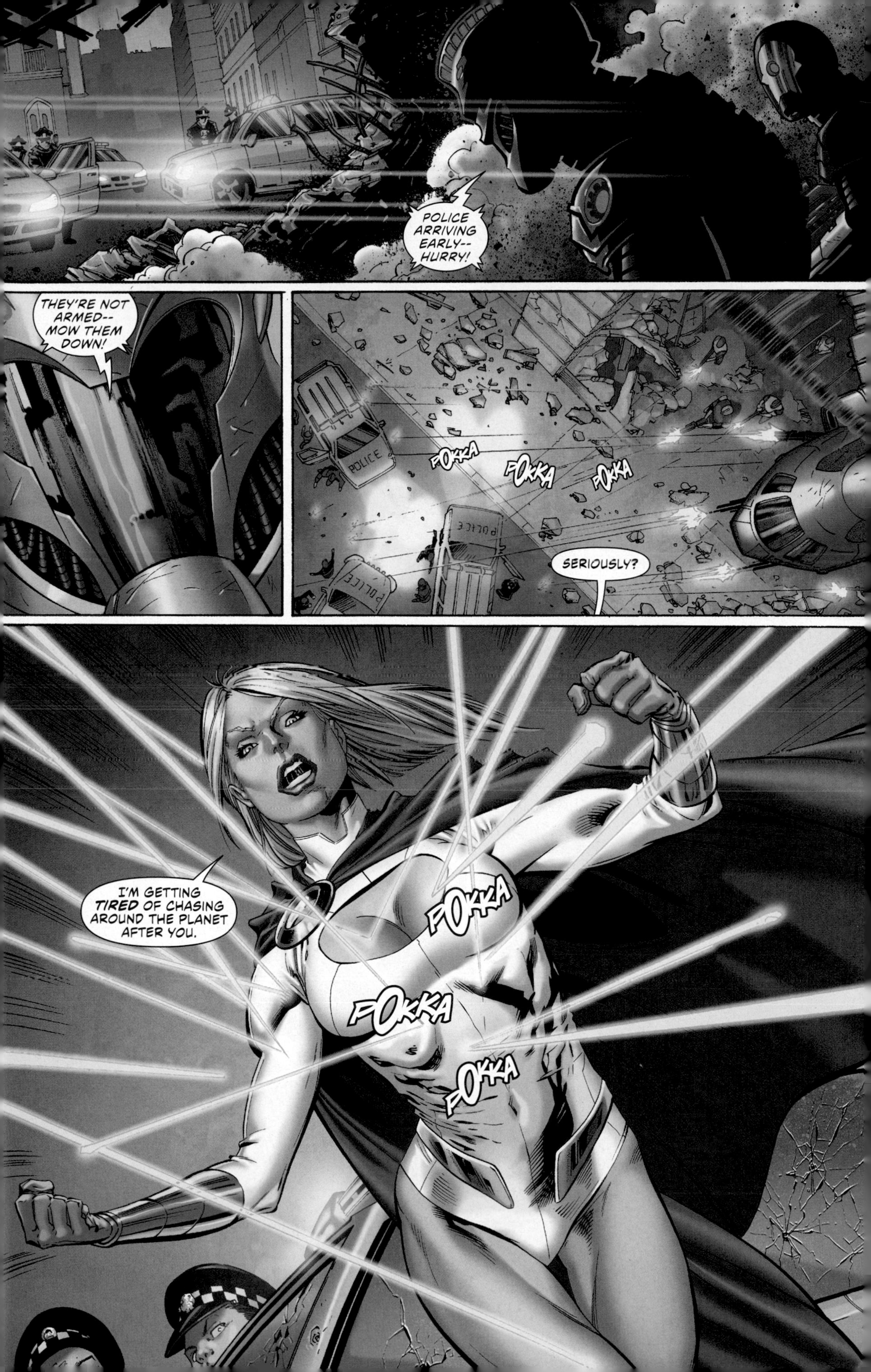
POLICE ARRIVING EARLY-- HURRY!
THEY'RE NOT ARMED-- MOW THEM DOWN!
POKKA
POKKA
POKKA
SERIOUSLY?
I'M GETTING *TIRED* OF CHASING AROUND THE PLANET AFTER YOU.
POKKA
POKKA
POKKA

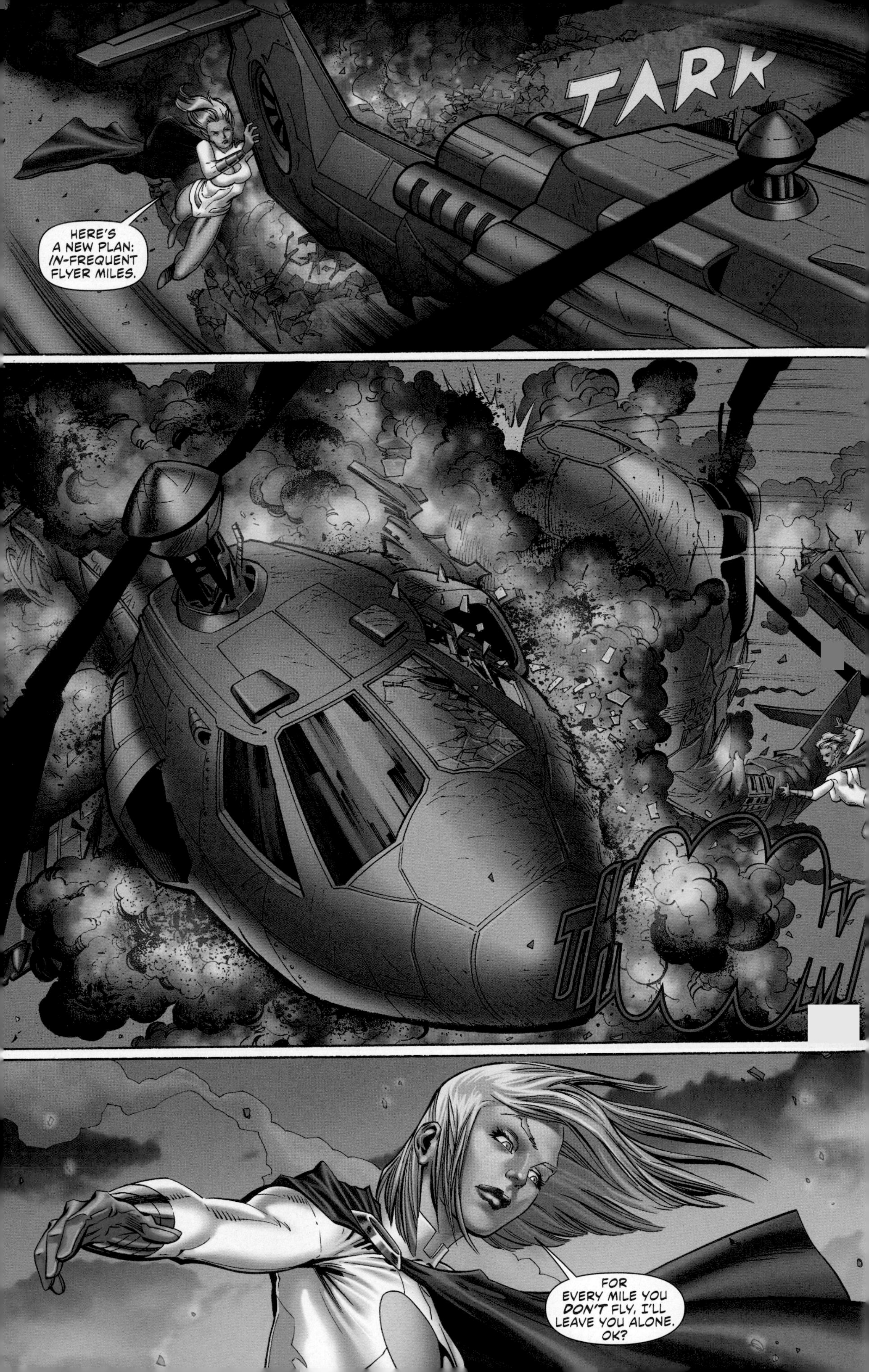
TARK
HERE'S A NEW PLAN: IN-FREQUENT FLYER MILES.
THOOM
FOR EVERY MILE YOU DON'T FLY, I'LL LEAVE YOU ALONE. OK?

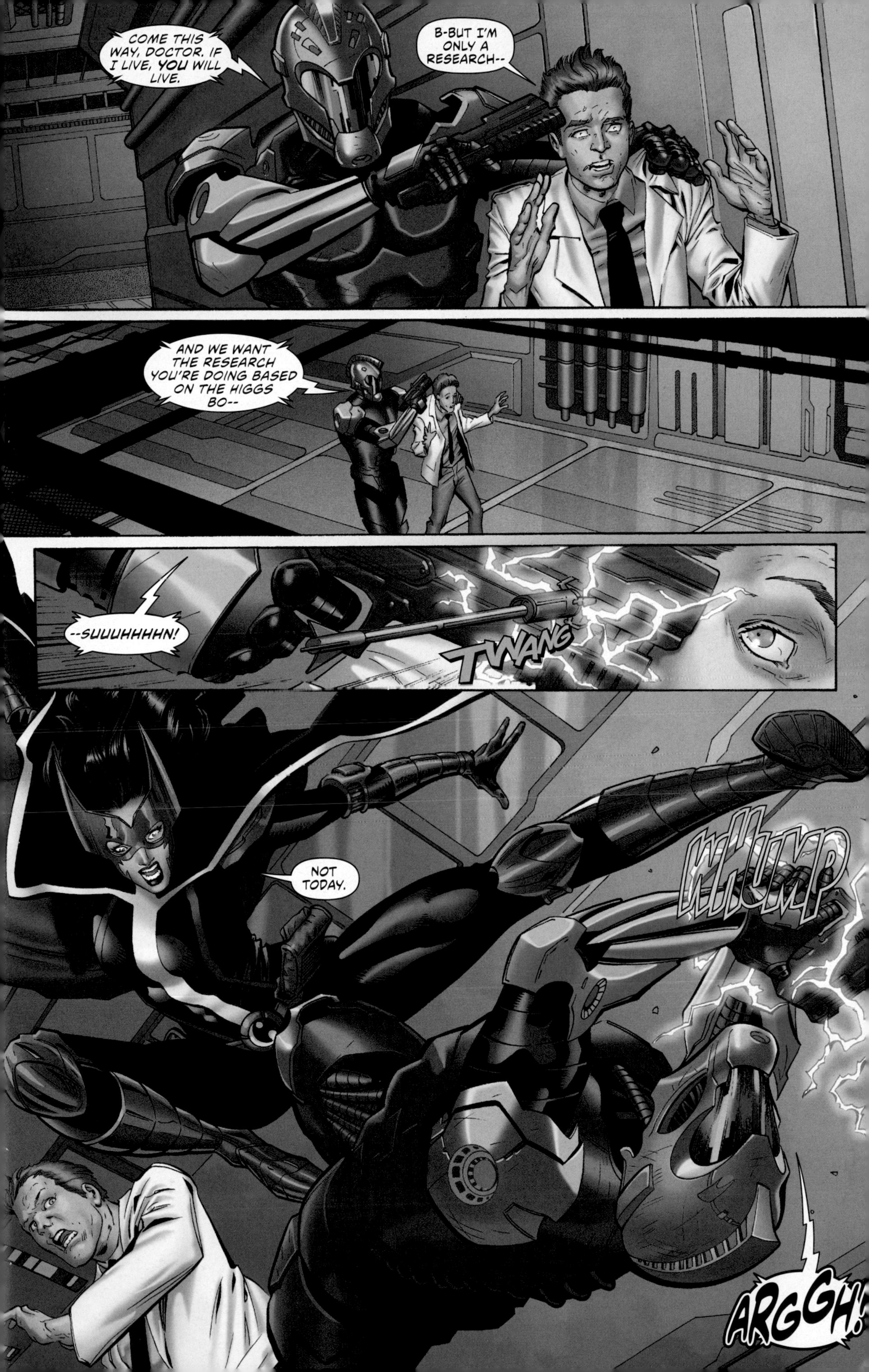
COME THIS WAY, DOCTOR. IF I LIVE, YOU WILL LIVE.
B-BUT I'M ONLY A RESEARCH--
AND WE WANT THE RESEARCH YOU'RE DOING BASED ON THE HIGGS BO--
--SUUUHHHHN!
TWANG
NOT TODAY.
WHUMP
ARGGH!

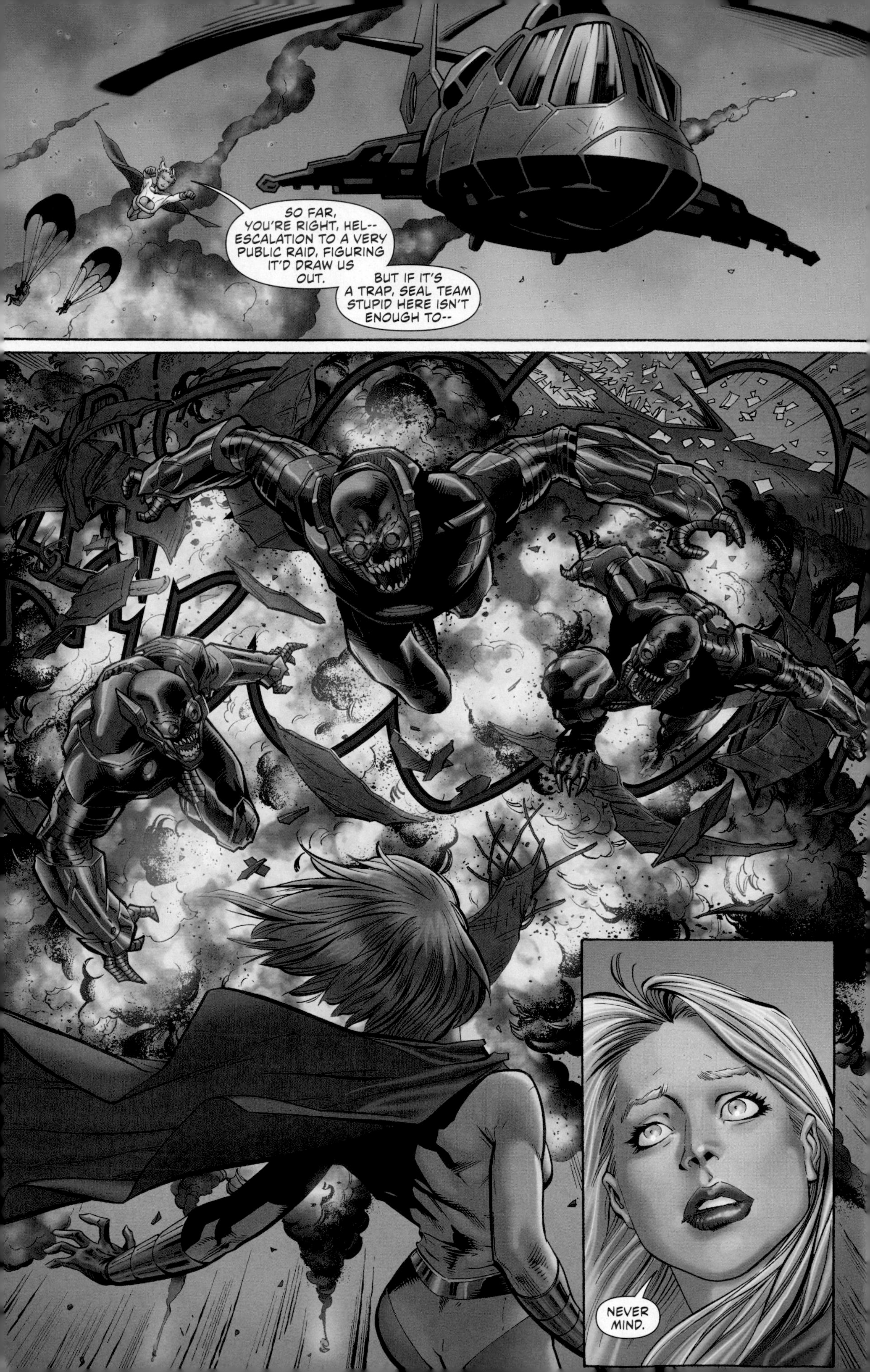
SO FAR, YOU'RE RIGHT, HEL-- ESCALATION TO A VERY PUBLIC RAID, FIGURING IT'D DRAW US OUT.
BUT IF IT'S A TRAP, SEAL TEAM STUPID HERE ISN'T ENOUGH TO--
NEVER MIND.

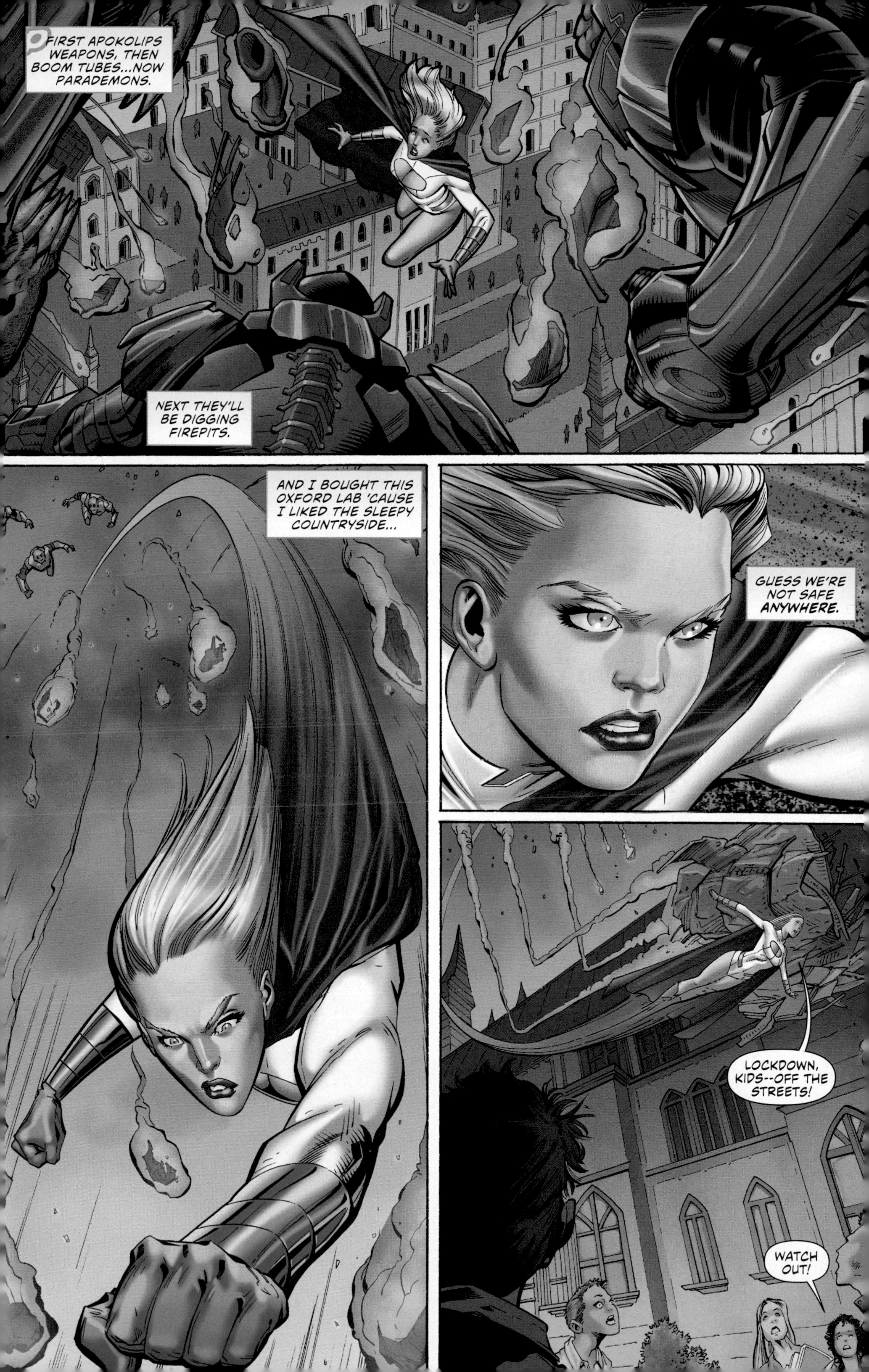
FIRST APOKOLIPS WEAPONS, THEN BOOM TUBES...NOW PARADEMONS.
NEXT THEY'LL BE DIGGING FIREPITS.
AND I BOUGHT THIS OXFORD LAB 'CAUSE I LIKED THE SLEEPY COUNTRYSIDE...
GUESS WE'RE NOT SAFE ANYWHERE.
LOCKDOWN, KIDS--OFF THE STREETS!
WATCH OUT!

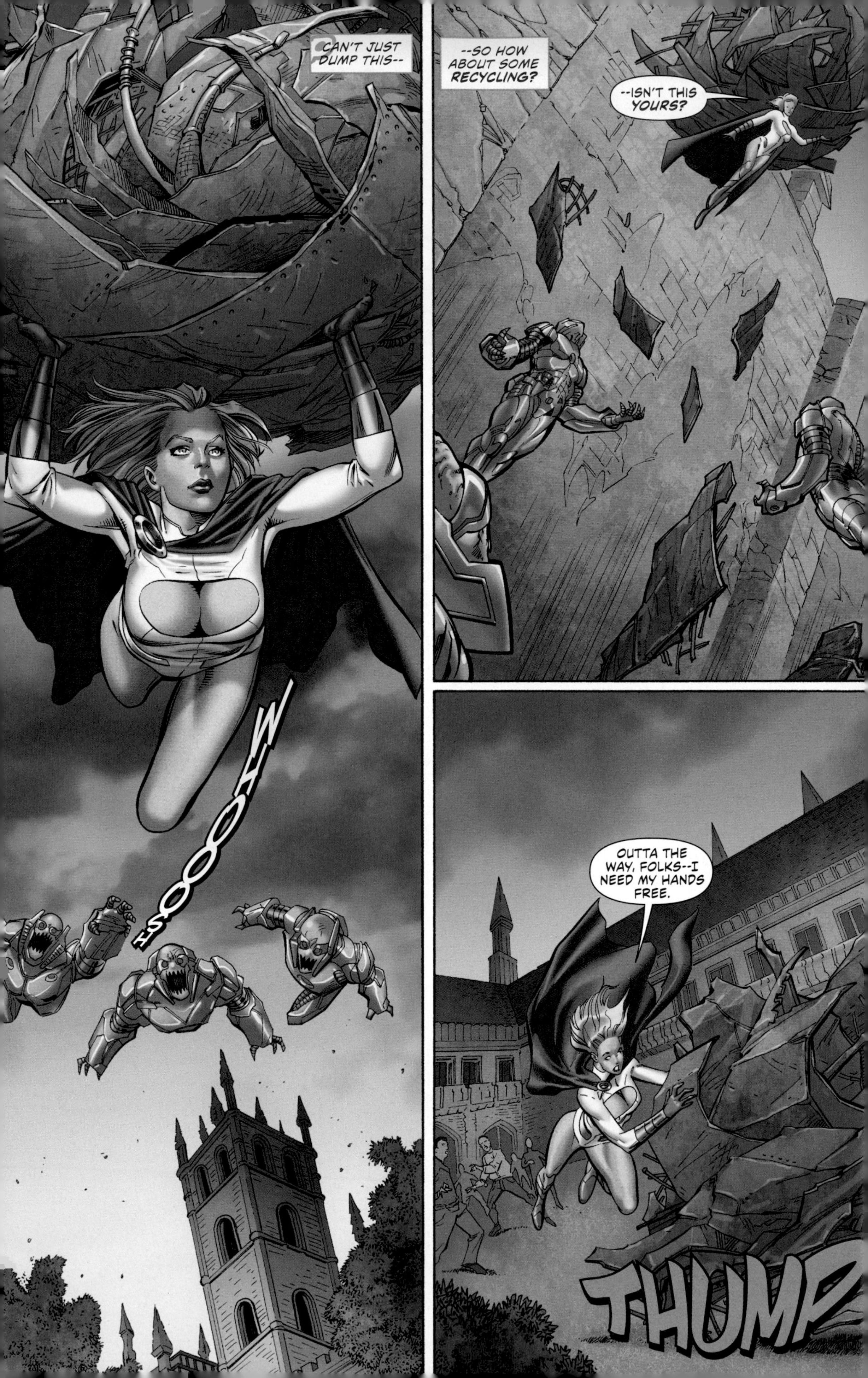
CAN'T JUST DUMP THIS--
WHOOOOOSH
--SO HOW ABOUT SOME RECYCLING?
--ISN'T THIS YOURS?
OUTTA THE WAY, FOLKS--I NEED MY HANDS FREE.
THUMP

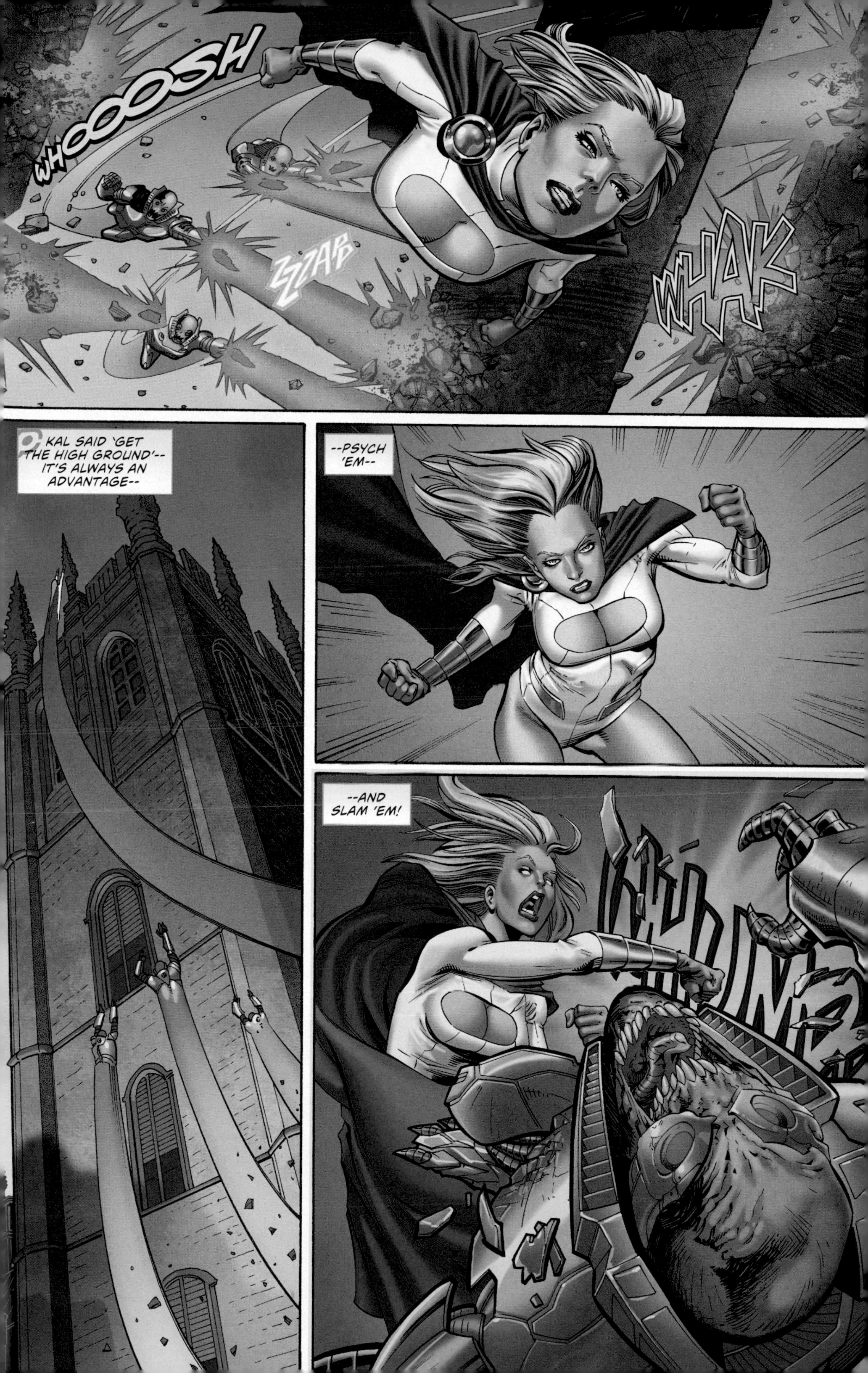
WHOOOOSH
ZZZAP
WHAK
KAL SAID 'GET THE HIGH GROUND'-- IT'S ALWAYS AN ADVANTAGE--
--PSYCH 'EM--
--AND SLAM 'EM!

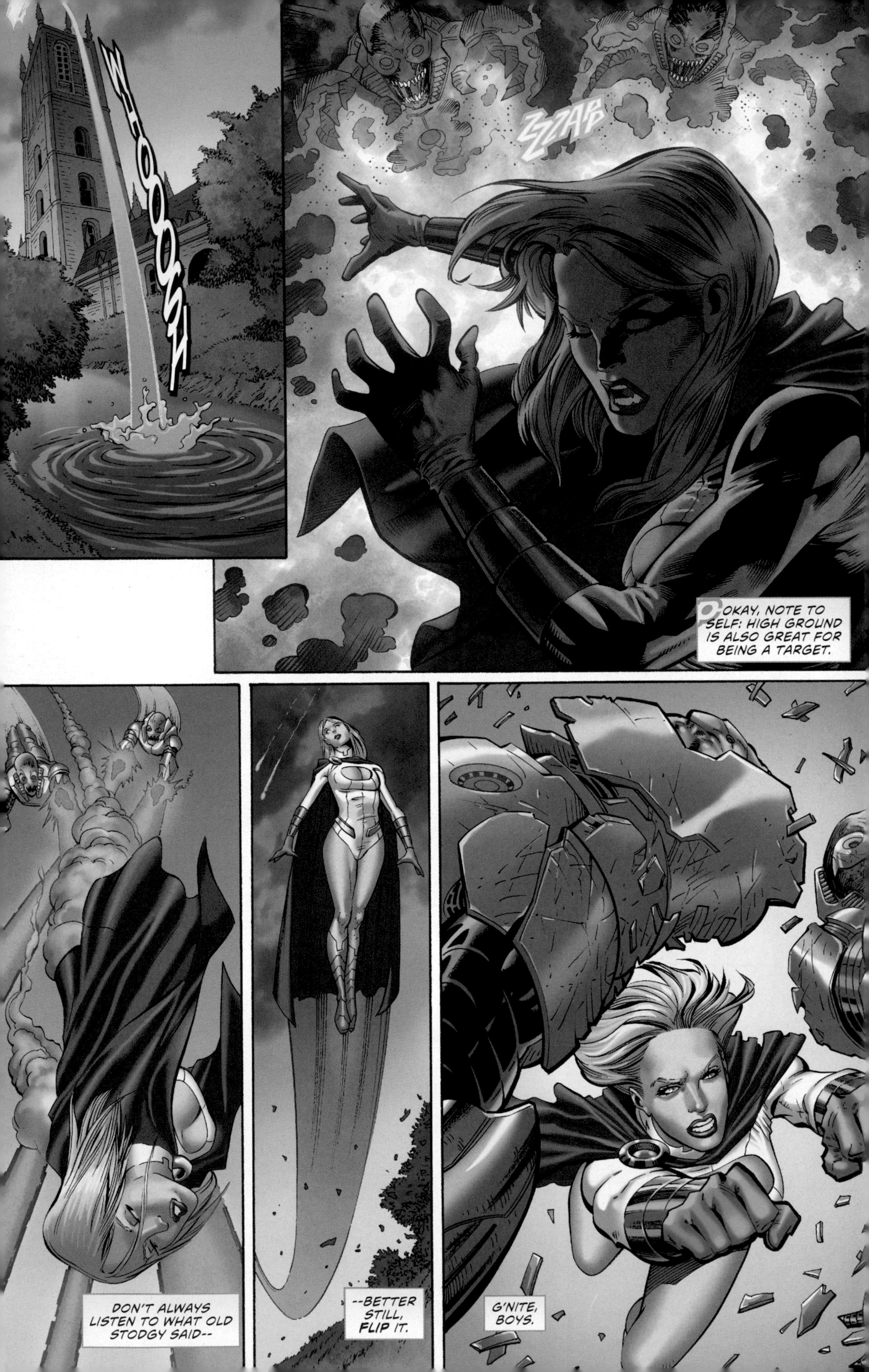
WHOOOOSH
ZZZAPP
OKAY, NOTE TO SELF: HIGH GROUND IS ALSO GREAT FOR BEING A TARGET.
DON'T ALWAYS LISTEN TO WHAT OLD STODGY SAID--
--BETTER STILL, FLIP IT.
G'NITE, BOYS.

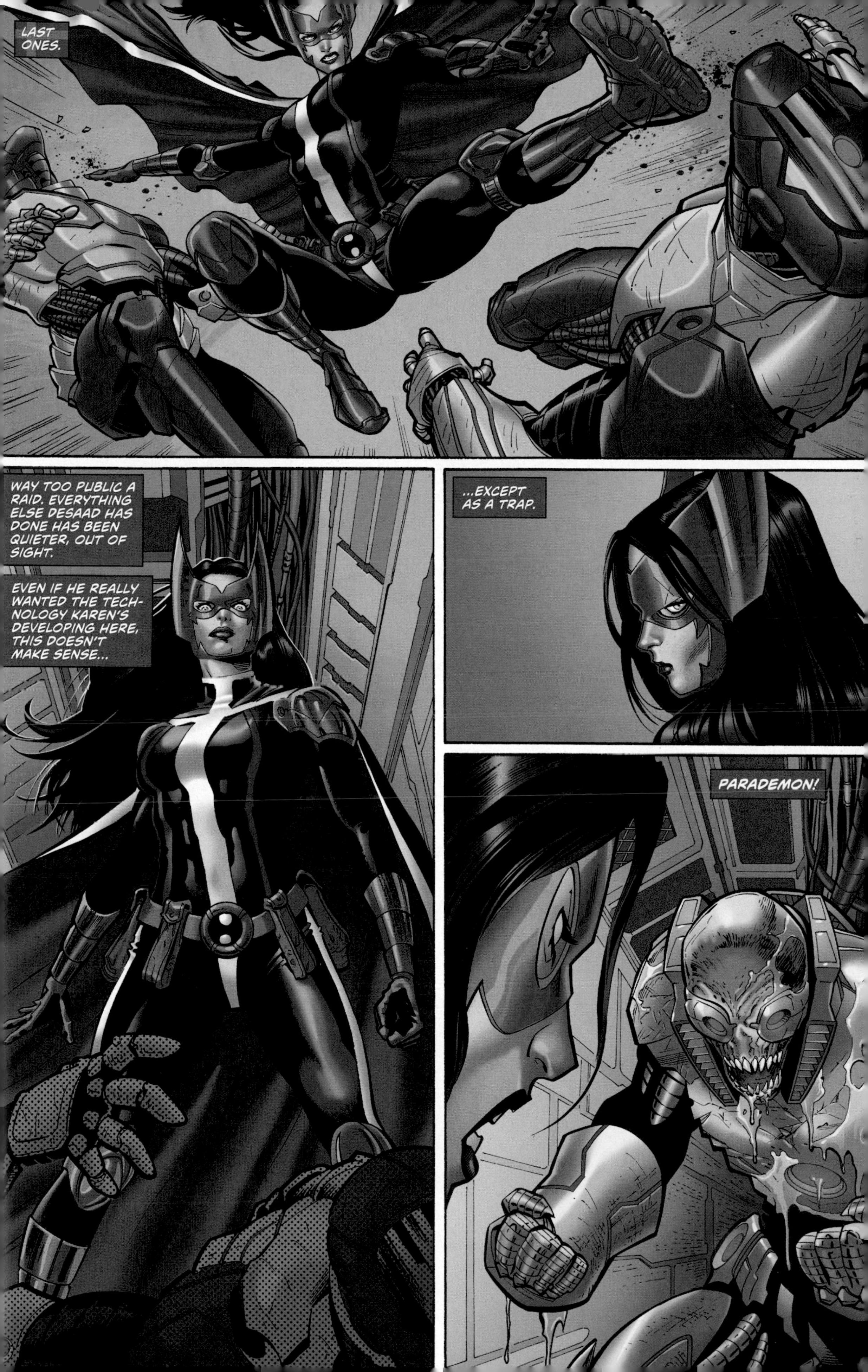
LAST ONES.
WAY TOO PUBLIC A RAID. EVERYTHING ELSE DESAAD HAS DONE HAS BEEN QUIETER, OUT OF SIGHT.
EVEN IF HE REALLY WANTED THE TECH-NOLOGY KAREN'S DEVELOPING HERE, THIS DOESN'T MAKE SENSE...
...EXCEPT AS A TRAP.
PARADEMON!

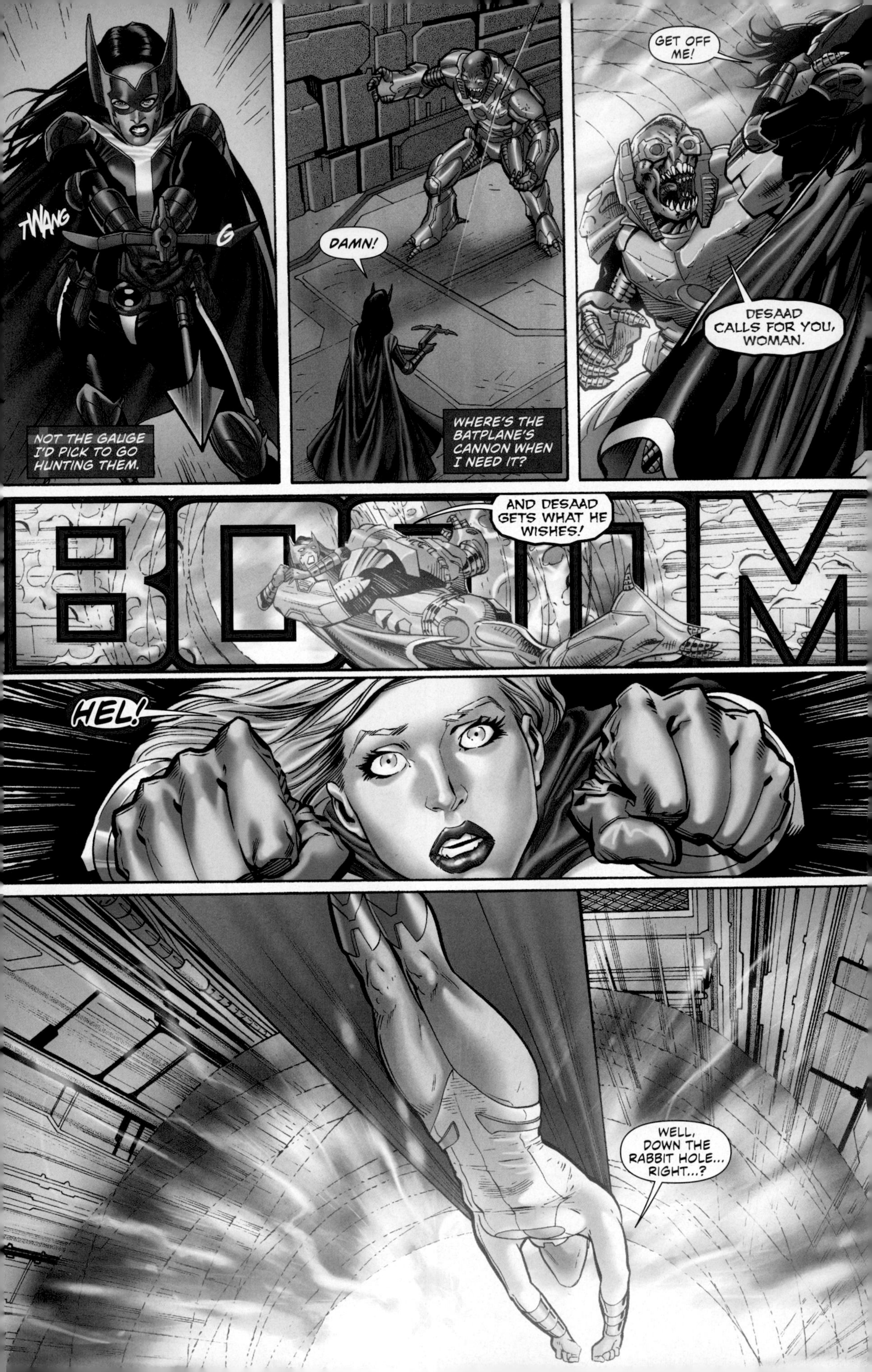
TWANG
G
NOT THE GAUGE I'D PICK TO GO HUNTING THEM.
DAMN!
WHERE'S THE BATPLANE'S CANNON WHEN I NEED IT?
GET OFF ME!
DESAAD CALLS FOR YOU, WOMAN.
BOOOM
AND DESAAD GETS WHAT HE WISHES!
HEL!
WELL, DOWN THE RABBIT HOLE... RIGHT...?

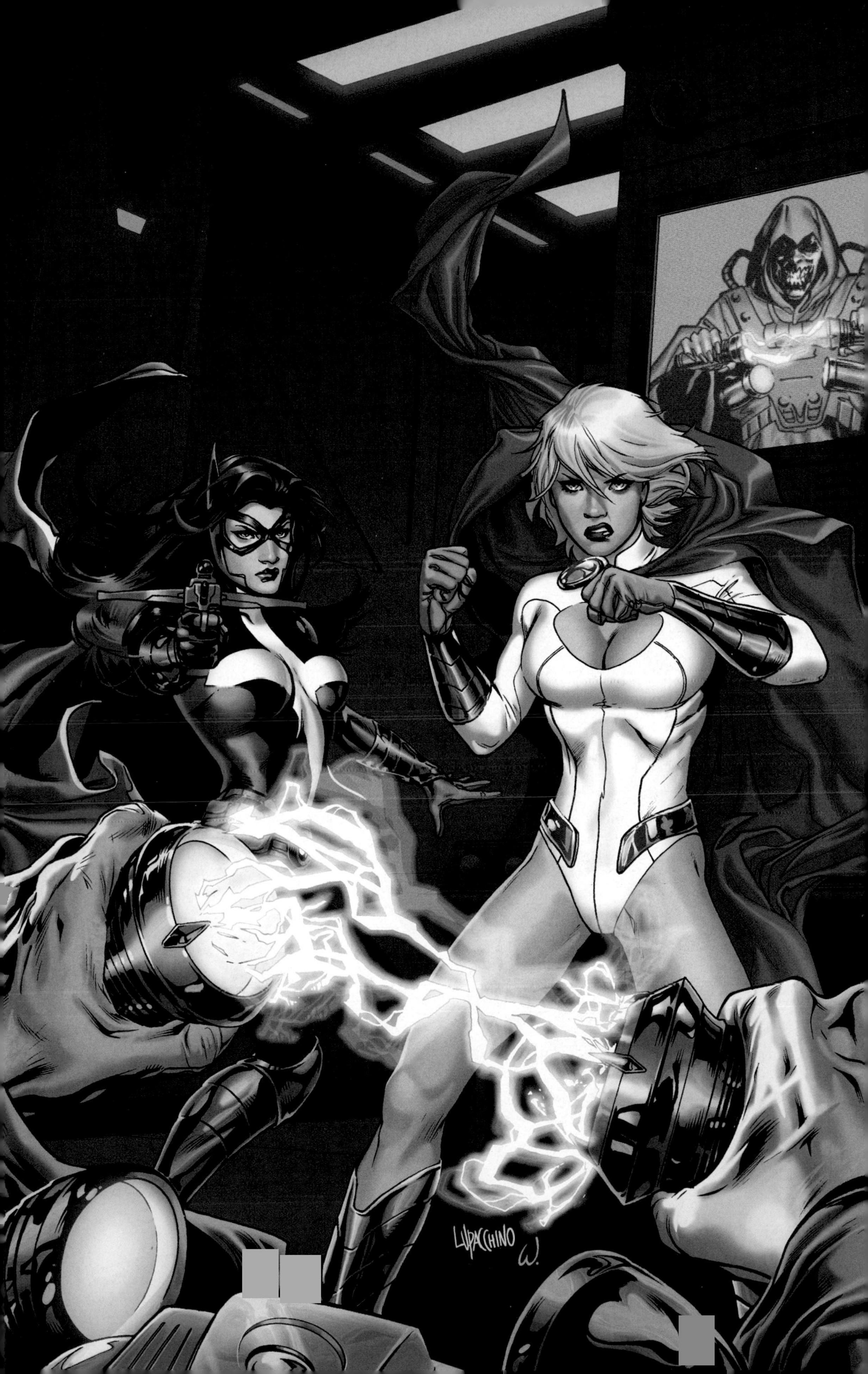
LUPACCHINO
W.

DOWN THE RABBIT HOLE

EMANUELA LUPACCHINO penciller **GUILLERMO ORTEGO** inker

cover art by **EMANUELA LUPACCHINO** with **JASON WRIGHT**

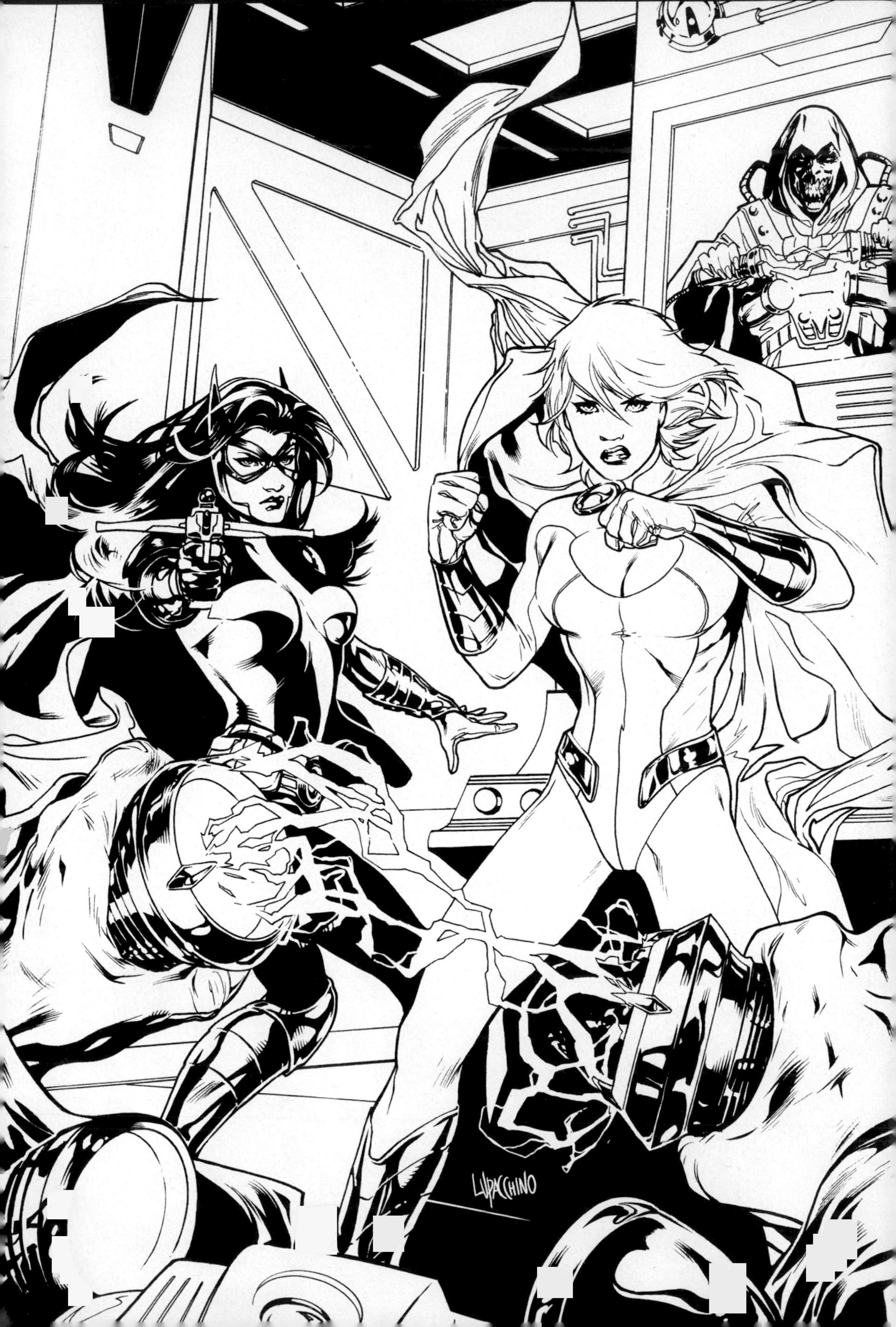
LUPACCHINO

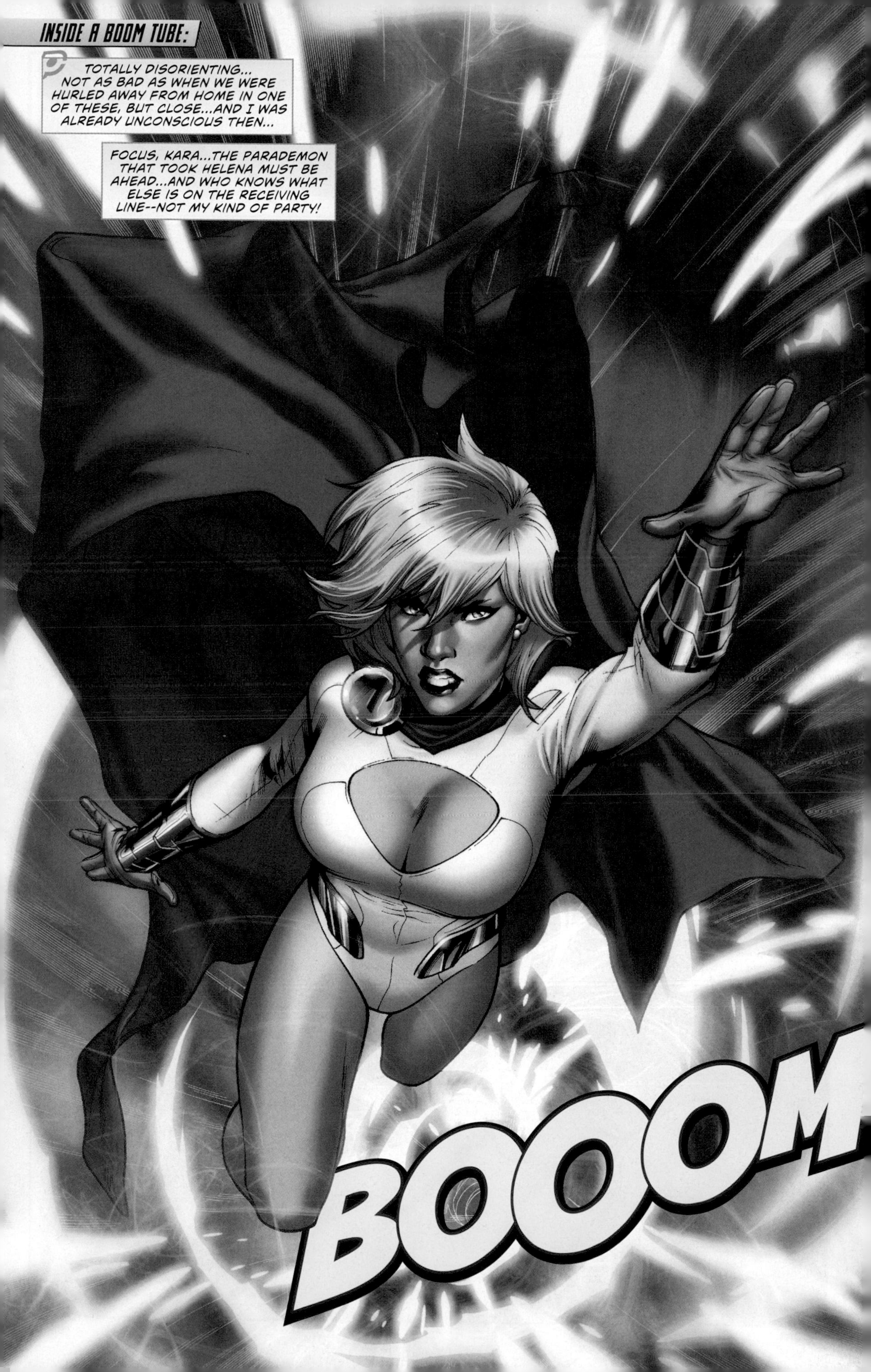
INSIDE A BOOM TUBE:
TOTALLY DISORIENTING... NOT AS BAD AS WHEN WE WERE HURLED AWAY FROM HOME IN ONE OF THESE, BUT CLOSE...AND I WAS ALREADY UNCONSCIOUS THEN...
FOCUS, KARA...THE PARADEMON THAT TOOK HELENA MUST BE AHEAD...AND WHO KNOWS WHAT ELSE IS ON THE RECEIVING LINE--NOT MY KIND OF PARTY!
BOOOM

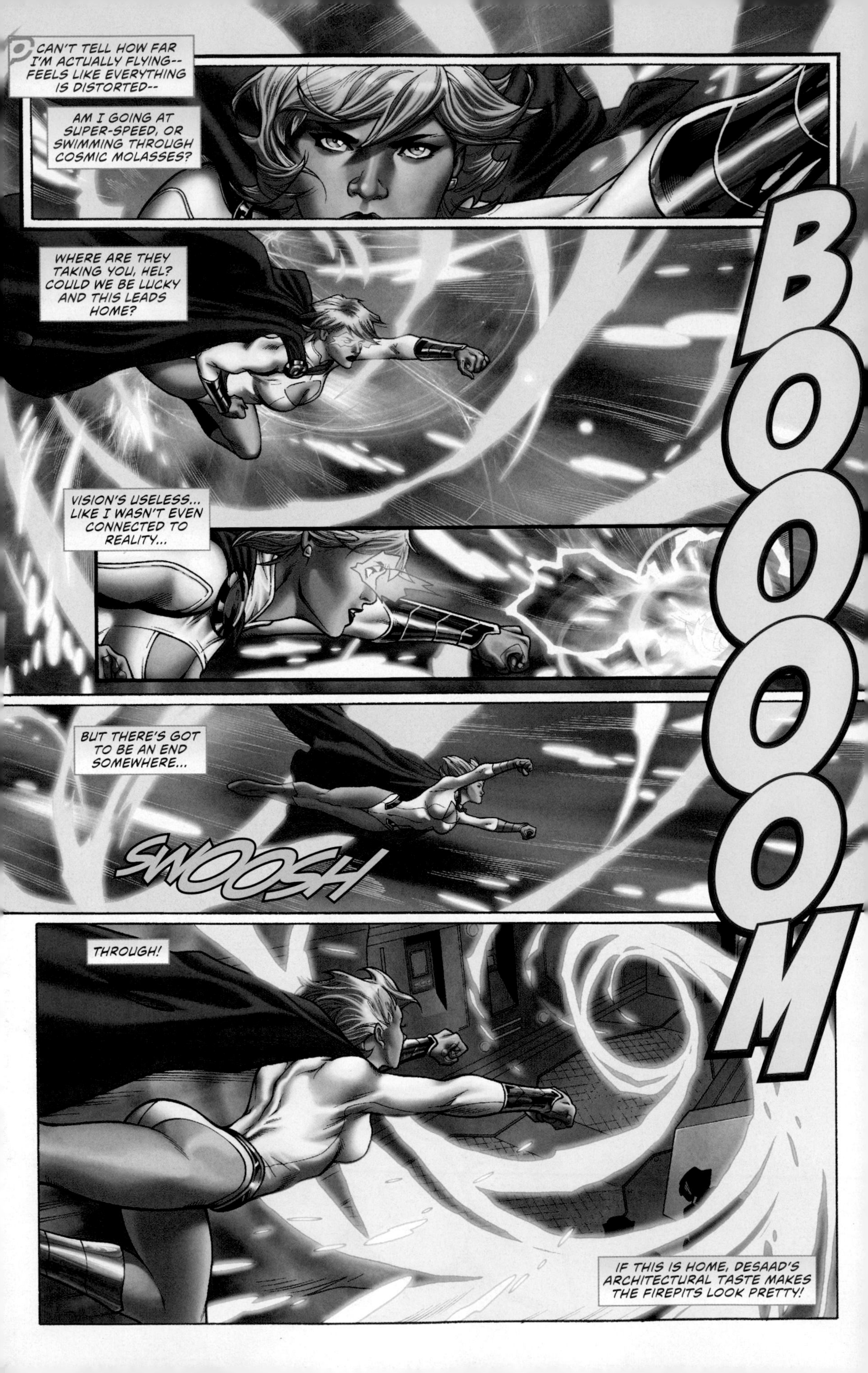
CAN'T TELL HOW FAR I'M ACTUALLY FLYING-- FEELS LIKE EVERYTHING IS DISTORTED--
AM I GOING AT SUPER-SPEED, OR SWIMMING THROUGH COSMIC MOLASSES?
WHERE ARE THEY TAKING YOU, HEL? COULD WE BE LUCKY AND THIS LEADS HOME?
VISION'S USELESS... LIKE I WASN'T EVEN CONNECTED TO REALITY...
BUT THERE'S GOT TO BE AN END SOMEWHERE...
SWOOSH
BOOOOOM
THROUGH!
IF THIS IS HOME, DESAAD'S ARCHITECTURAL TASTE MAKES THE FIREPITS LOOK PRETTY!

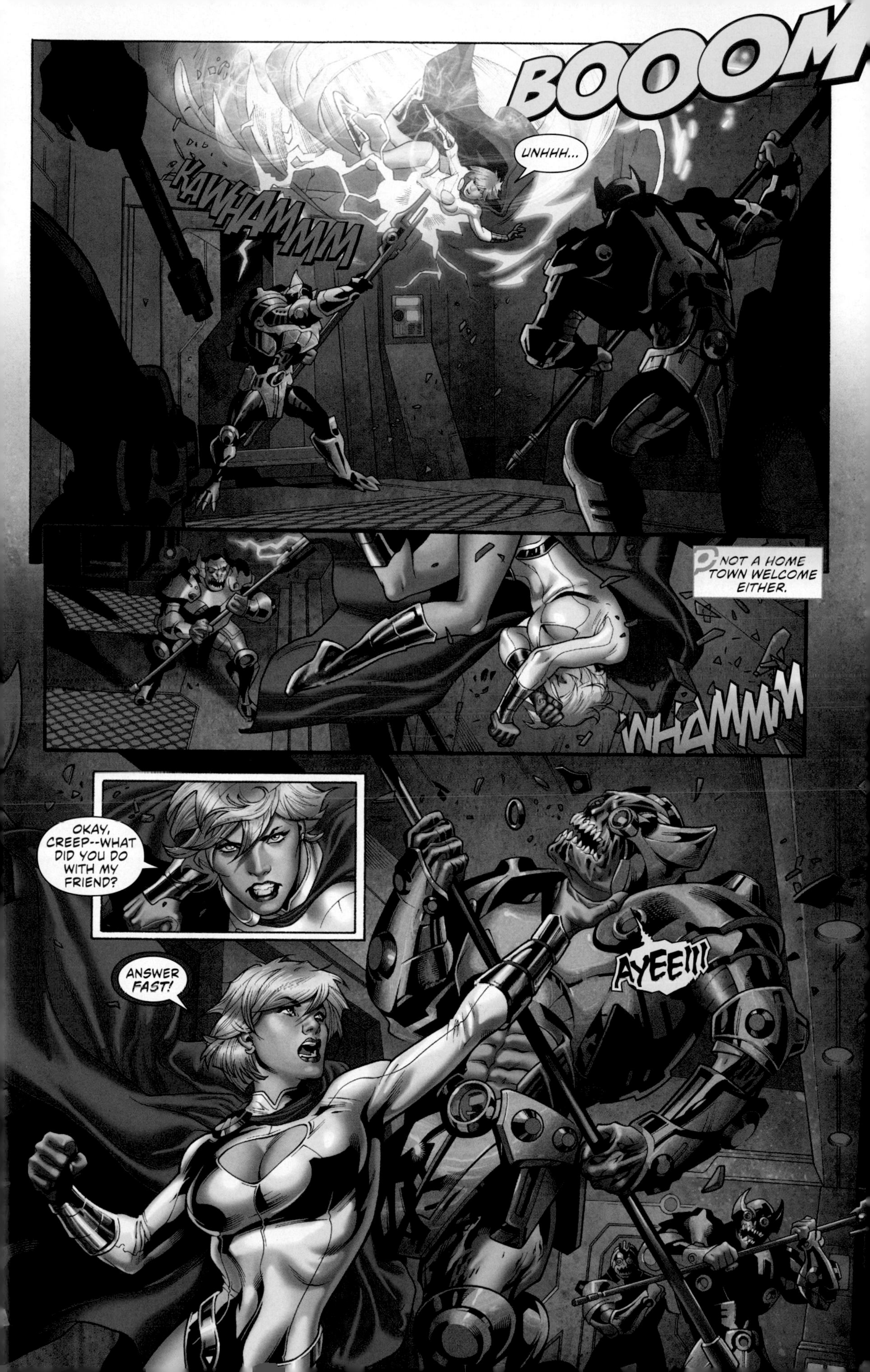
BOOOOM
KAWHAMMM
UNHHH...
NOT A HOME TOWN WELCOME EITHER.
WHAMMM
OKAY, CREEP--WHAT DID YOU DO WITH MY FRIEND?
ANSWER FAST!
AYEE!!!

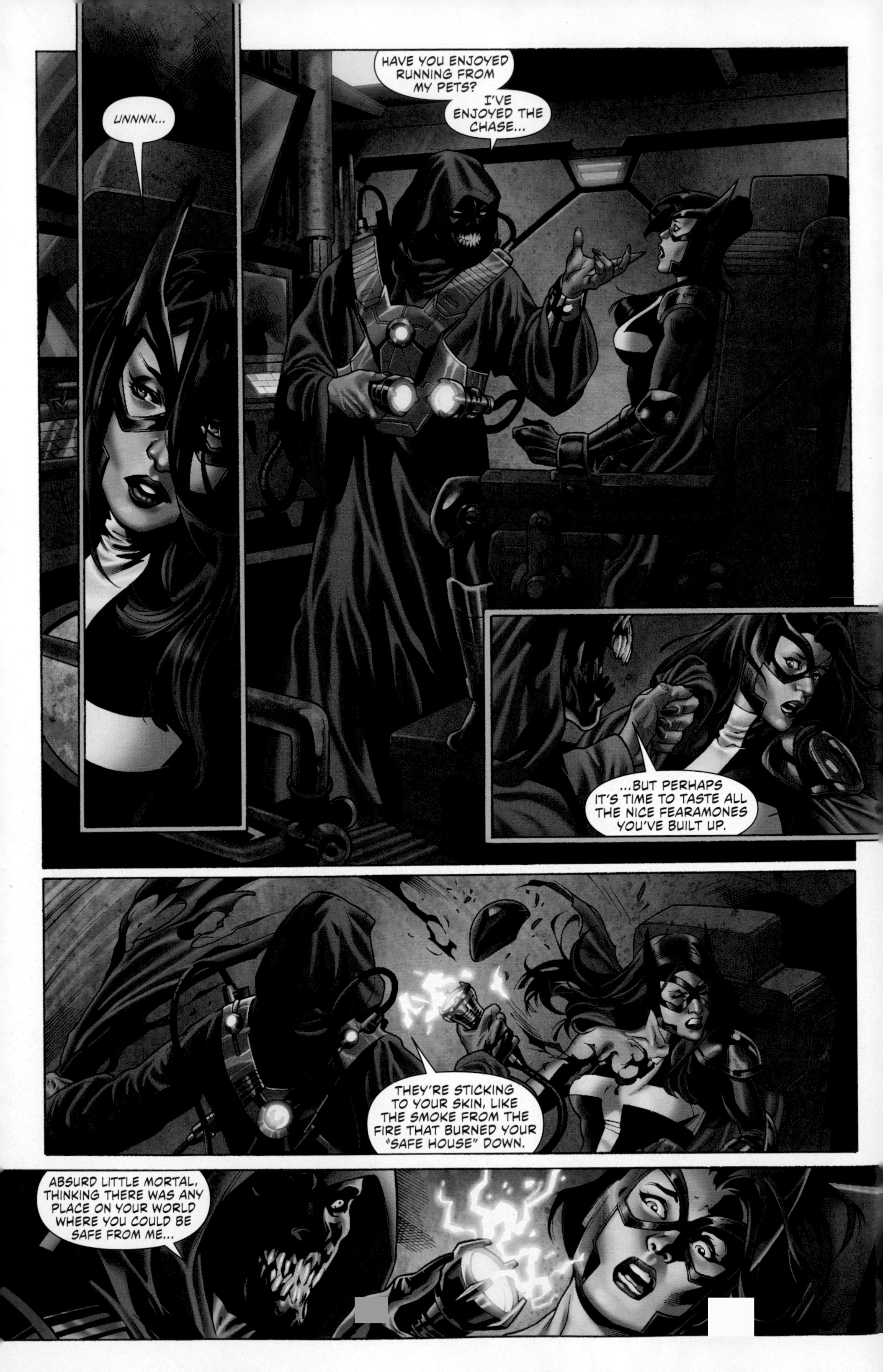
UNNNN...
HAVE YOU ENJOYED RUNNING FROM MY PETS?
I'VE ENJOYED THE CHASE...
...BUT PERHAPS IT'S TIME TO TASTE ALL THE NICE FEARAMONES YOU'VE BUILT UP.
THEY'RE STICKING TO YOUR SKIN, LIKE THE SMOKE FROM THE FIRE THAT BURNED YOUR "SAFE HOUSE" DOWN.
ABSURD LITTLE MORTAL, THINKING THERE WAS ANY PLACE ON YOUR WORLD WHERE YOU COULD BE SAFE FROM ME...

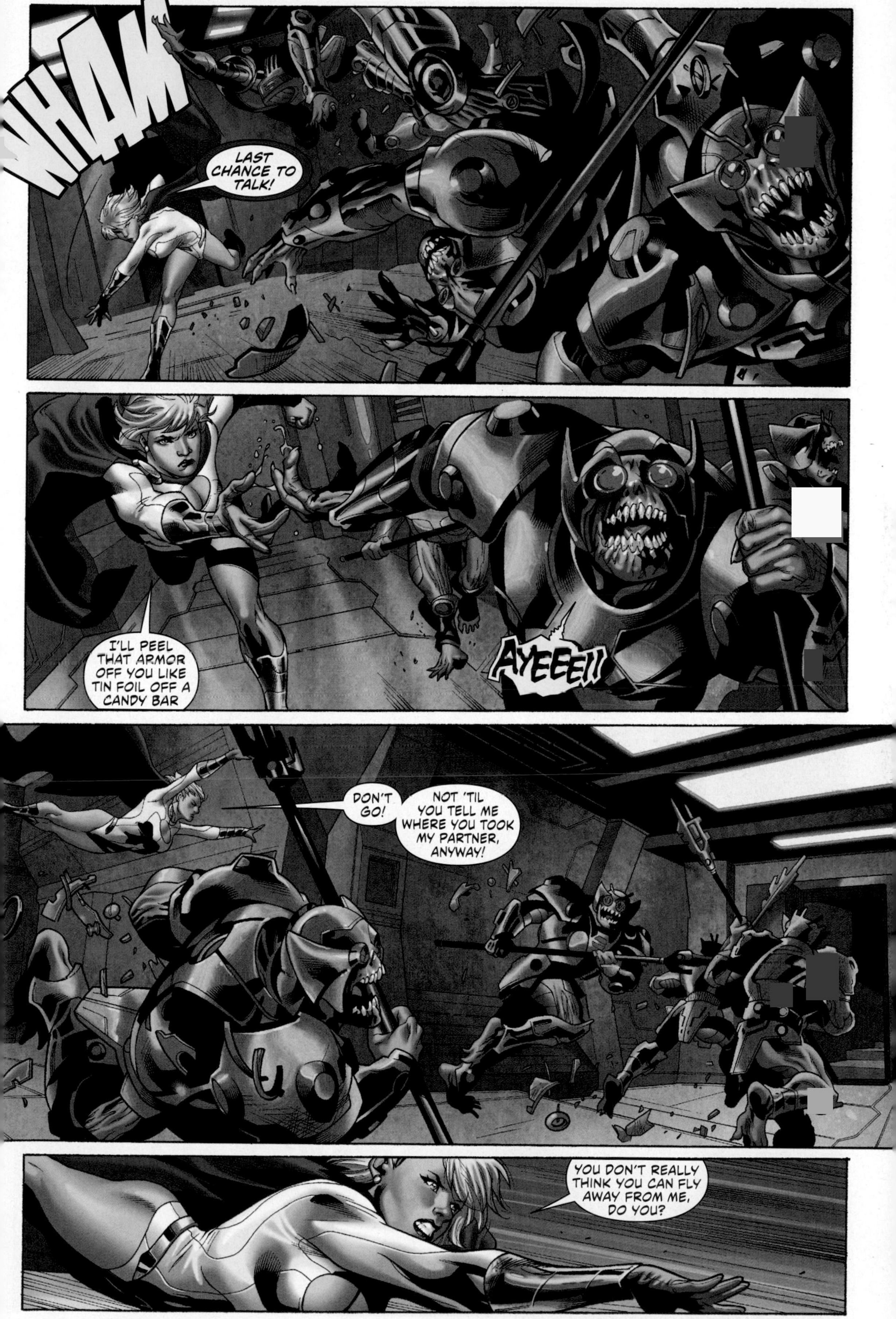
WHAM
LAST CHANCE TO TALK!
I'LL PEEL THAT ARMOR OFF YOU LIKE TIN FOIL OFF A CANDY BAR
AYEEE!!
DON'T GO!
NOT 'TIL YOU TELL ME WHERE YOU TOOK MY PARTNER, ANYWAY!
YOU DON'T REALLY THINK YOU CAN FLY AWAY FROM ME, DO YOU?

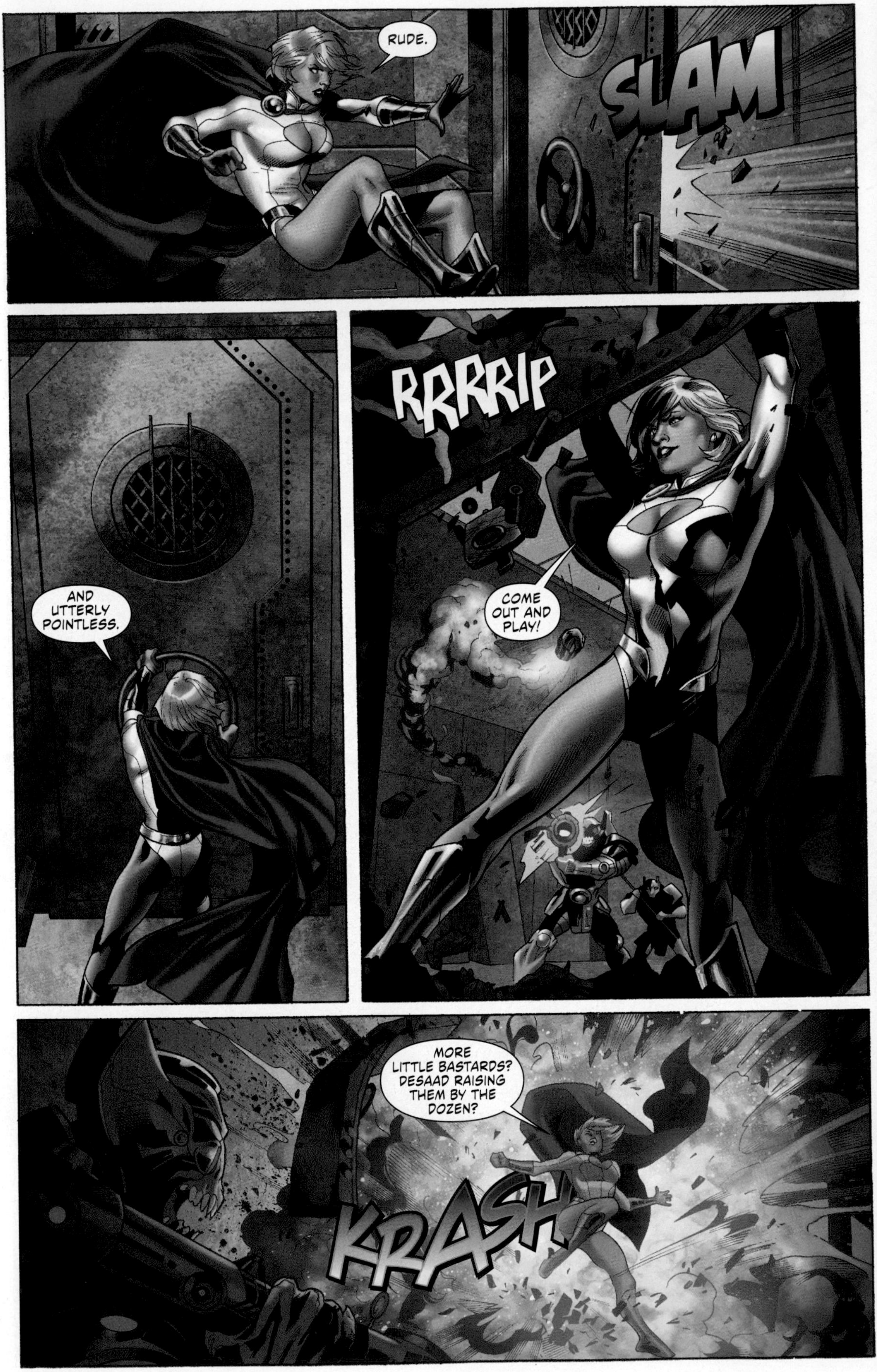
RUDE.
SLAM
AND UTTERLY POINTLESS.
RRRRIP
COME OUT AND PLAY!
MORE LITTLE BASTARDS? DESAAD RAISING THEM BY THE DOZEN?
KRASH

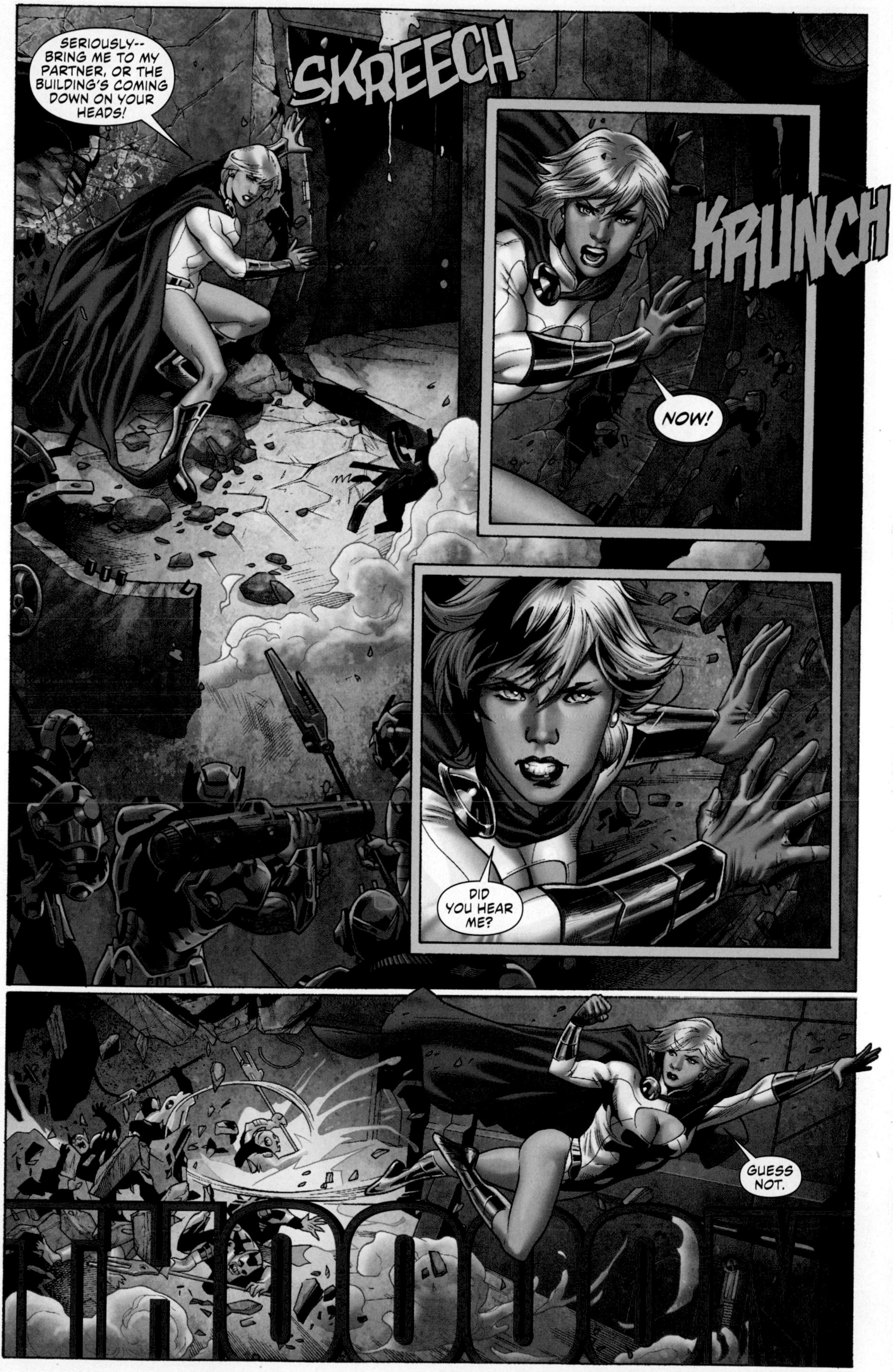
SERIOUSLY-- BRING ME TO MY PARTNER, OR THE BUILDING'S COMING DOWN ON YOUR HEADS!
SKREECH
KRUNCH
NOW!
DID YOU HEAR ME?
GUESS NOT.

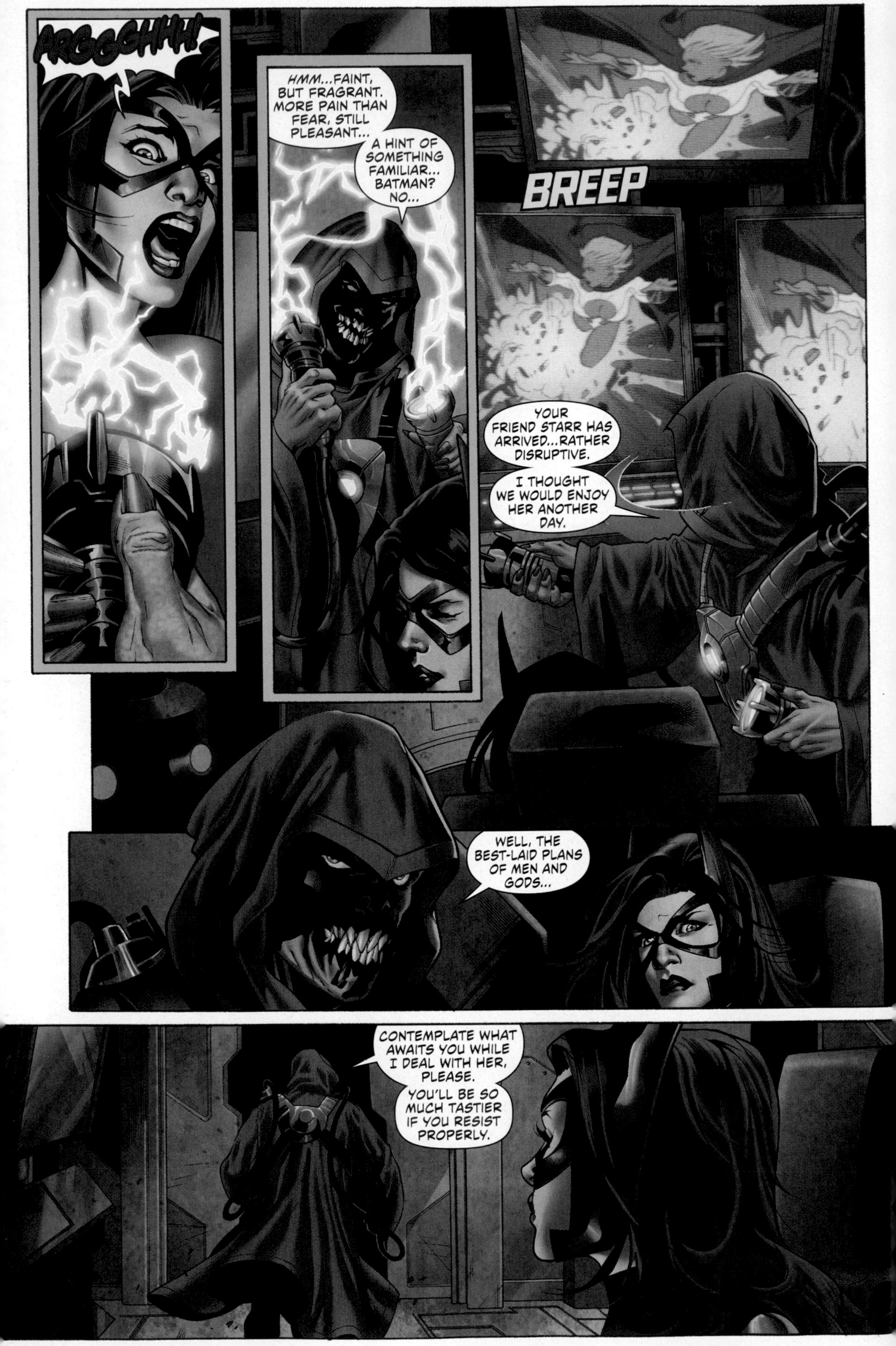
ARGGGHHH!
HMM...FAINT, BUT FRAGRANT. MORE PAIN THAN FEAR, STILL PLEASANT...
A HINT OF SOMETHING FAMILIAR... BATMAN? NO...
BREEP
YOUR FRIEND STARR HAS ARRIVED...RATHER DISRUPTIVE.
I THOUGHT WE WOULD ENJOY HER ANOTHER DAY.
WELL, THE BEST-LAID PLANS OF MEN AND GODS...
CONTEMPLATE WHAT AWAITS YOU WHILE I DEAL WITH HER, PLEASE.
YOU'LL BE SO MUCH TASTIER IF YOU RESIST PROPERLY.

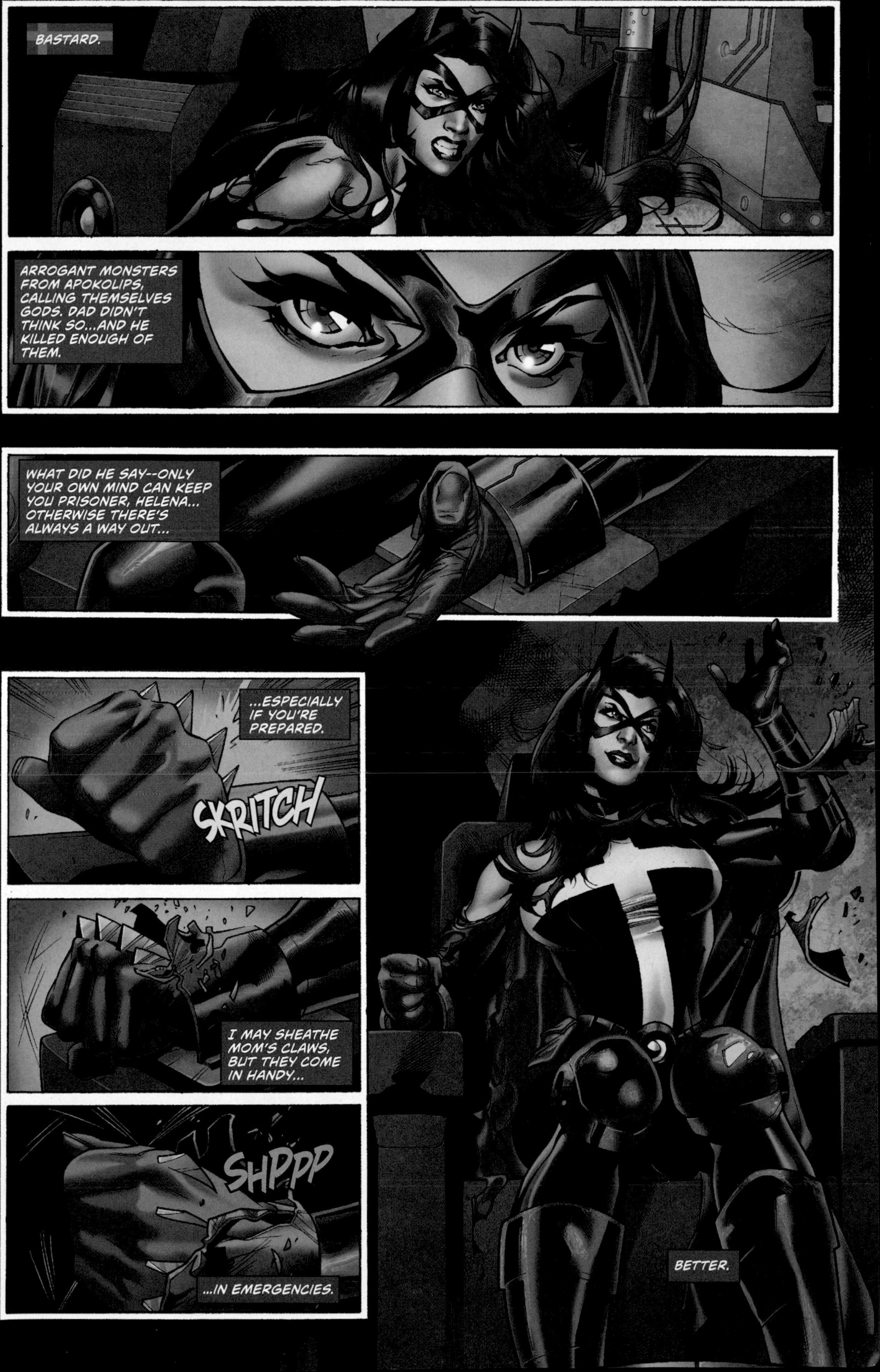
BASTARD.
ARROGANT MONSTERS FROM APOKOLIPS, CALLING THEMSELVES GODS. DAD DIDN'T THINK SO...AND HE KILLED ENOUGH OF THEM.
WHAT DID HE SAY--ONLY YOUR OWN MIND CAN KEEP YOU PRISONER, HELENA... OTHERWISE THERE'S ALWAYS A WAY OUT...
...ESPECIALLY IF YOU'RE PREPARED.
SKRITCH
I MAY SHEATHE MOM'S CLAWS, BUT THEY COME IN HANDY...
SHPPP
...IN EMERGENCIES.
BETTER.

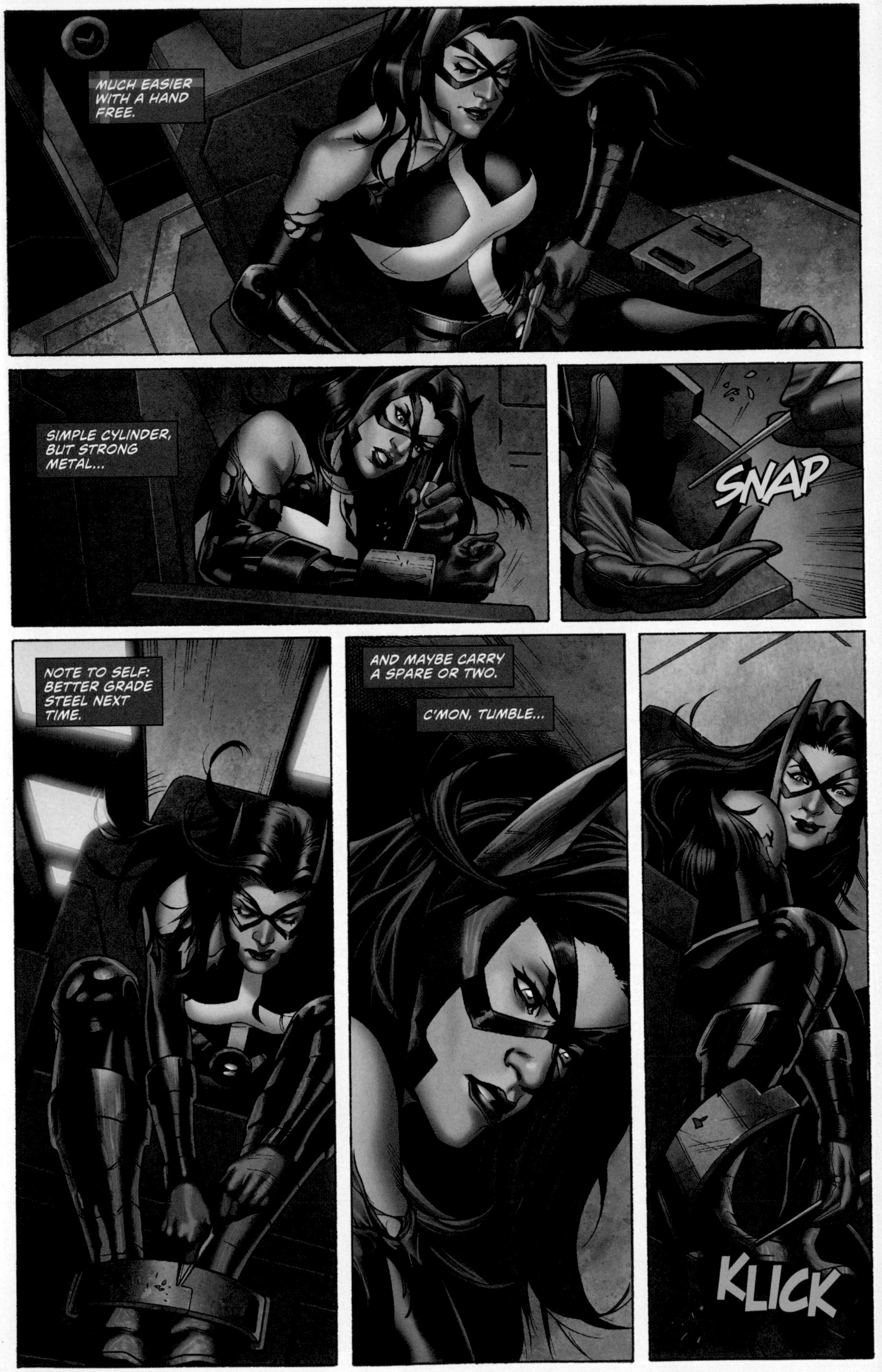
MUCH EASIER WITH A HAND FREE.
SIMPLE CYLINDER, BUT STRONG METAL...
SNAP
NOTE TO SELF: BETTER GRADE STEEL NEXT TIME.
AND MAYBE CARRY A SPARE OR TWO.
C'MON, TUMBLE...
KLICK

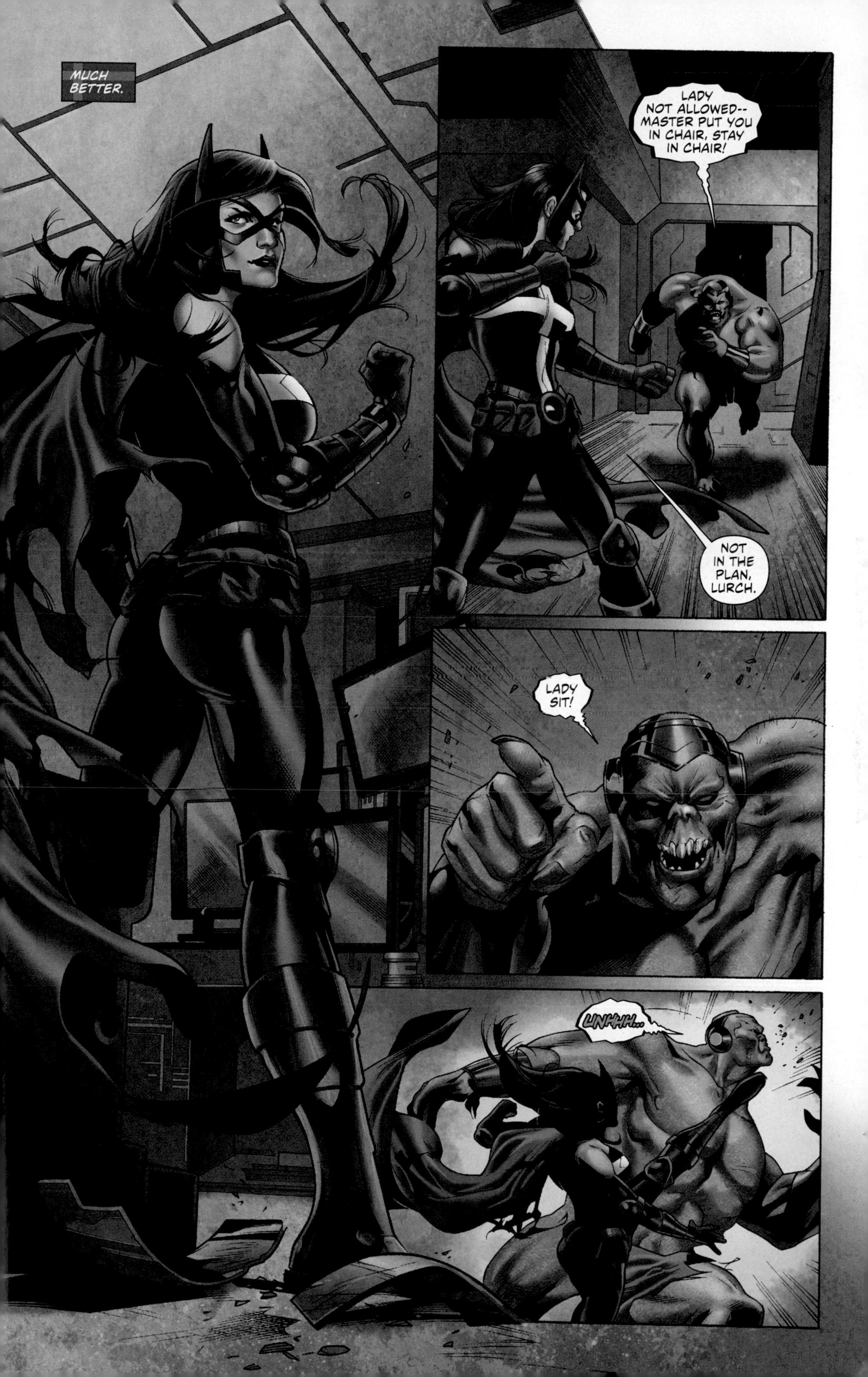
MUCH BETTER.
LADY NOT ALLOWED--MASTER PUT YOU IN CHAIR, STAY IN CHAIR!
NOT IN THE PLAN, LURCH.
LADY SIT!
UNHHH...

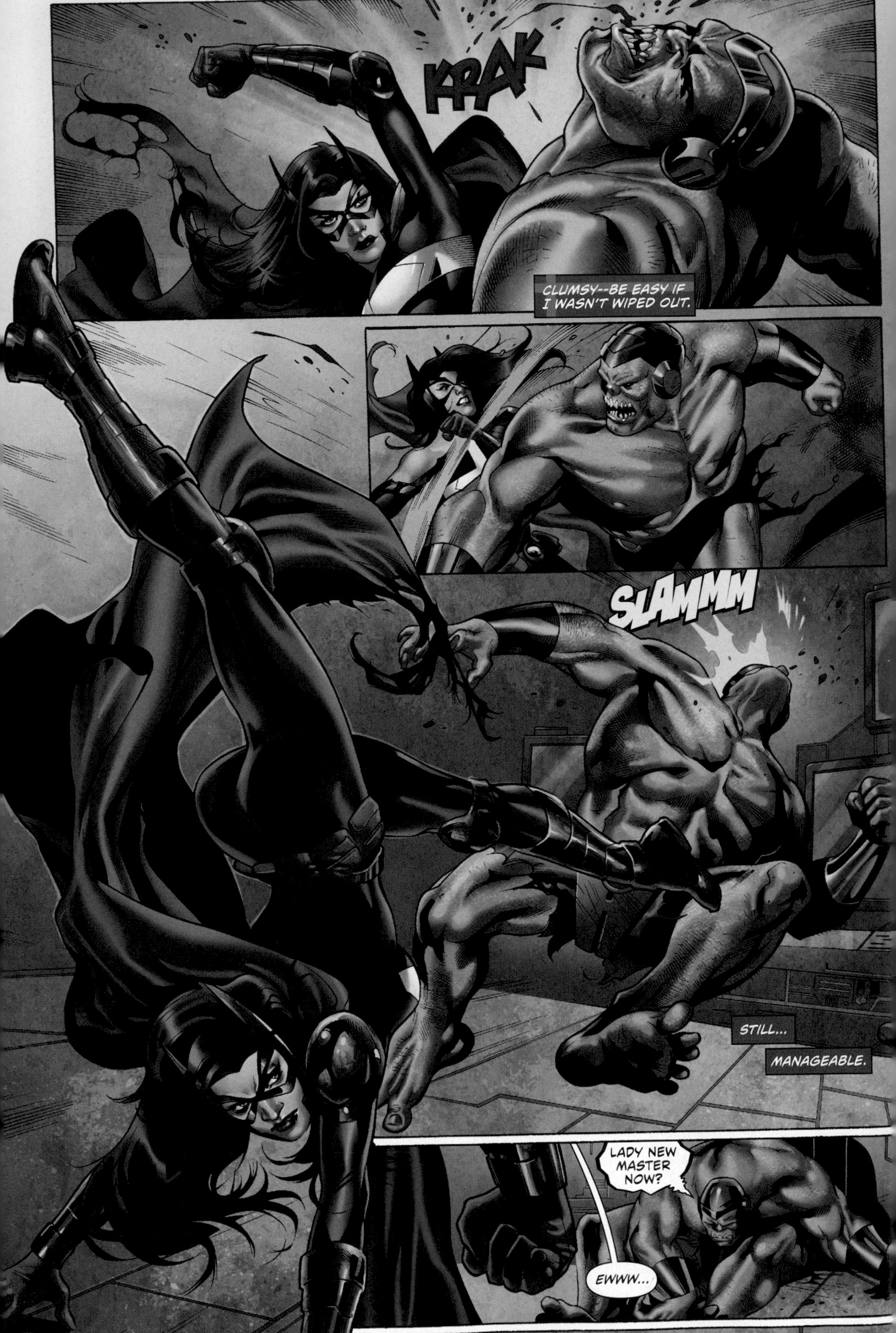
KRAK
CLUMSY--BE EASY IF I WASN'T WIPED OUT.
SLAMMM
STILL...
MANAGEABLE.
LADY NEW MASTER NOW?
EWWW...

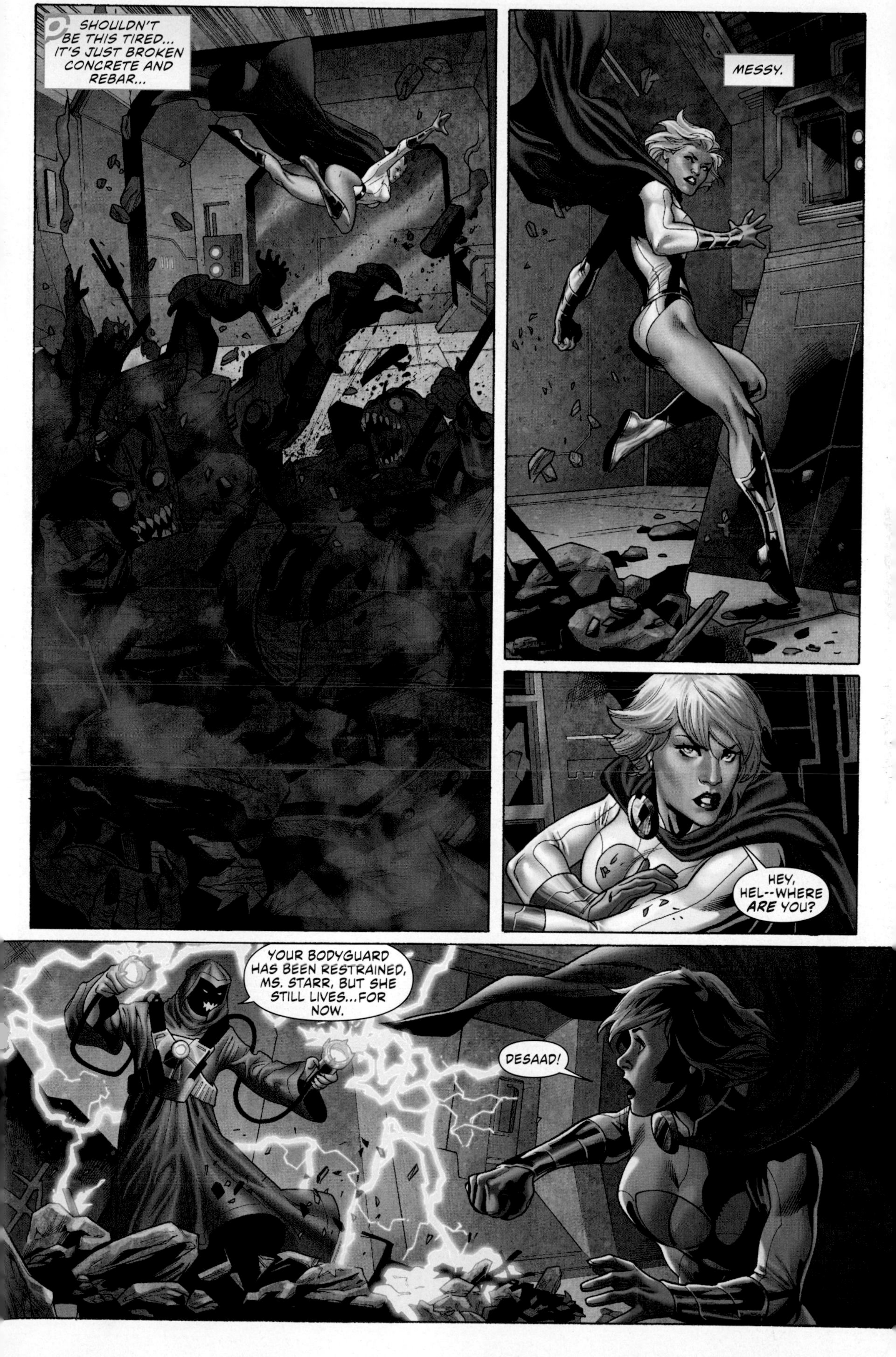
SHOULDN'T BE THIS TIRED... IT'S JUST BROKEN CONCRETE AND REBAR...
MESSY.
HEY, HEL--WHERE *ARE* YOU?
YOUR BODYGUARD HAS BEEN RESTRAINED, MS. STARR, BUT SHE STILL LIVES...FOR NOW.
DESAAD!

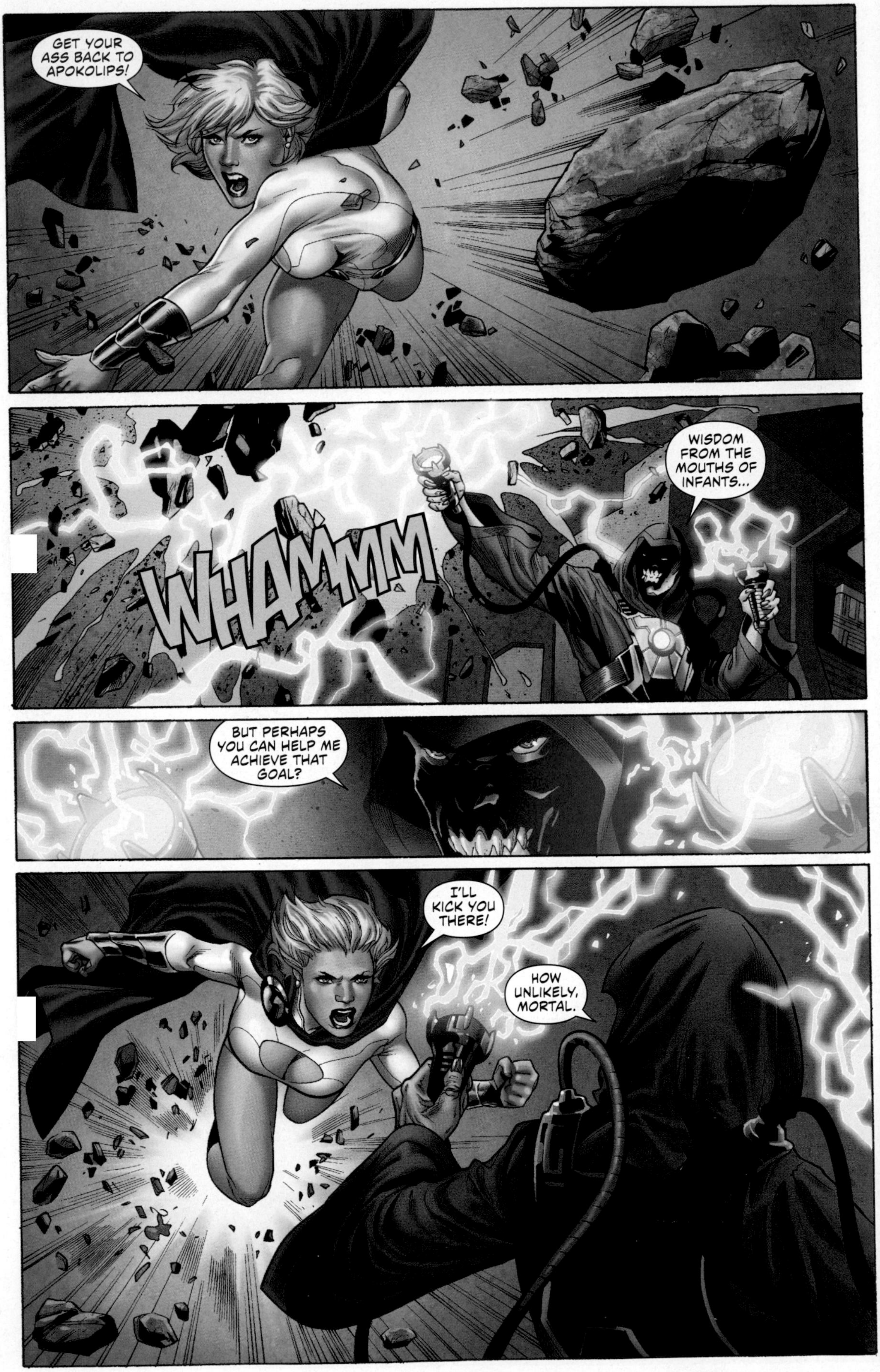
GET YOUR ASS BACK TO APOKOLIPS!
WHAMMMM
WISDOM FROM THE MOUTHS OF INFANTS...
BUT PERHAPS YOU CAN HELP ME ACHIEVE THAT GOAL?
I'LL KICK YOU THERE!
HOW UNLIKELY, MORTAL.

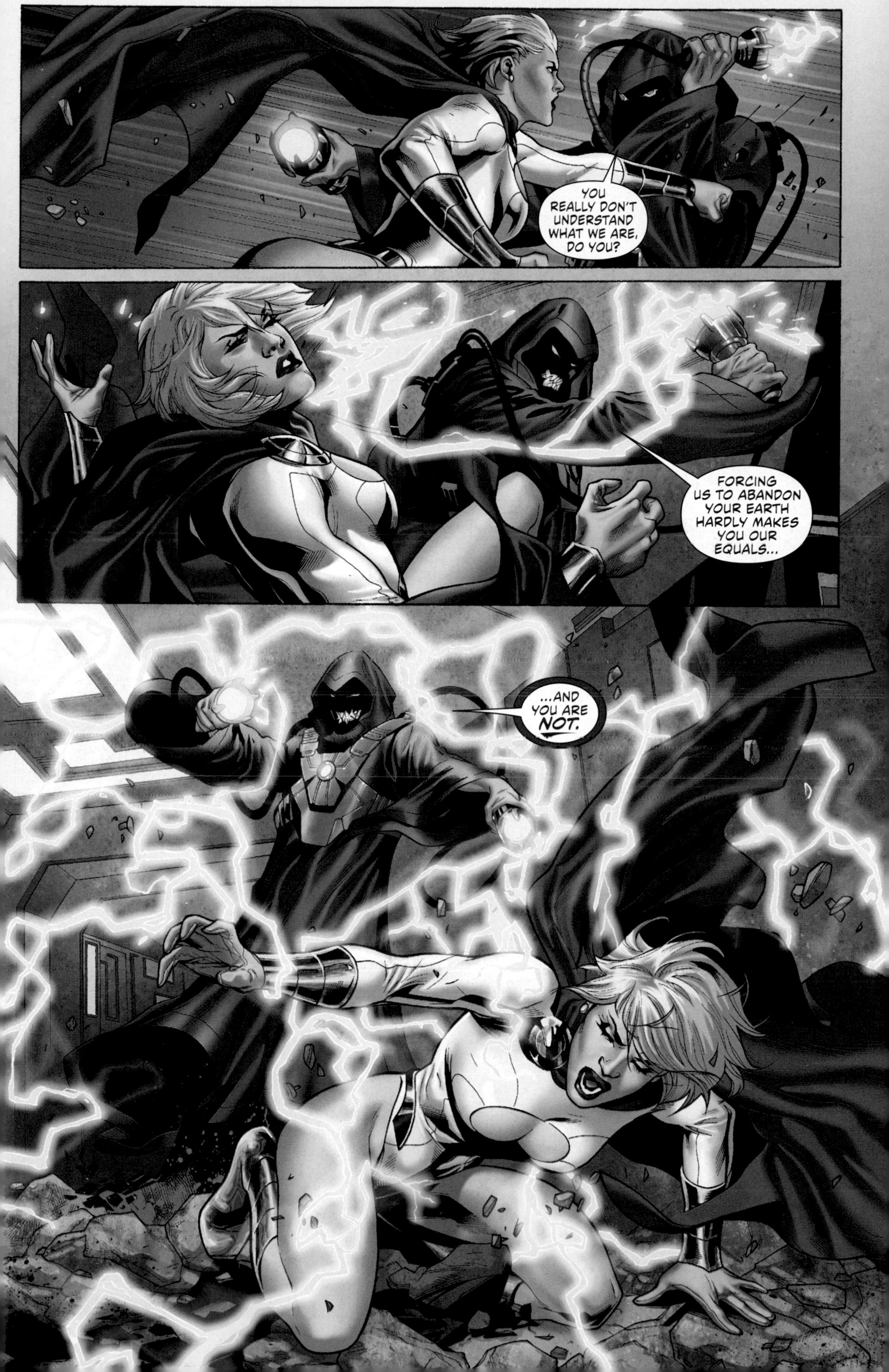
YOU REALLY DON'T UNDERSTAND WHAT WE ARE, DO YOU?
FORCING US TO ABANDON YOUR EARTH HARDLY MAKES YOU OUR EQUALS...
...AND YOU ARE NOT.

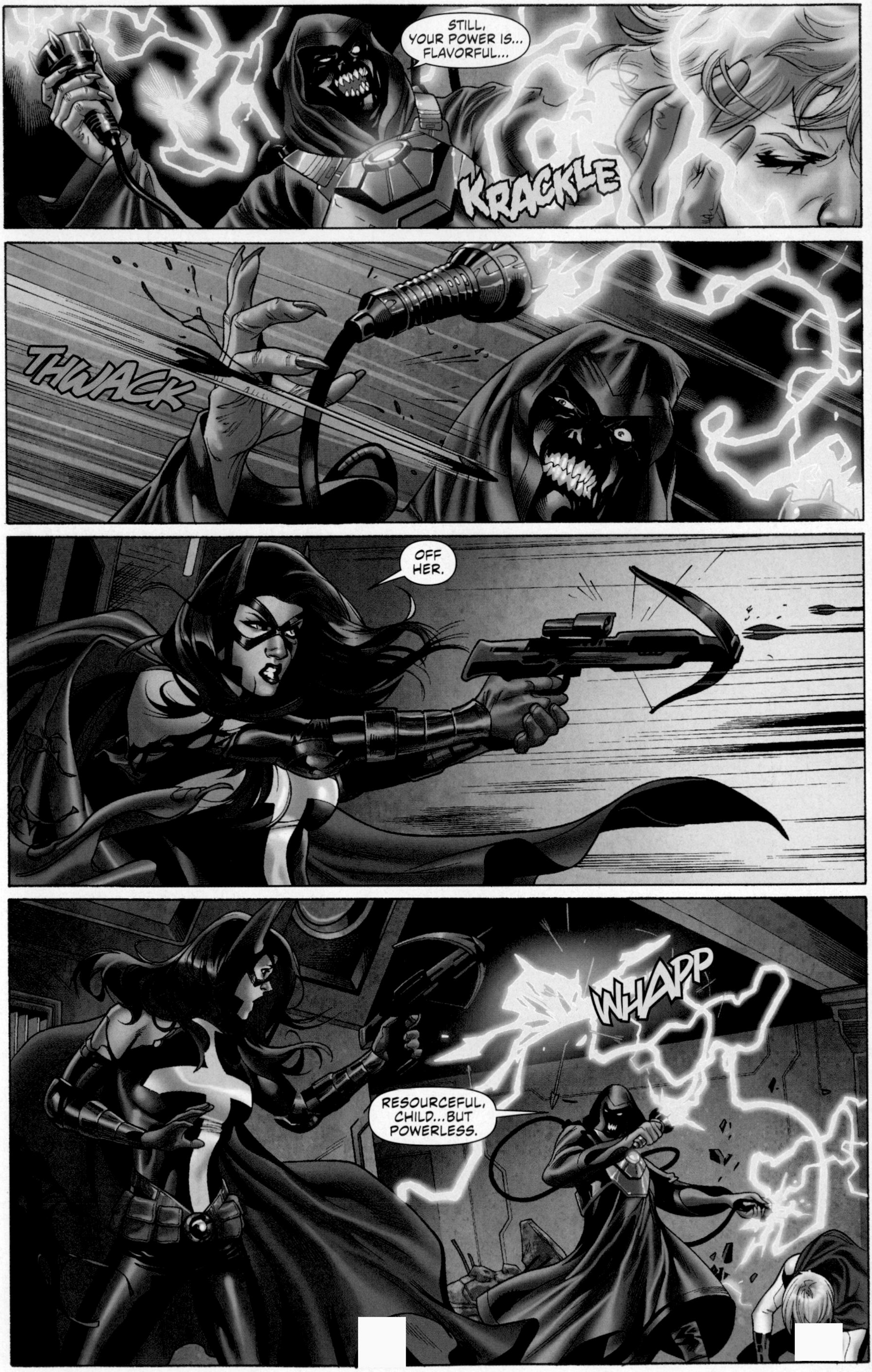
STILL, YOUR POWER IS... FLAVORFUL...
KRACKLE
THWACK
OFF HER.
WHAPP
RESOURCEFUL, CHILD...BUT POWERLESS.

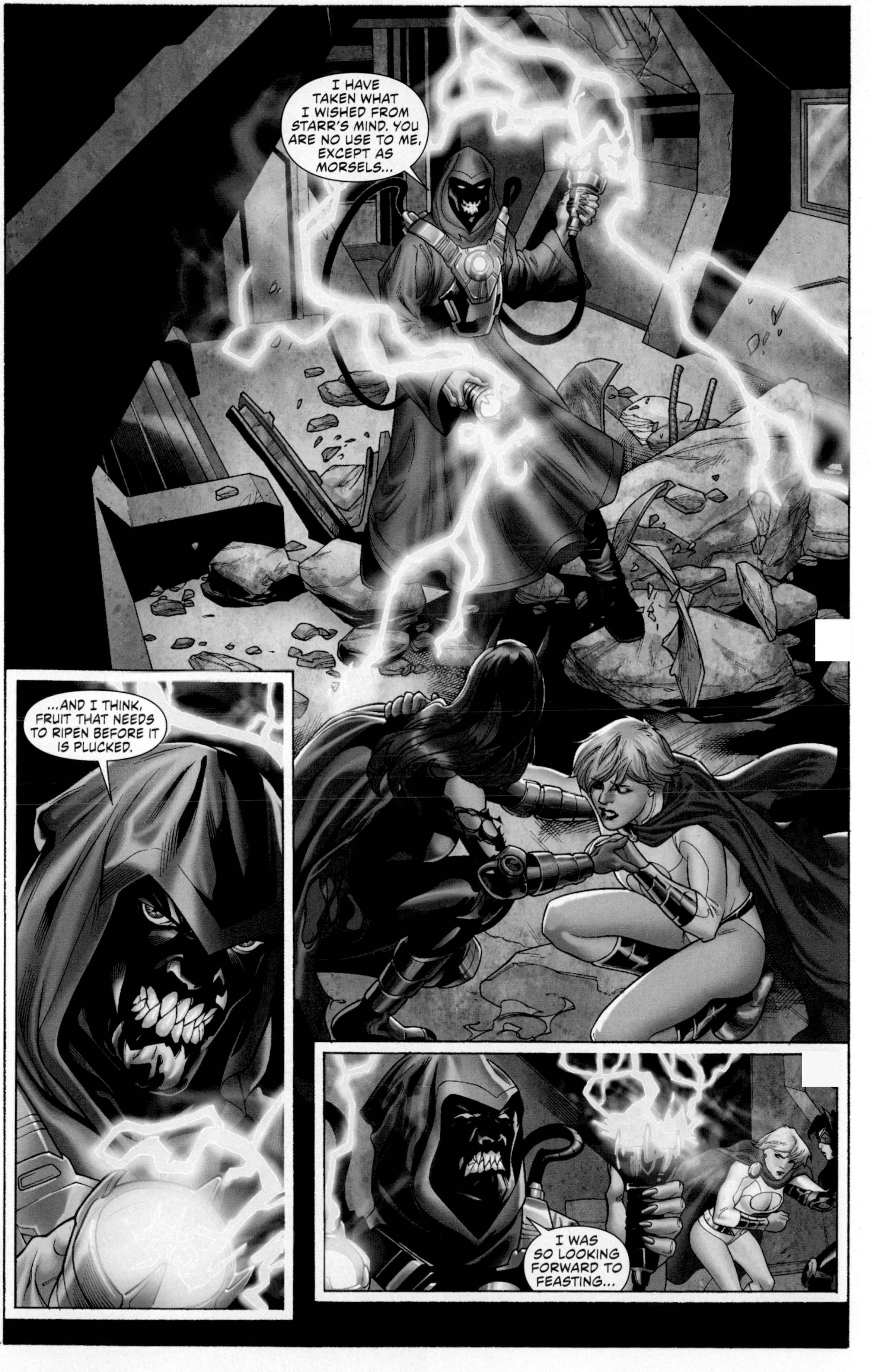
I HAVE TAKEN WHAT I WISHED FROM STARR'S MIND. YOU ARE NO USE TO ME, EXCEPT AS MORSELS...
...AND I THINK, FRUIT THAT NEEDS TO RIPEN BEFORE IT IS PLUCKED.
I WAS SO LOOKING FORWARD TO FEASTING...

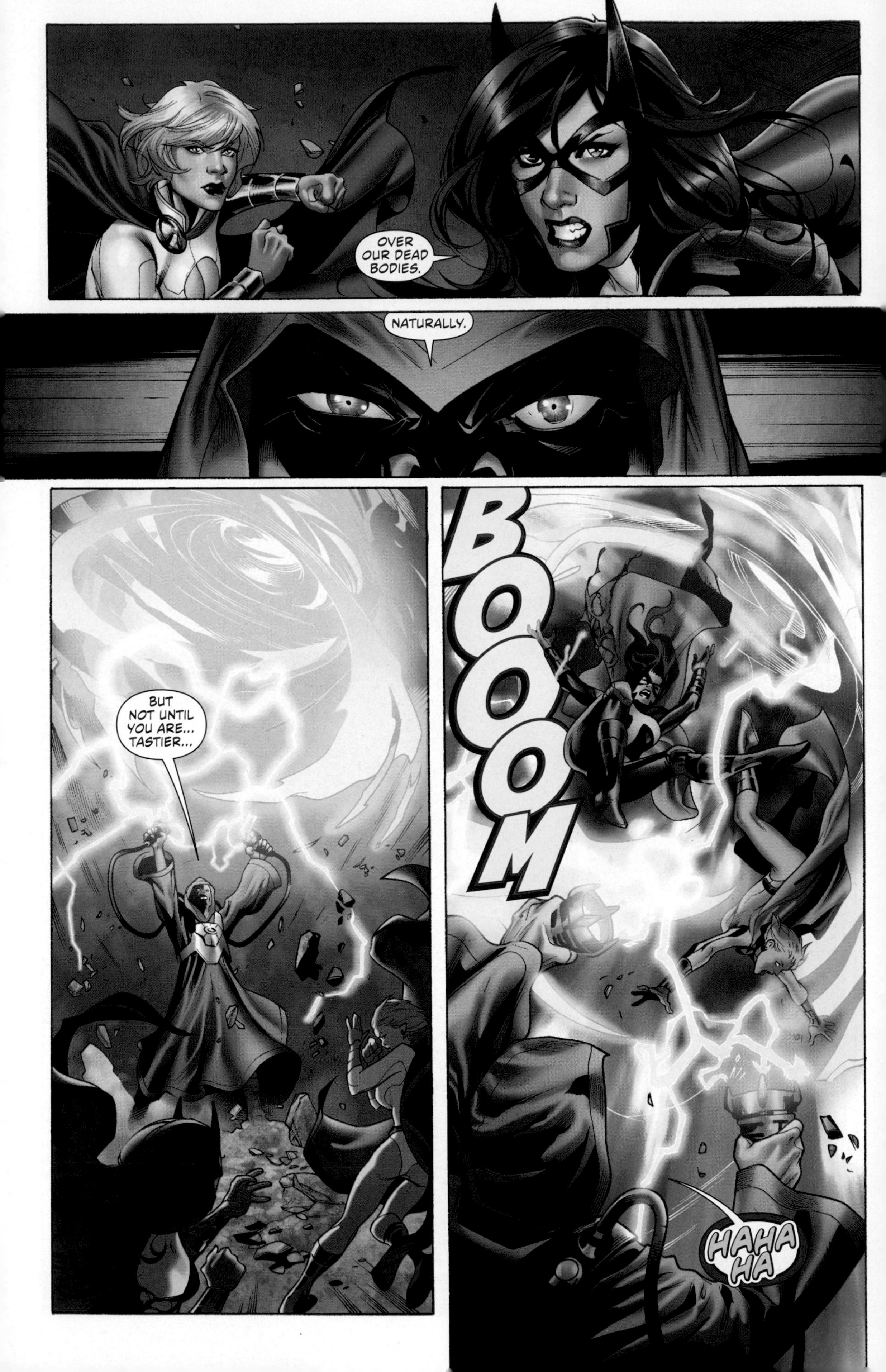
OVER OUR DEAD BODIES.
NATURALLY.
BUT NOT UNTIL YOU ARE... TASTIER...
BOOOOM
HAHAHA

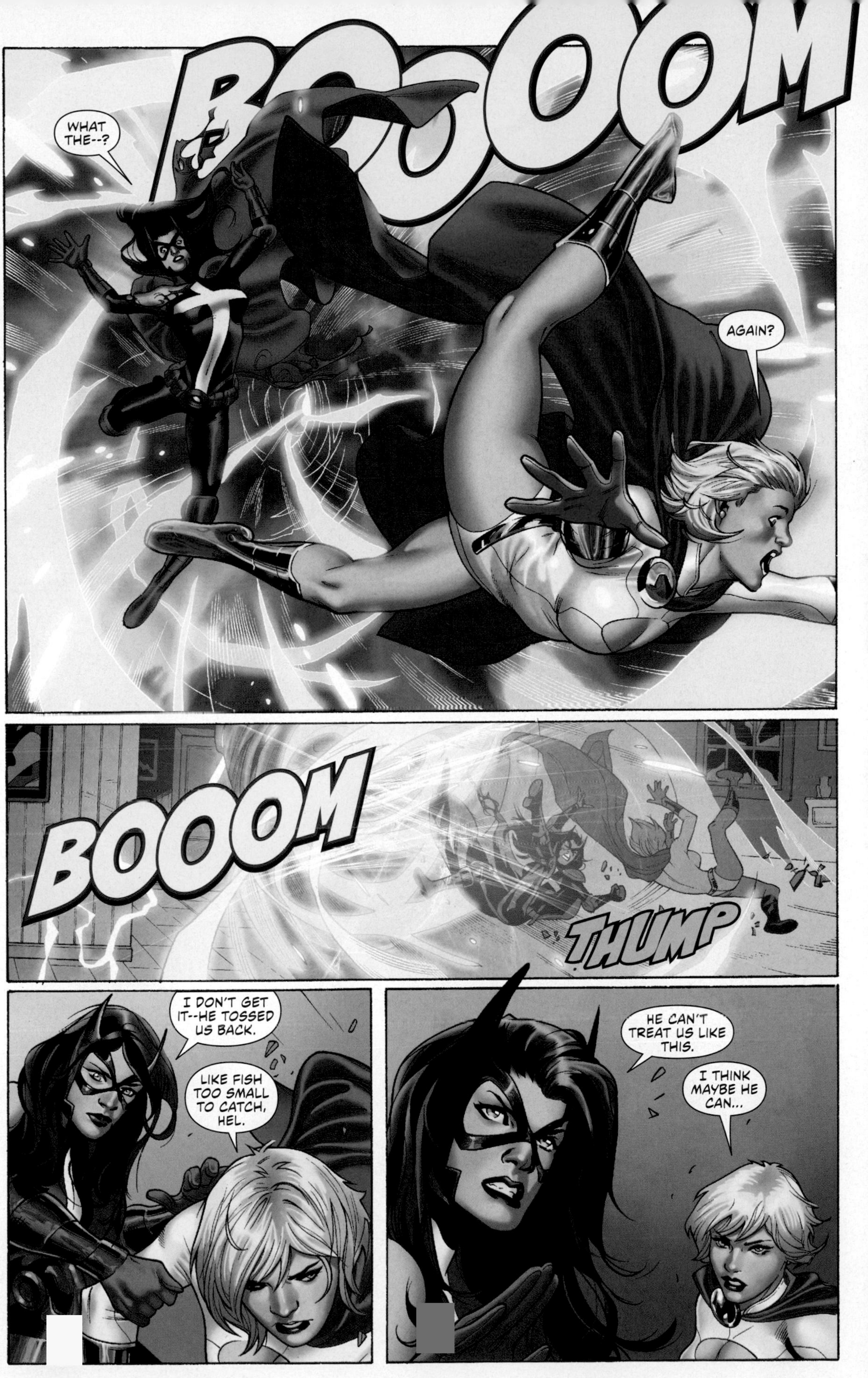
BOOOOM
WHAT THE--?
AGAIN?
BOOOM
THUMP
I DON'T GET IT--HE TOSSED US BACK.
LIKE FISH TOO SMALL TO CATCH, HEL.
HE CAN'T TREAT US LIKE THIS.
I THINK MAYBE HE CAN...

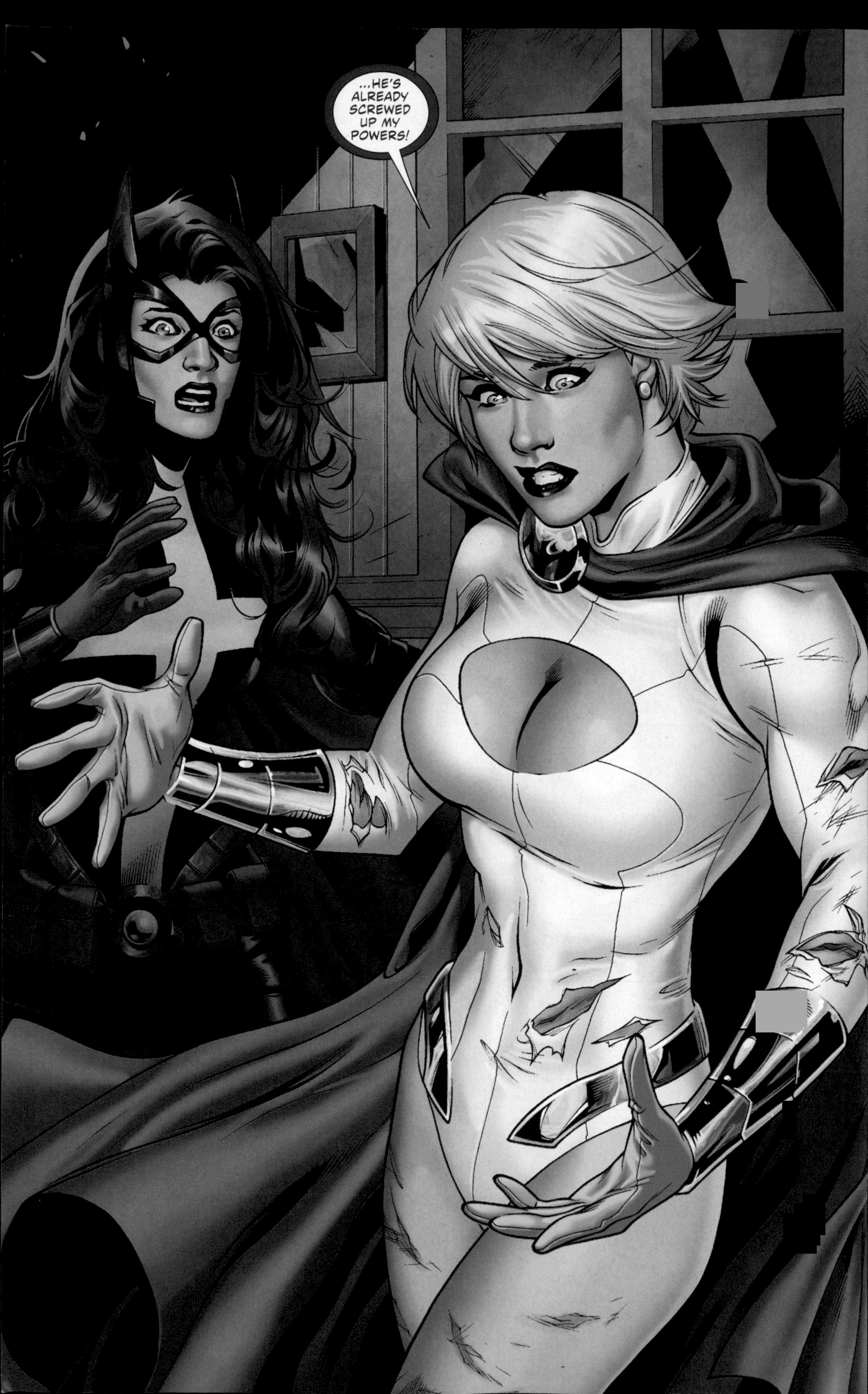
...HE'S ALREADY SCREWED UP MY POWERS!

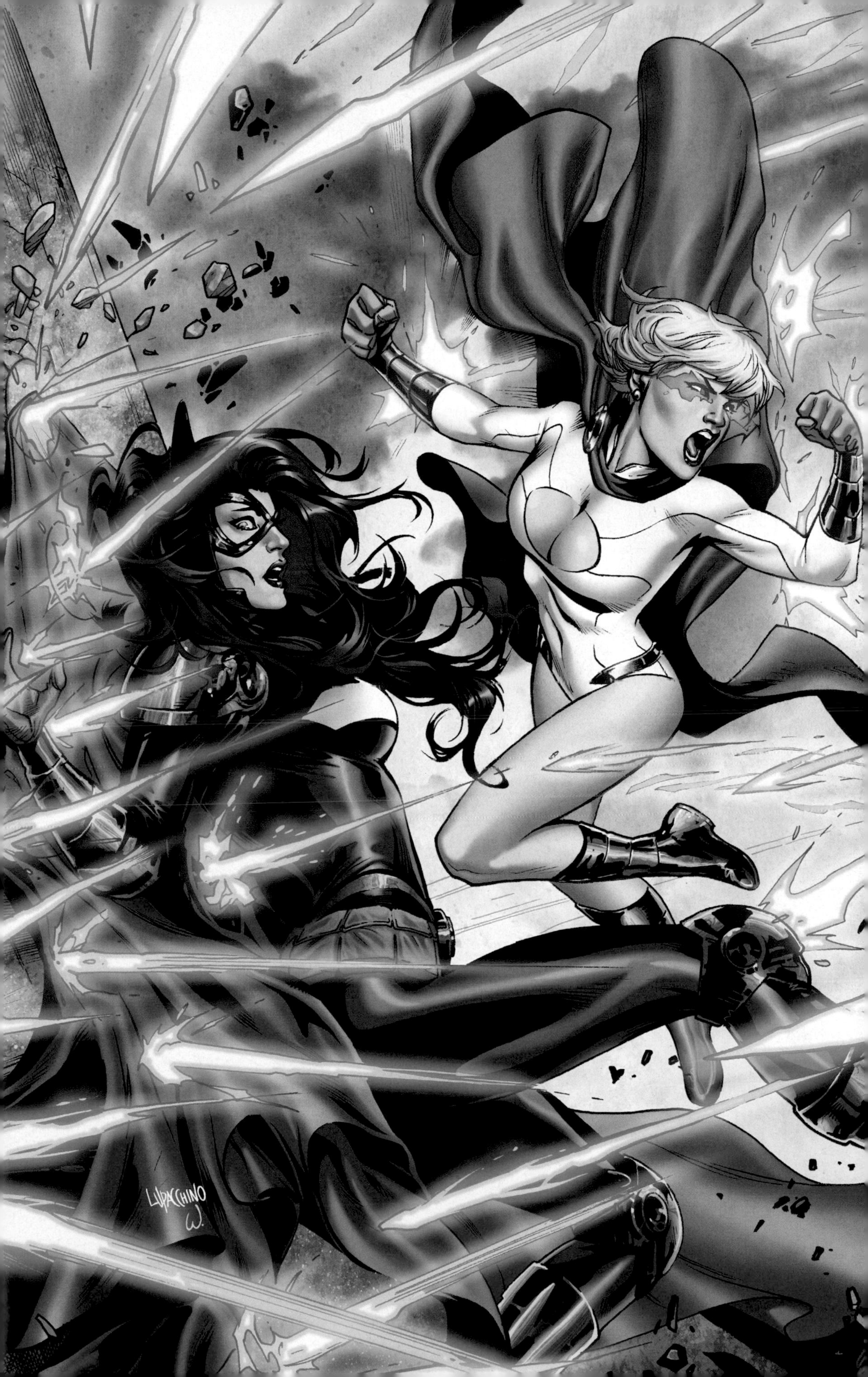
LUPACCHINO
W.

QUESTIONS

SCOTT MCDANIEL breakdowns **R.B. SILVA** penciller **JOE WEEMS** inker

cover art by **EMANUELA LUPACCHINO** with **JASON WRIGHT**

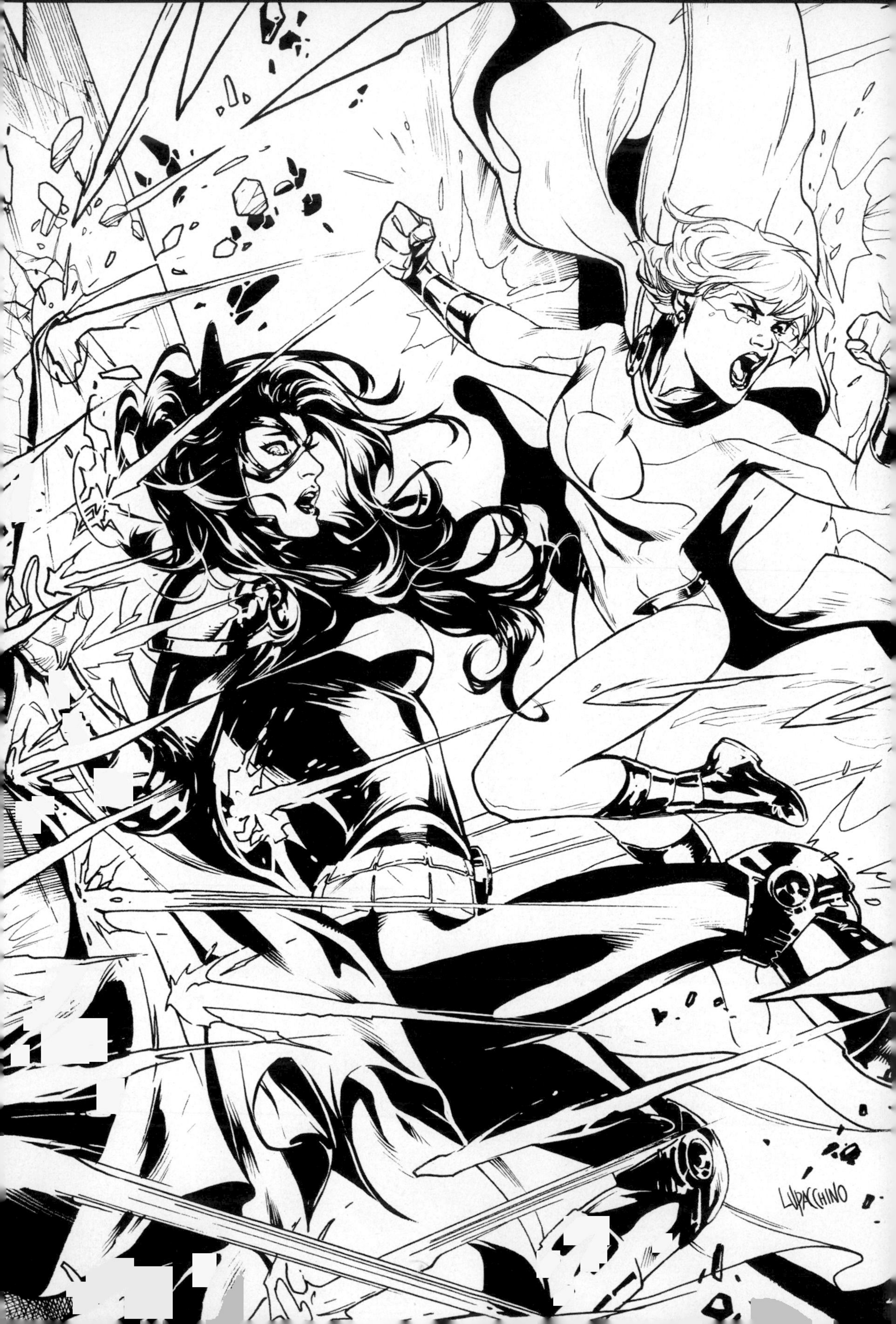
LUPACCHINO

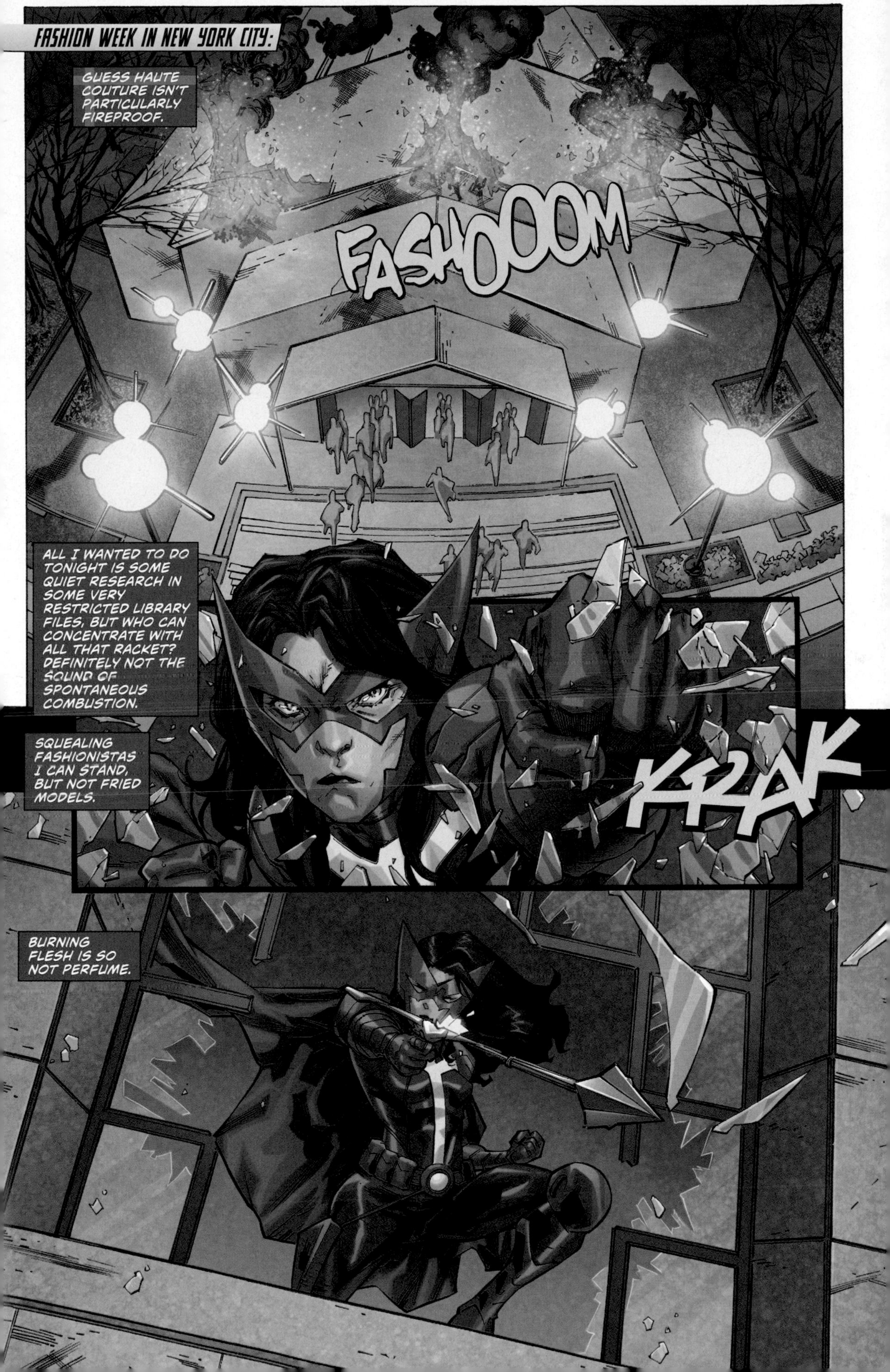
FASHION WEEK IN NEW YORK CITY:
GUESS HAUTE COUTURE ISN'T PARTICULARLY FIREPROOF.
FASHOOOM
ALL I WANTED TO DO TONIGHT IS SOME QUIET RESEARCH IN SOME VERY RESTRICTED LIBRARY FILES, BUT WHO CAN CONCENTRATE WITH ALL THAT RACKET? DEFINITELY NOT THE SOUND OF SPONTANEOUS COMBUSTION.
SQUEALING FASHIONISTAS I CAN STAND, BUT NOT FRIED MODELS.
KRAK
BURNING FLESH IS SO NOT PERFUME.

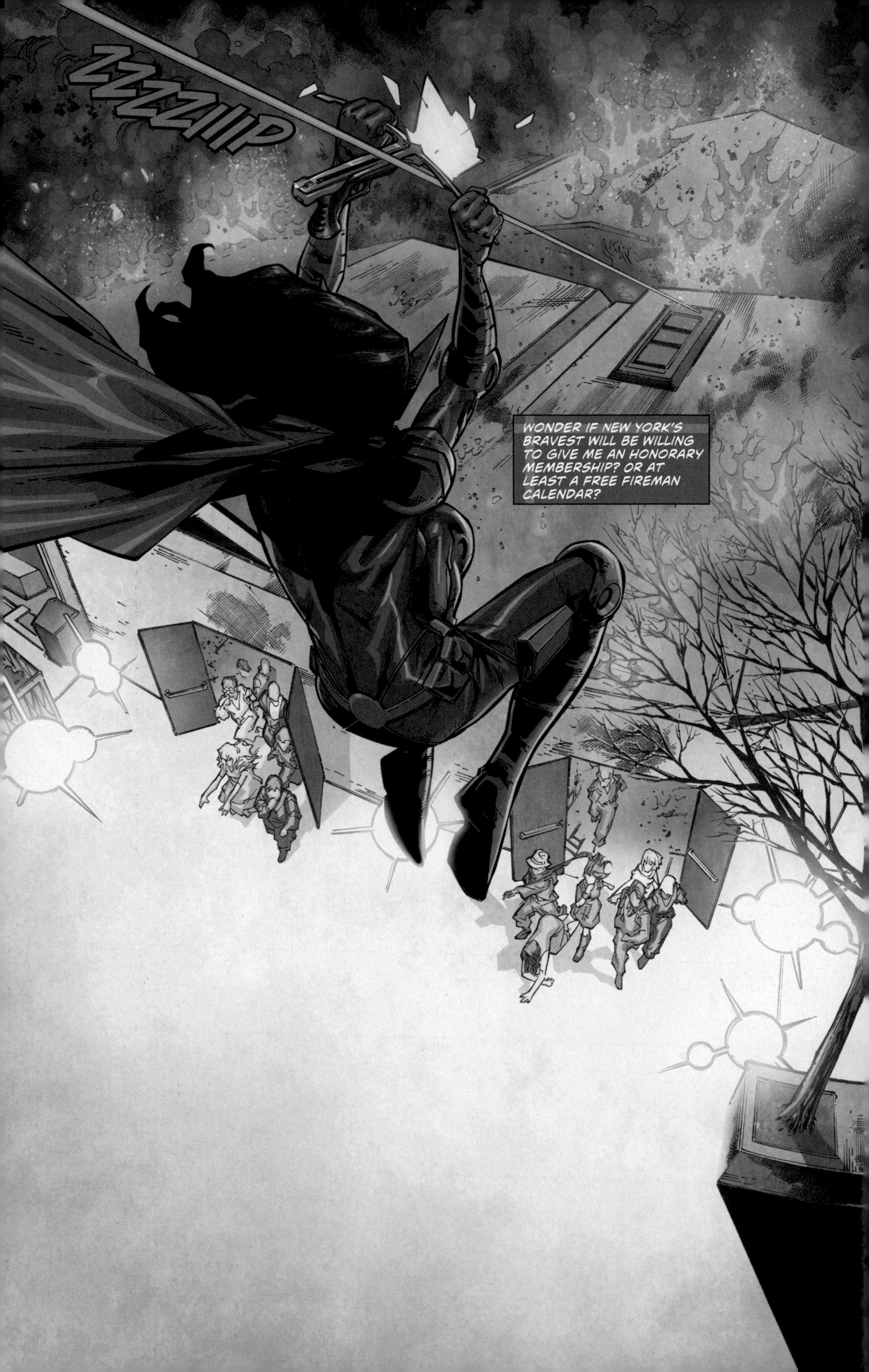
ZZZZIIIP
WONDER IF NEW YORK'S BRAVEST WILL BE WILLING TO GIVE ME AN HONORARY MEMBERSHIP? OR AT LEAST A FREE FIREMAN CALENDAR?

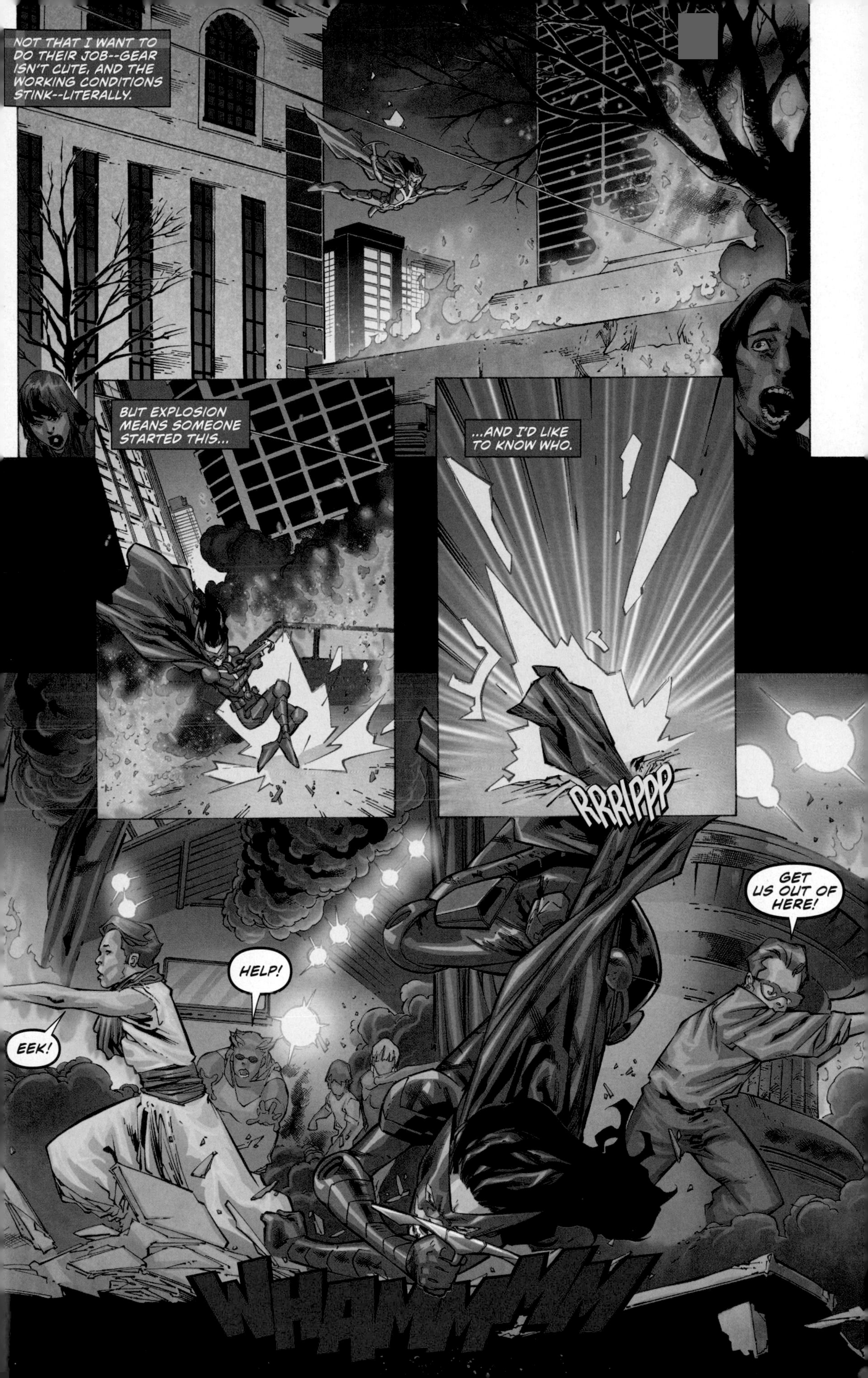
NOT THAT I WANT TO DO THEIR JOB--GEAR ISN'T CUTE, AND THE WORKING CONDITIONS STINK--LITERALLY.
BUT EXPLOSION MEANS SOMEONE STARTED THIS...
...AND I'D LIKE TO KNOW WHO.
RRRIPPP
GET US OUT OF HERE!
HELP!
EEK!
WHAMMMM

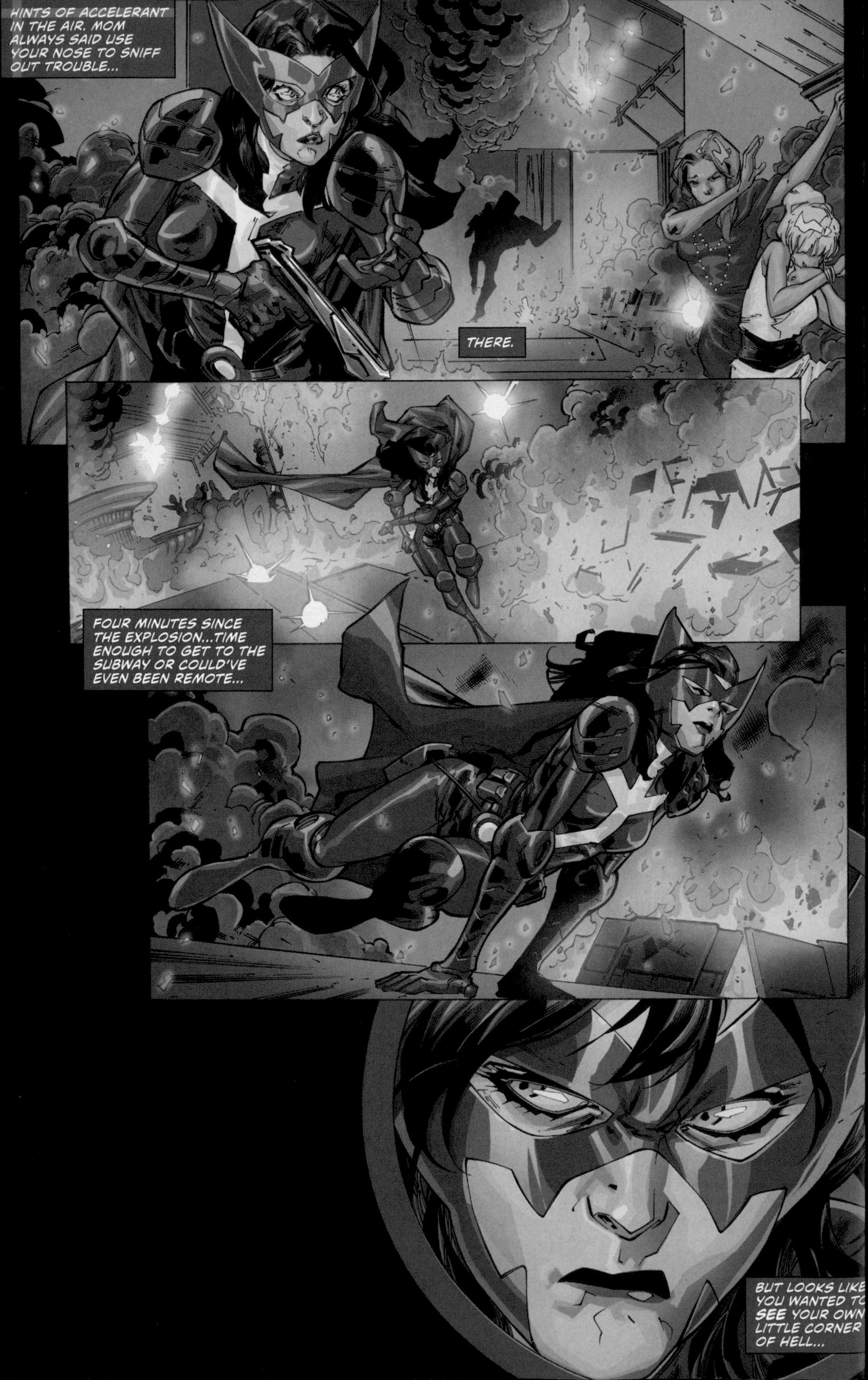
HINTS OF ACCELERANT IN THE AIR. MOM ALWAYS SAID USE YOUR NOSE TO SNIFF OUT TROUBLE...
THERE.
FOUR MINUTES SINCE THE EXPLOSION...TIME ENOUGH TO GET TO THE SUBWAY OR COULD'VE EVEN BEEN REMOTE...
BUT LOOKS LIKE YOU WANTED TO SEE YOUR OWN LITTLE CORNER OF HELL...

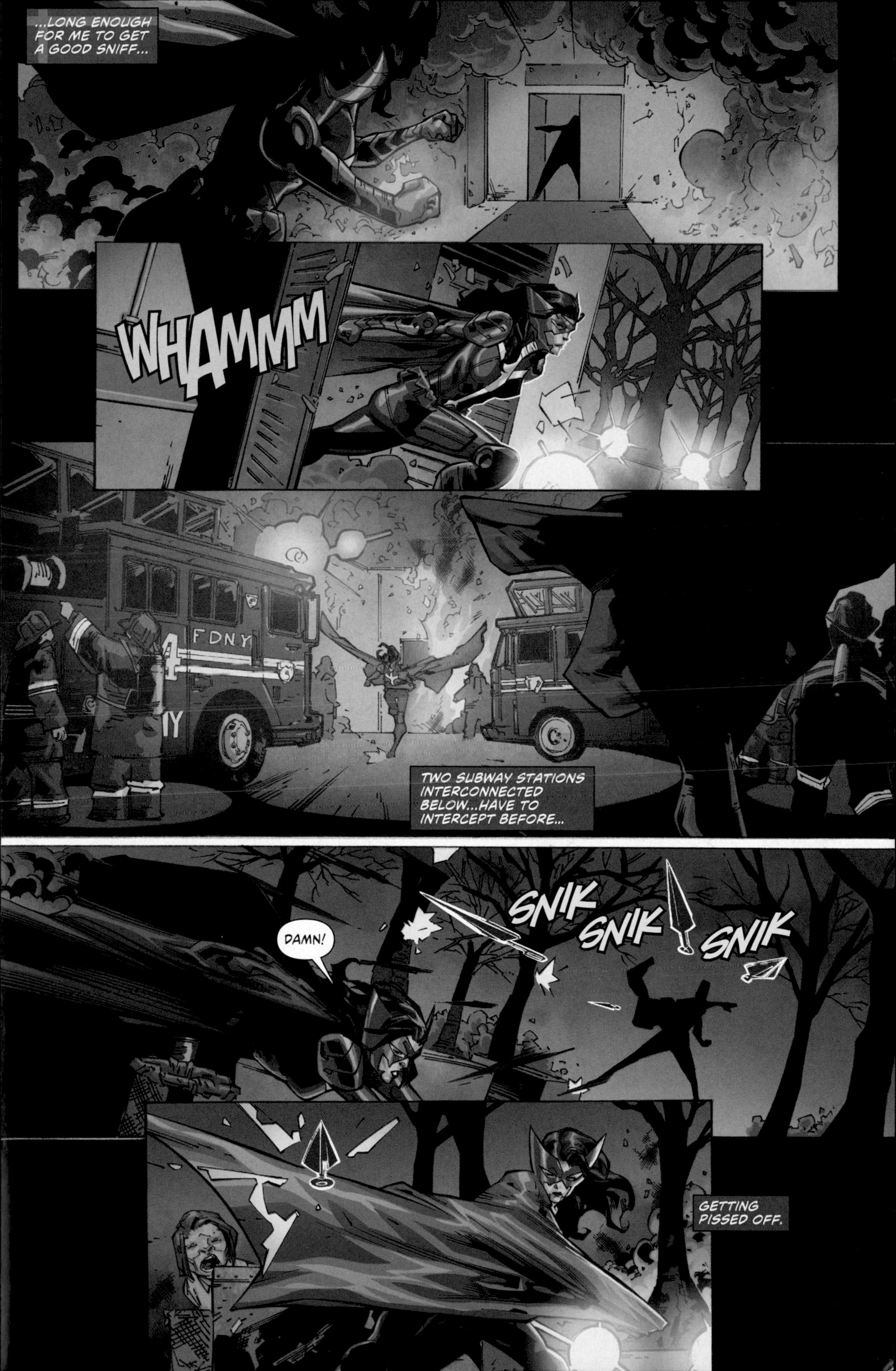
...LONG ENOUGH FOR ME TO GET A GOOD SNIFF...
WHAMMM
FDNY
TWO SUBWAY STATIONS INTERCONNECTED BELOW...HAVE TO INTERCEPT BEFORE...
DAMN!
SNIK
SNIK
SNIK
GETTING PISSED OFF.

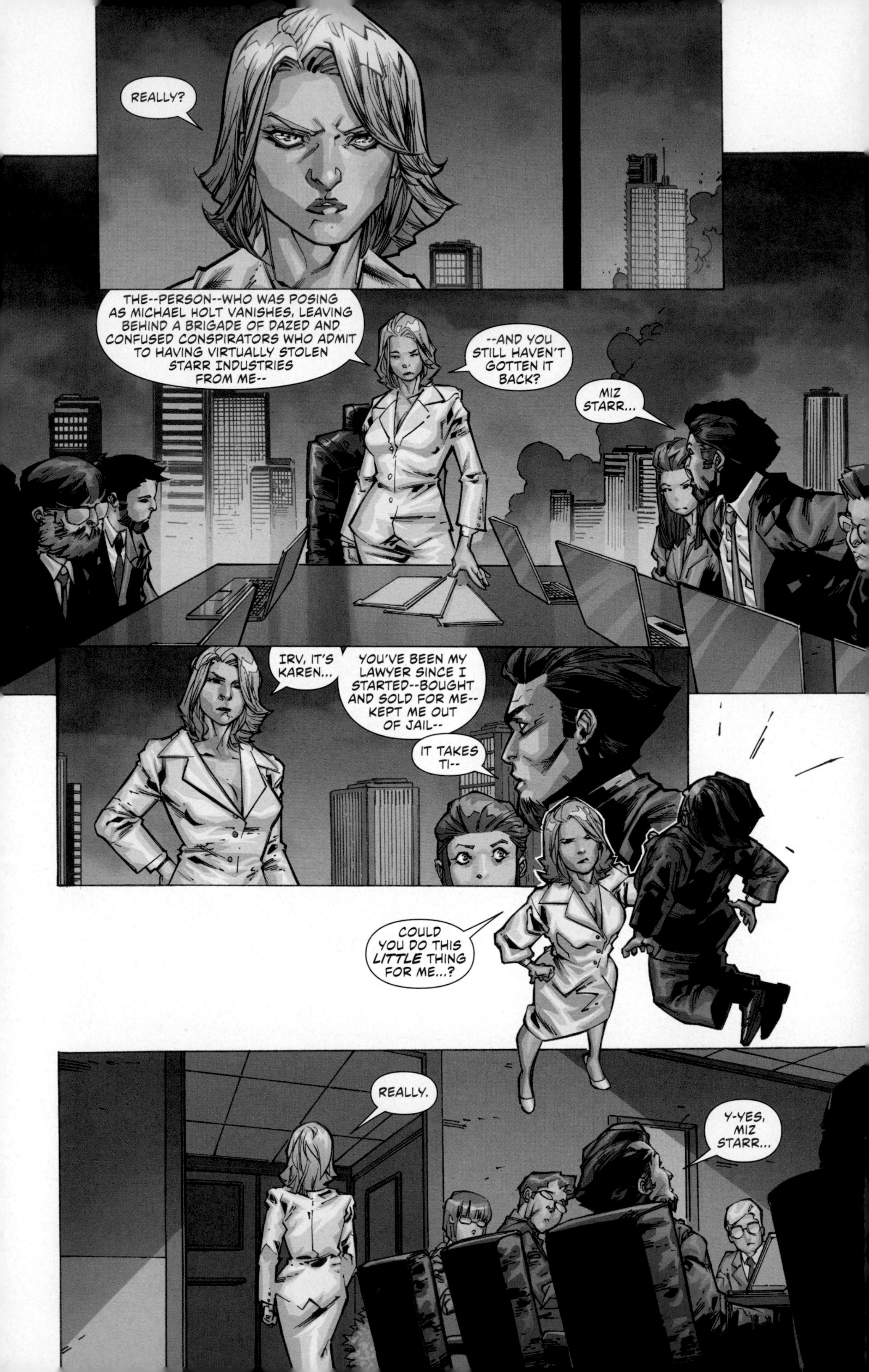
REALLY?
THE--PERSON--WHO WAS POSING AS MICHAEL HOLT VANISHES, LEAVING BEHIND A BRIGADE OF DAZED AND CONFUSED CONSPIRATORS WHO ADMIT TO HAVING VIRTUALLY STOLEN STARR INDUSTRIES FROM ME--
--AND YOU STILL HAVEN'T GOTTEN IT BACK?
MIZ STARR...
IRV, IT'S KAREN...
YOU'VE BEEN MY LAWYER SINCE I STARTED--BOUGHT AND SOLD FOR ME--KEPT ME OUT OF JAIL--
IT TAKES TI--
COULD YOU DO THIS *LITTLE* THING FOR ME...?
REALLY.
Y-YES, MIZ STARR...

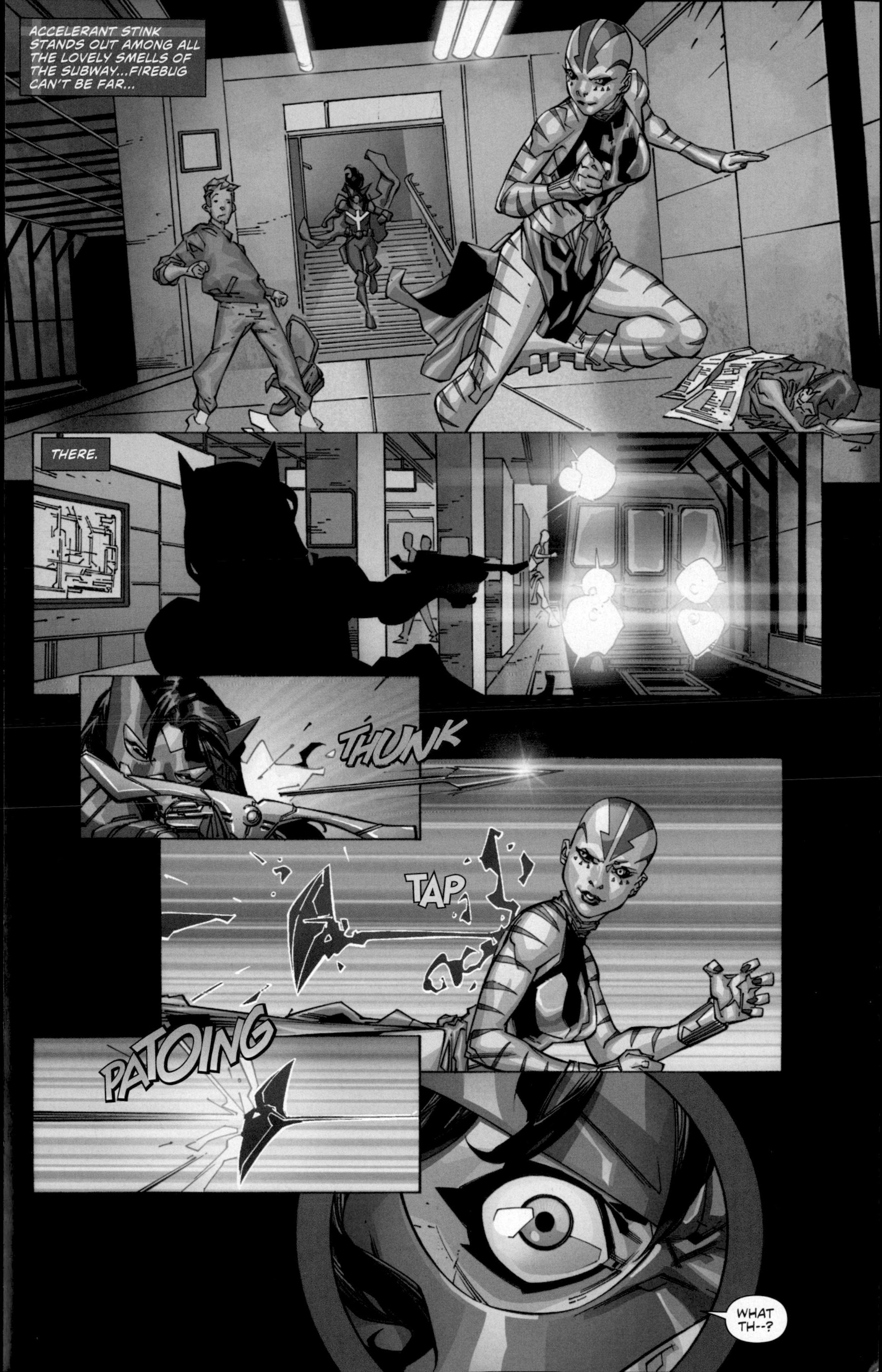

ACCELERANT STINK STANDS OUT AMONG ALL THE LOVELY SMELLS OF THE SUBWAY...FIREBUG CAN'T BE FAR...
THERE.
THUNK
TAP
PATOING
WHAT TH--?

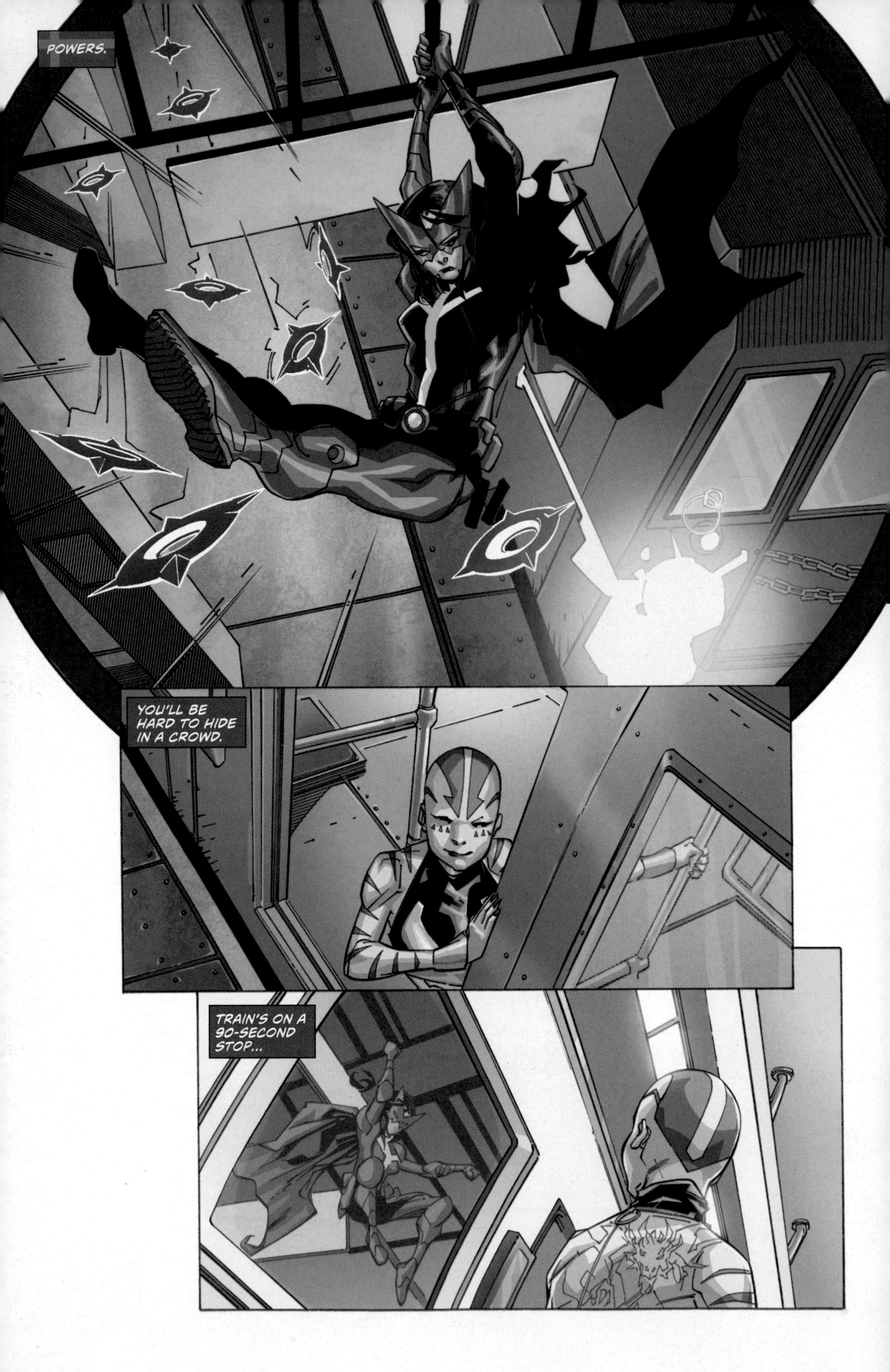
POWERS.
YOU'LL BE HARD TO HIDE IN A CROWD.
TRAIN'S ON A 90-SECOND STOP...

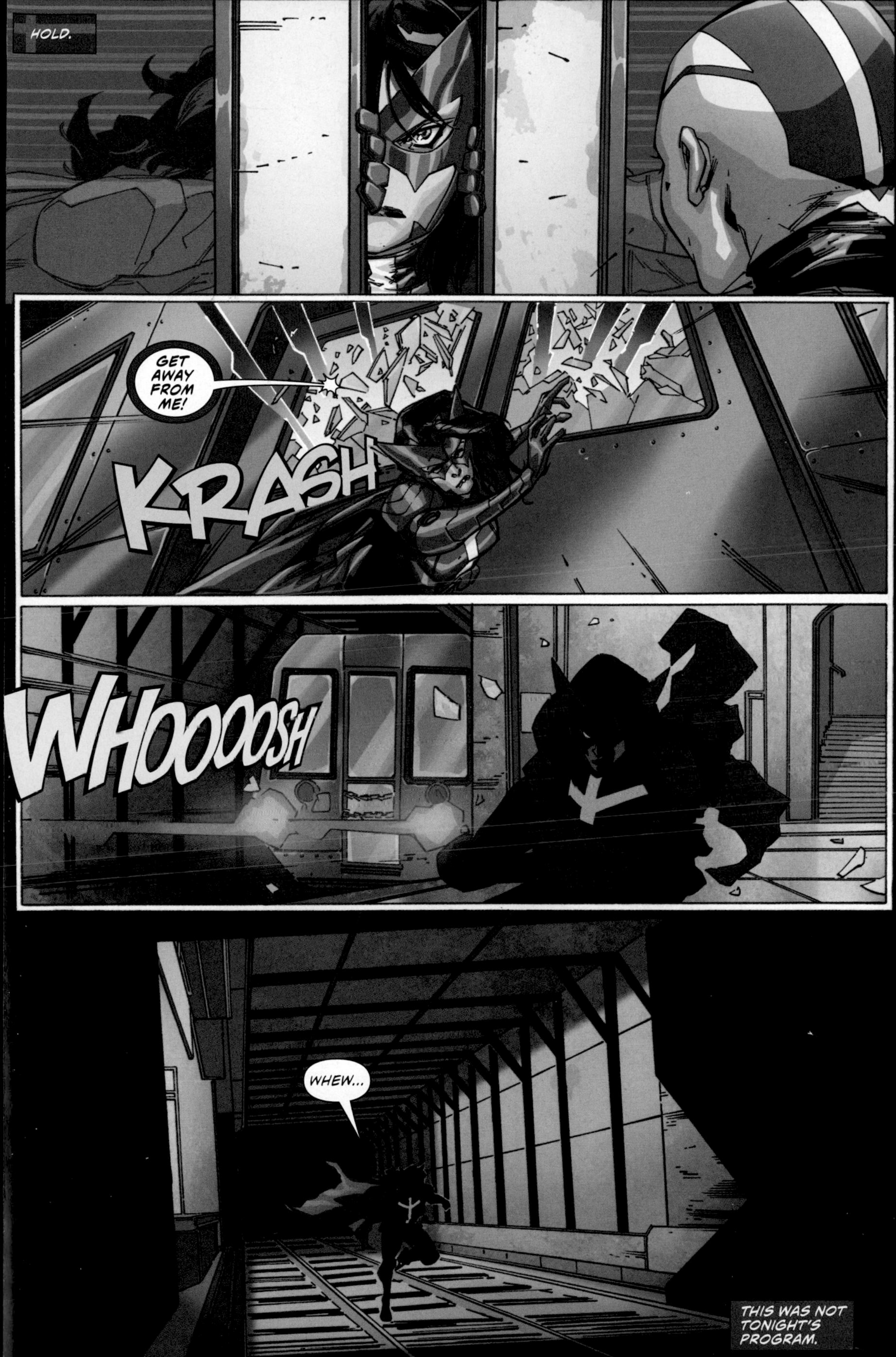
HOLD.
GET AWAY FROM ME!
KRASH
WHOOOOSH
WHEW...
THIS WAS NOT TONIGHT'S PROGRAM.

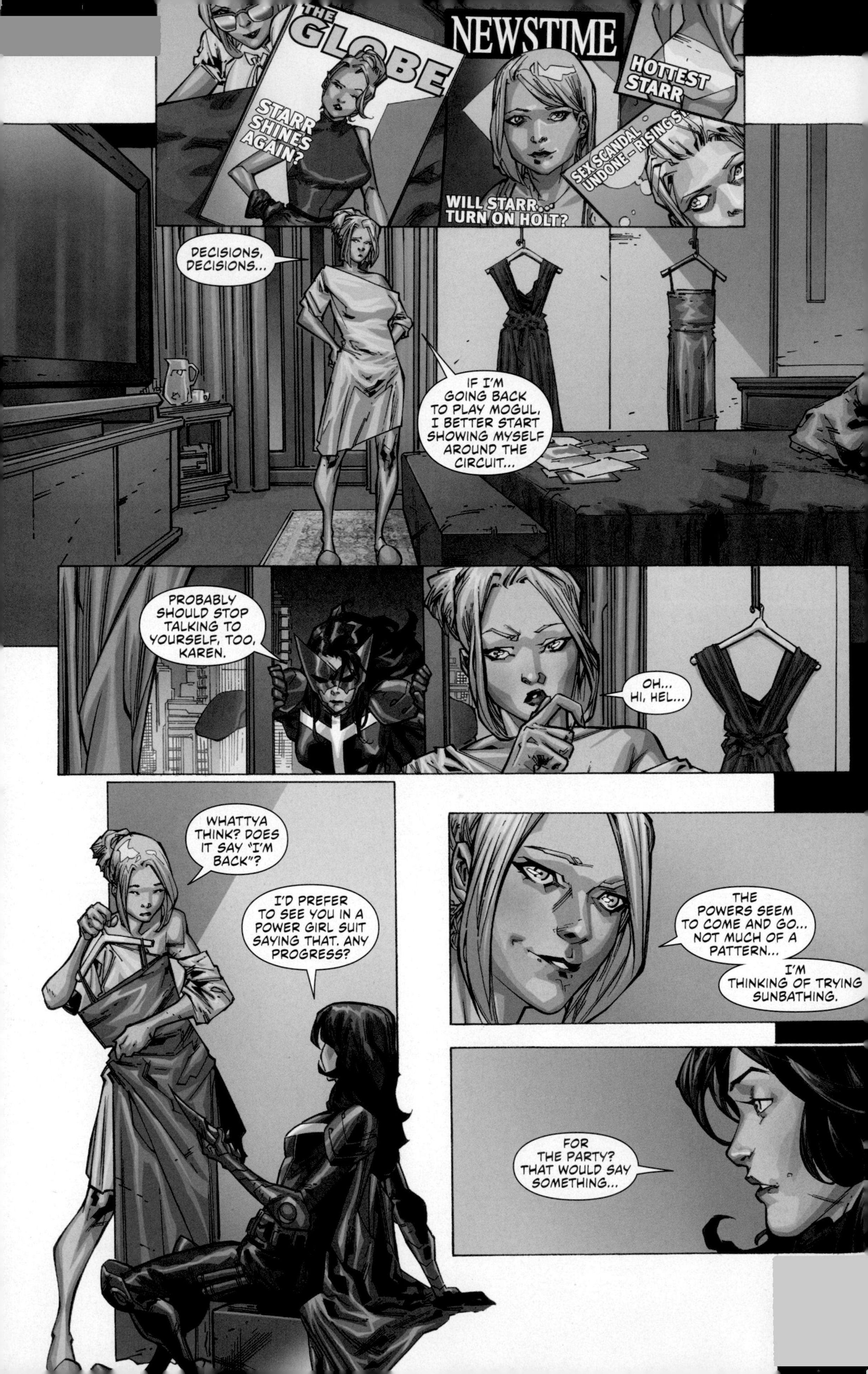
THE GLOBE
STARR SHINES AGAIN?
NEWSTIME
WILL STARR... TURN ON HOLT?
HOTTEST STARR
SEX SCANDAL UNDONE—RISING S
DECISIONS, DECISIONS...
IF I'M GOING BACK TO PLAY MOGUL, I BETTER START SHOWING MYSELF AROUND THE CIRCUIT...
PROBABLY SHOULD STOP TALKING TO YOURSELF, TOO, KAREN.
OH... HI, HEL...
WHATTYA THINK? DOES IT SAY "I'M BACK"?
I'D PREFER TO SEE YOU IN A POWER GIRL SUIT SAYING THAT. ANY PROGRESS?
THE POWERS SEEM TO COME AND GO... NOT MUCH OF A PATTERN...
I'M THINKING OF TRYING SUNBATHING.
FOR THE PARTY? THAT WOULD SAY SOMETHING...

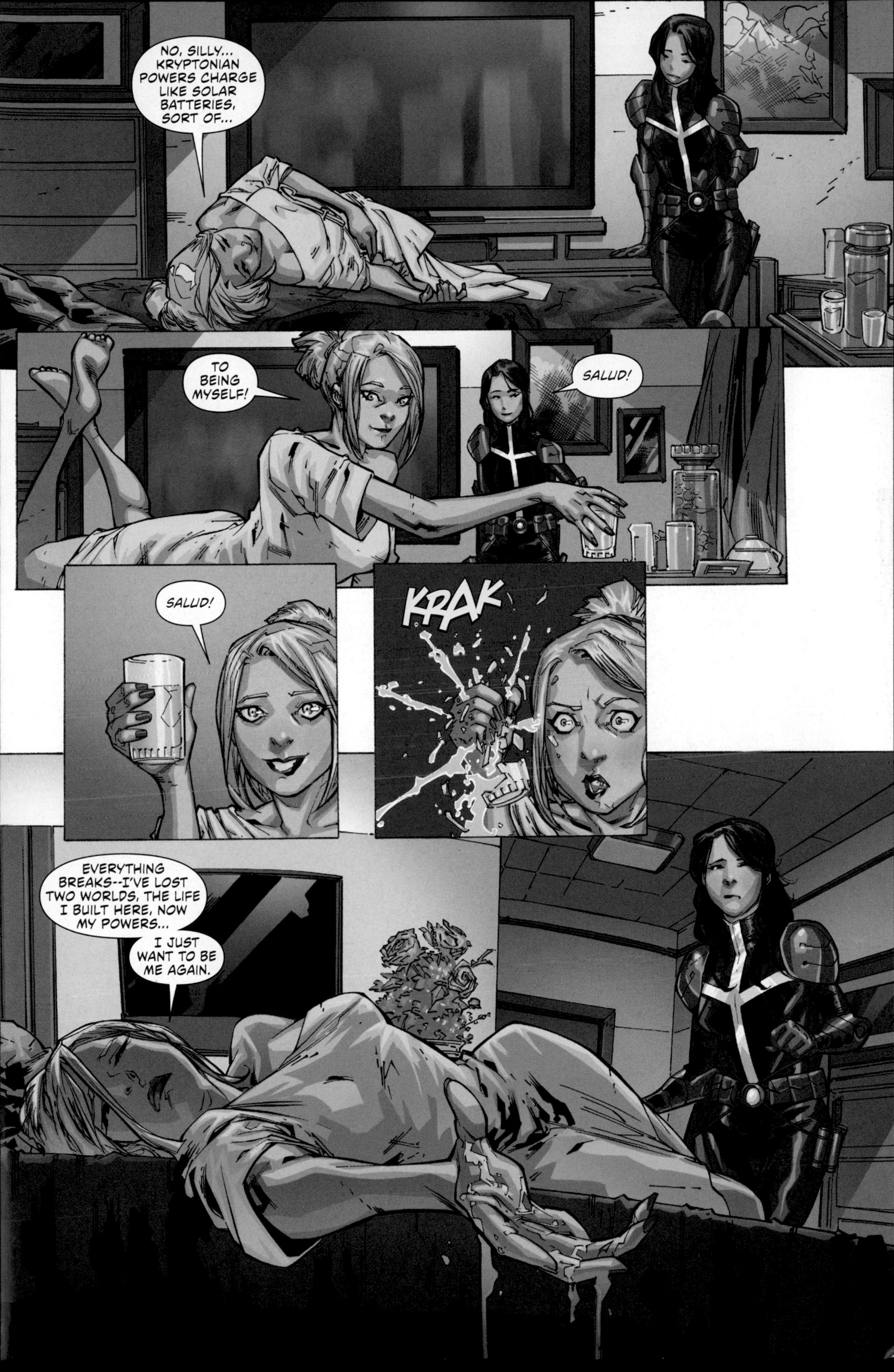

NO, SILLY... KRYPTONIAN POWERS CHARGE LIKE SOLAR BATTERIES, SORT OF...
TO BEING MYSELF!
SALUD!
SALUD!
KRAK
EVERYTHING BREAKS--I'VE LOST TWO WORLDS, THE LIFE I BUILT HERE, NOW MY POWERS...
I JUST WANT TO BE ME AGAIN.

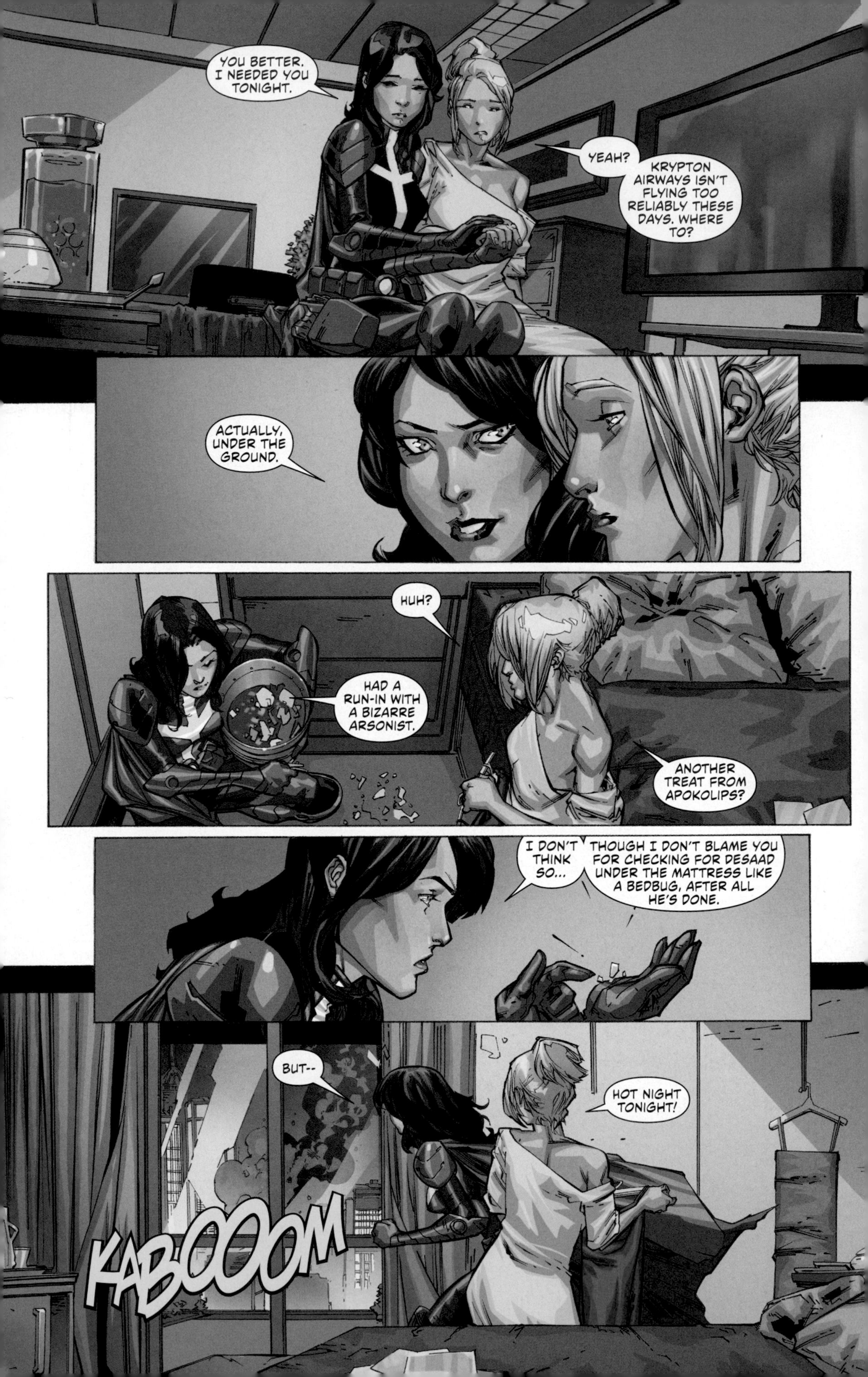
YOU BETTER. I NEEDED YOU TONIGHT.
YEAH?
KRYPTON AIRWAYS ISN'T FLYING TOO RELIABLY THESE DAYS. WHERE TO?
ACTUALLY, UNDER THE GROUND.
HUH?
HAD A RUN-IN WITH A BIZARRE ARSONIST.
ANOTHER TREAT FROM APOKOLIPS?
I DON'T THINK SO...
THOUGH I DON'T BLAME YOU FOR CHECKING FOR DESAAD UNDER THE MATTRESS LIKE A BEDBUG, AFTER ALL HE'S DONE.
BUT--
HOT NIGHT TONIGHT!
KABOOOM

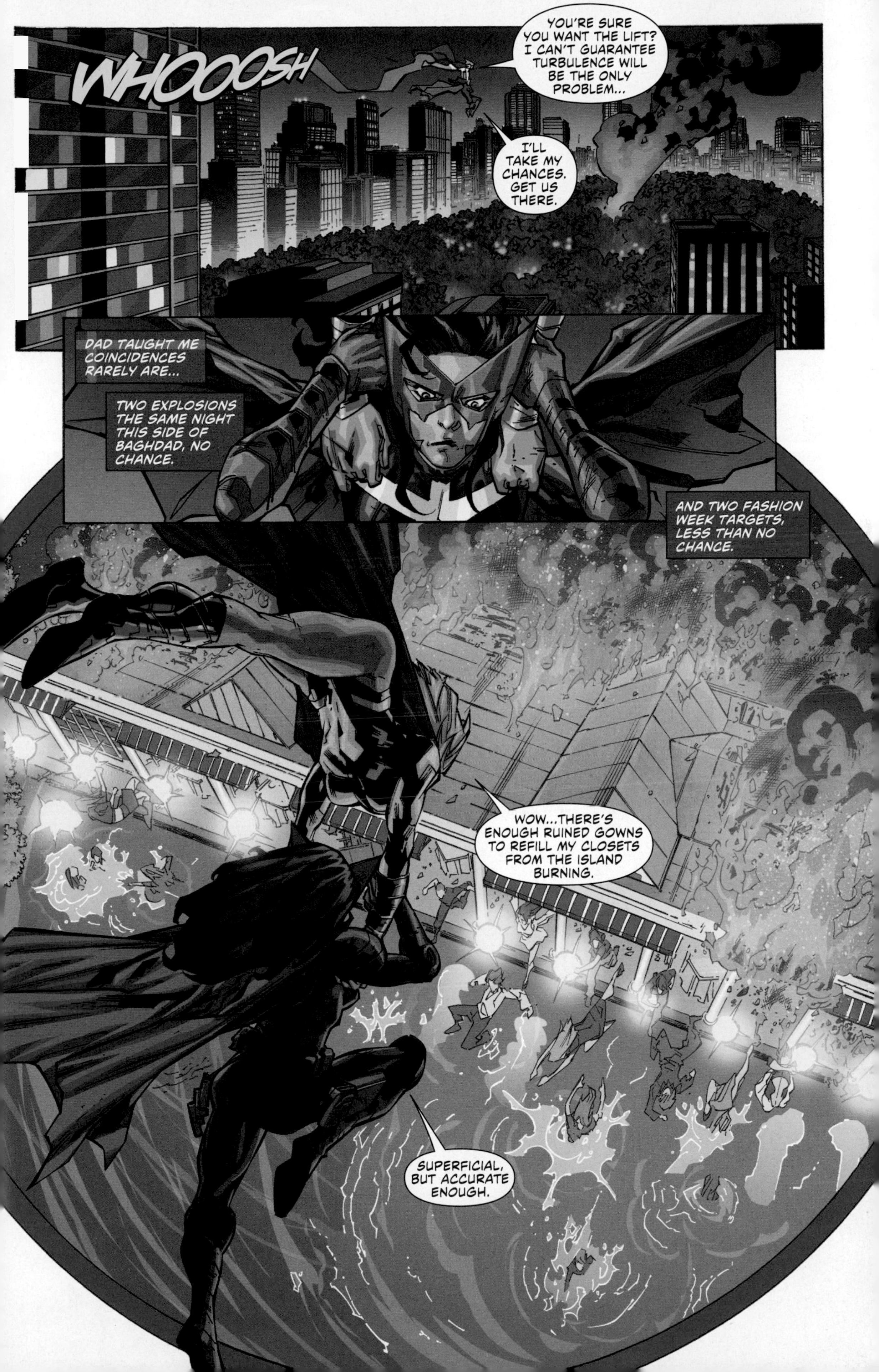
WHOOOOSH
YOU'RE SURE YOU WANT THE LIFT? I CAN'T GUARANTEE TURBULENCE WILL BE THE ONLY PROBLEM...
I'LL TAKE MY CHANCES. GET US THERE.
DAD TAUGHT ME COINCIDENCES RARELY ARE...
TWO EXPLOSIONS THE SAME NIGHT THIS SIDE OF BAGHDAD, NO CHANCE.
AND TWO FASHION WEEK TARGETS, LESS THAN NO CHANCE.
WOW...THERE'S ENOUGH RUINED GOWNS TO REFILL MY CLOSETS FROM THE ISLAND BURNING.
SUPERFICIAL, BUT ACCURATE ENOUGH.

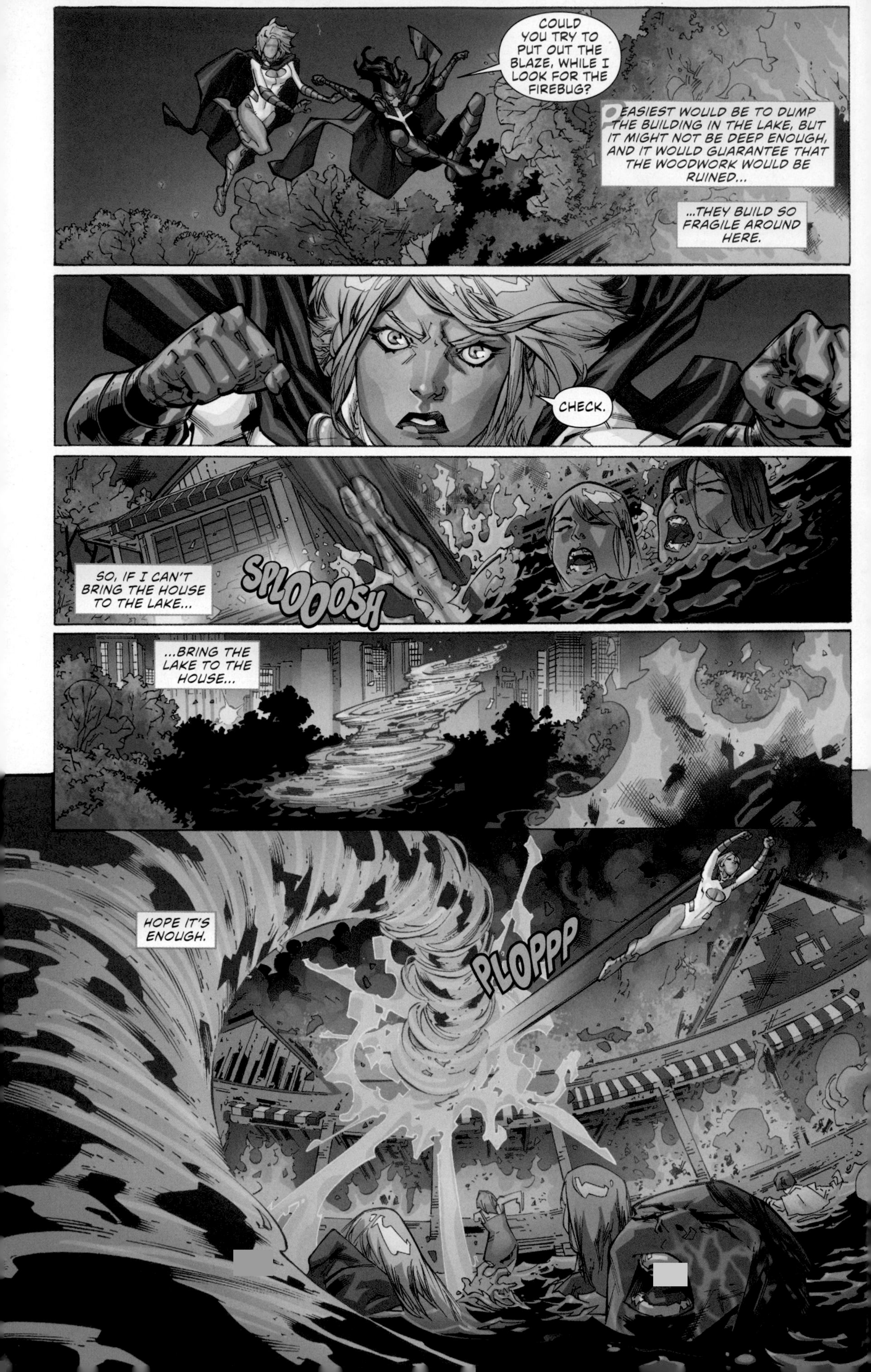
COULD YOU TRY TO PUT OUT THE BLAZE, WHILE I LOOK FOR THE FIREBUG?
EASIEST WOULD BE TO DUMP THE BUILDING IN THE LAKE, BUT IT MIGHT NOT BE DEEP ENOUGH, AND IT WOULD GUARANTEE THAT THE WOODWORK WOULD BE RUINED...
...THEY BUILD SO FRAGILE AROUND HERE.
CHECK.
SO, IF I CAN'T BRING THE HOUSE TO THE LAKE...
SPLOOOOSH
...BRING THE LAKE TO THE HOUSE...
HOPE IT'S ENOUGH.
PLOPPP

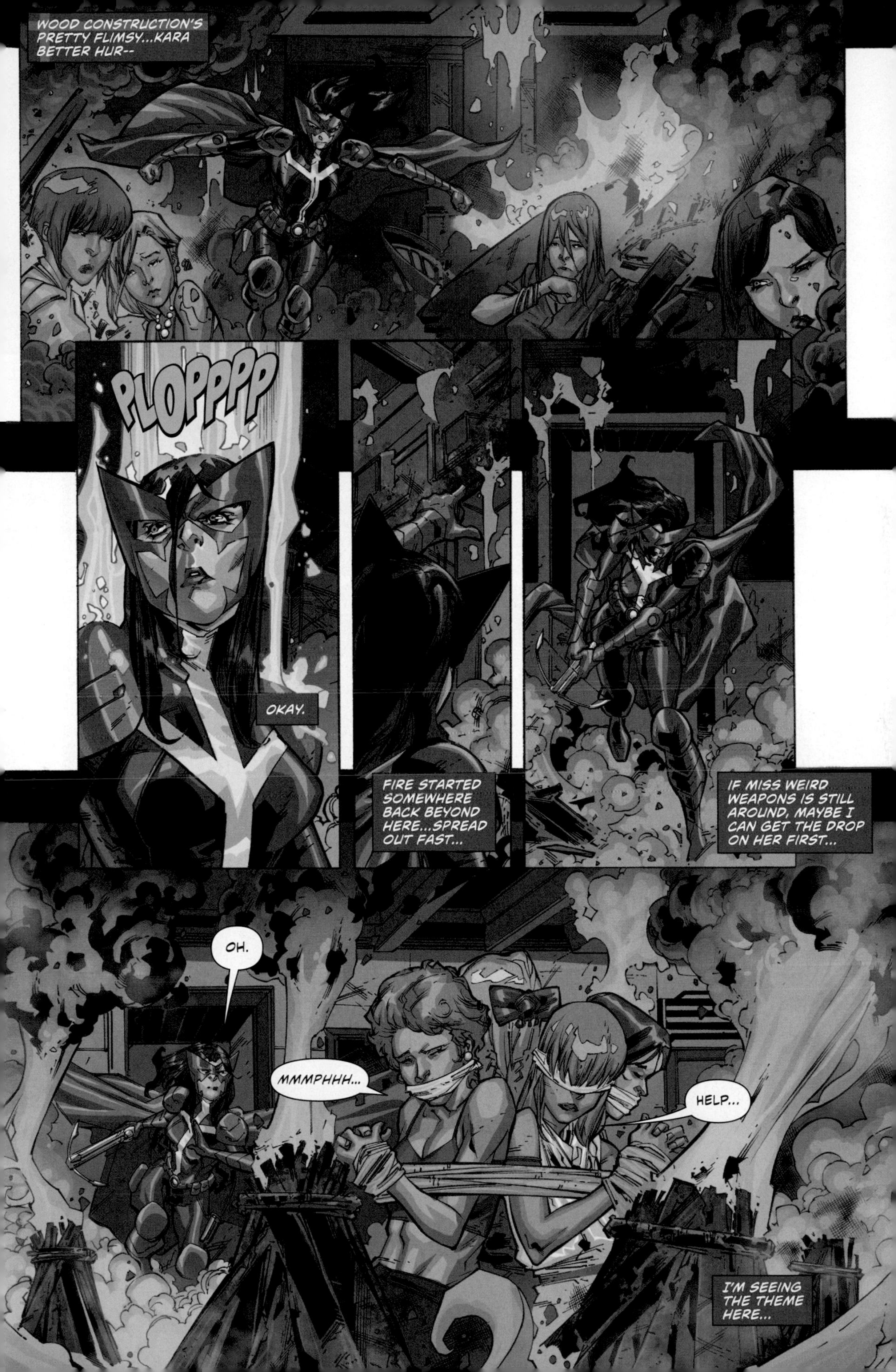
WOOD CONSTRUCTION'S PRETTY FLIMSY...KARA BETTER HUR--
PLOPPPP
OKAY.
FIRE STARTED SOMEWHERE BACK BEYOND HERE...SPREAD OUT FAST...
IF MISS WEIRD WEAPONS IS STILL AROUND, MAYBE I CAN GET THE DROP ON HER FIRST...
OH.
MMMPHHH...
HELP...
I'M SEEING THE THEME HERE...

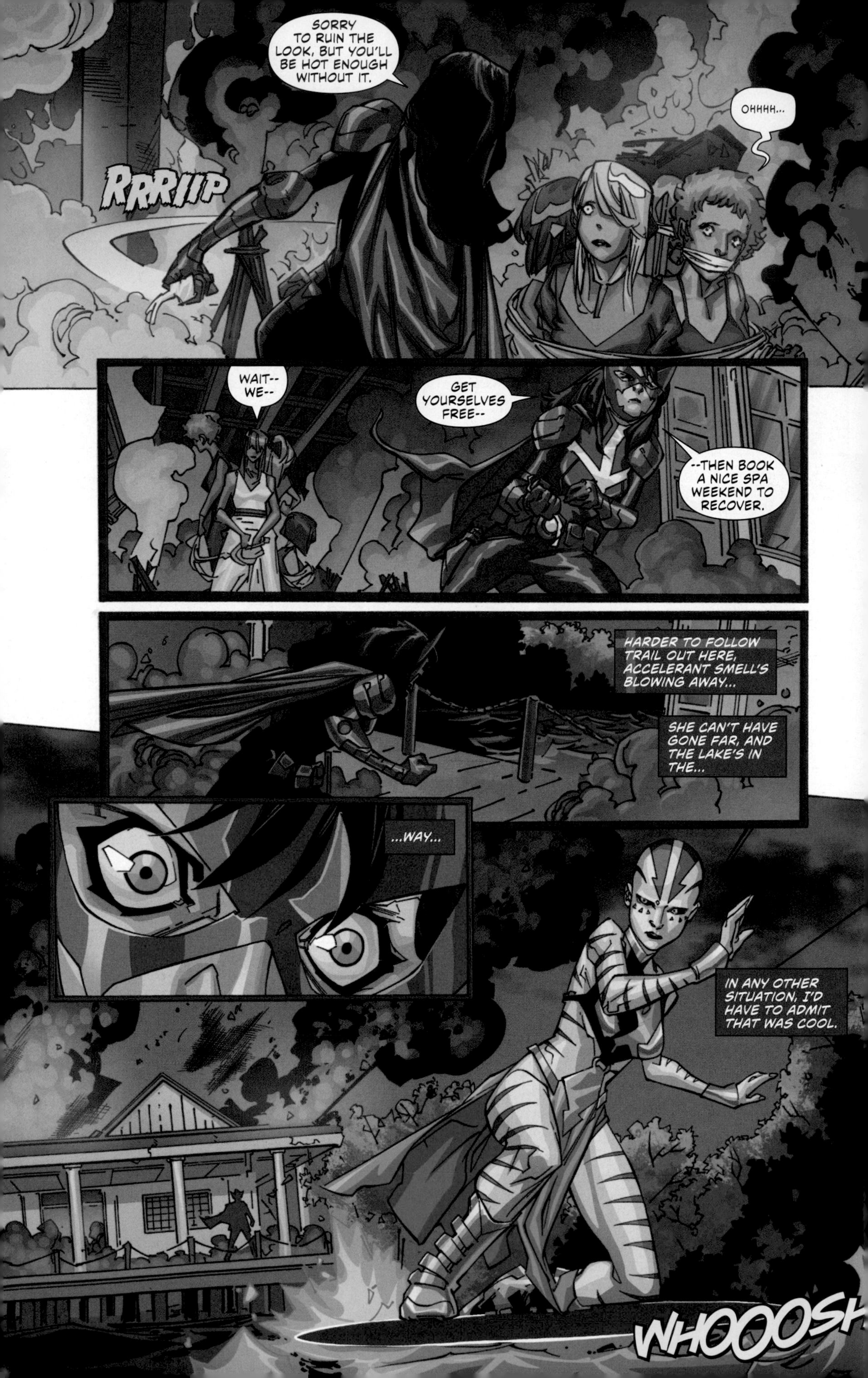
SORRY TO RUIN THE LOOK, BUT YOU'LL BE HOT ENOUGH WITHOUT IT.
RRRIIP
OHHHH...
WAIT-- WE--
GET YOURSELVES FREE--
--THEN BOOK A NICE SPA WEEKEND TO RECOVER.
HARDER TO FOLLOW TRAIL OUT HERE, ACCELERANT SMELL'S BLOWING AWAY...
SHE CAN'T HAVE GONE FAR, AND THE LAKE'S IN THE...
...WAY...
IN ANY OTHER SITUATION, I'D HAVE TO ADMIT THAT WAS COOL.
WHOOOSH

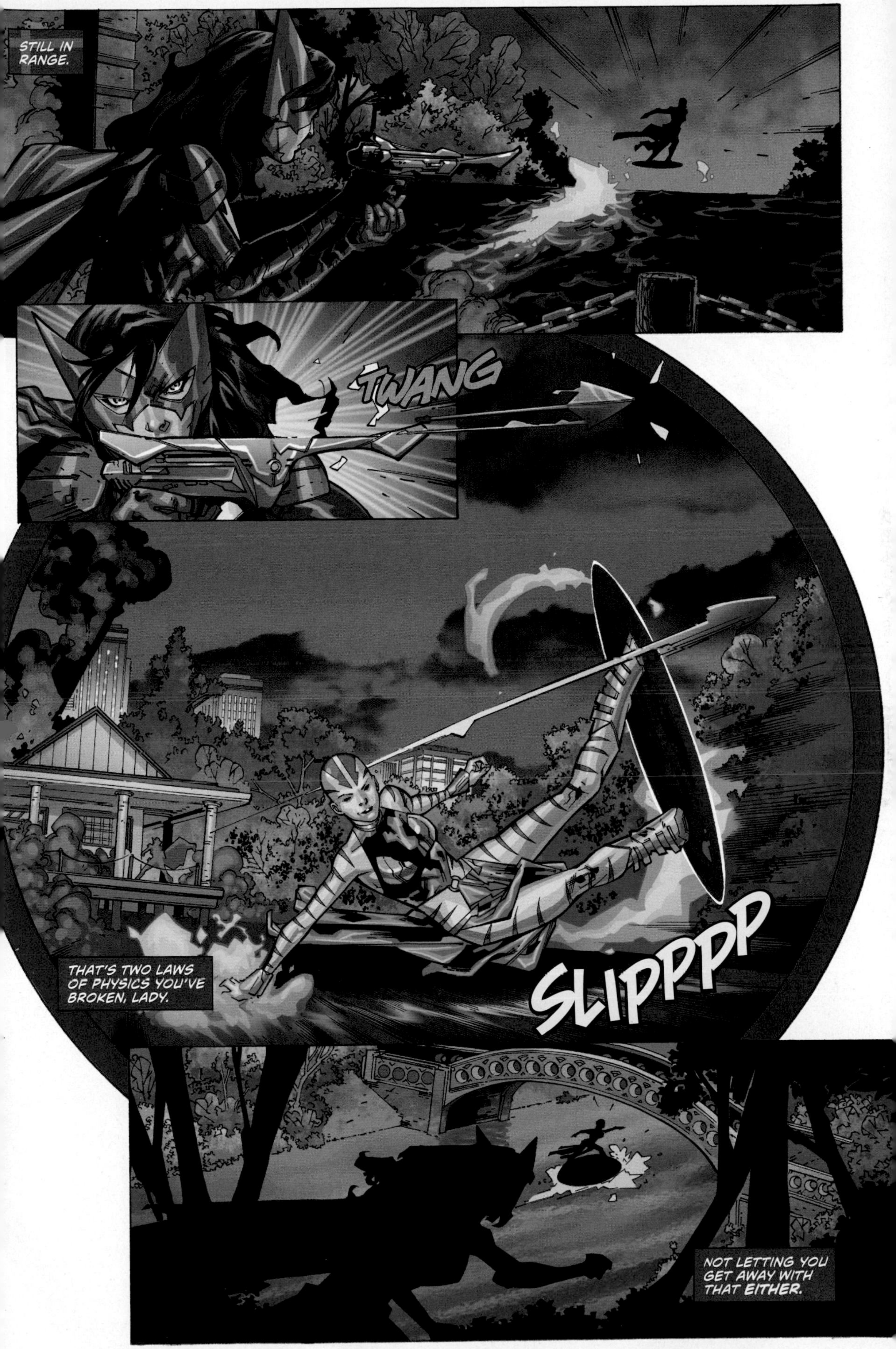
STILL IN RANGE.
TWANG
THAT'S TWO LAWS OF PHYSICS YOU'VE BROKEN, LADY.
SLIPPPP
NOT LETTING YOU GET AWAY WITH THAT EITHER.

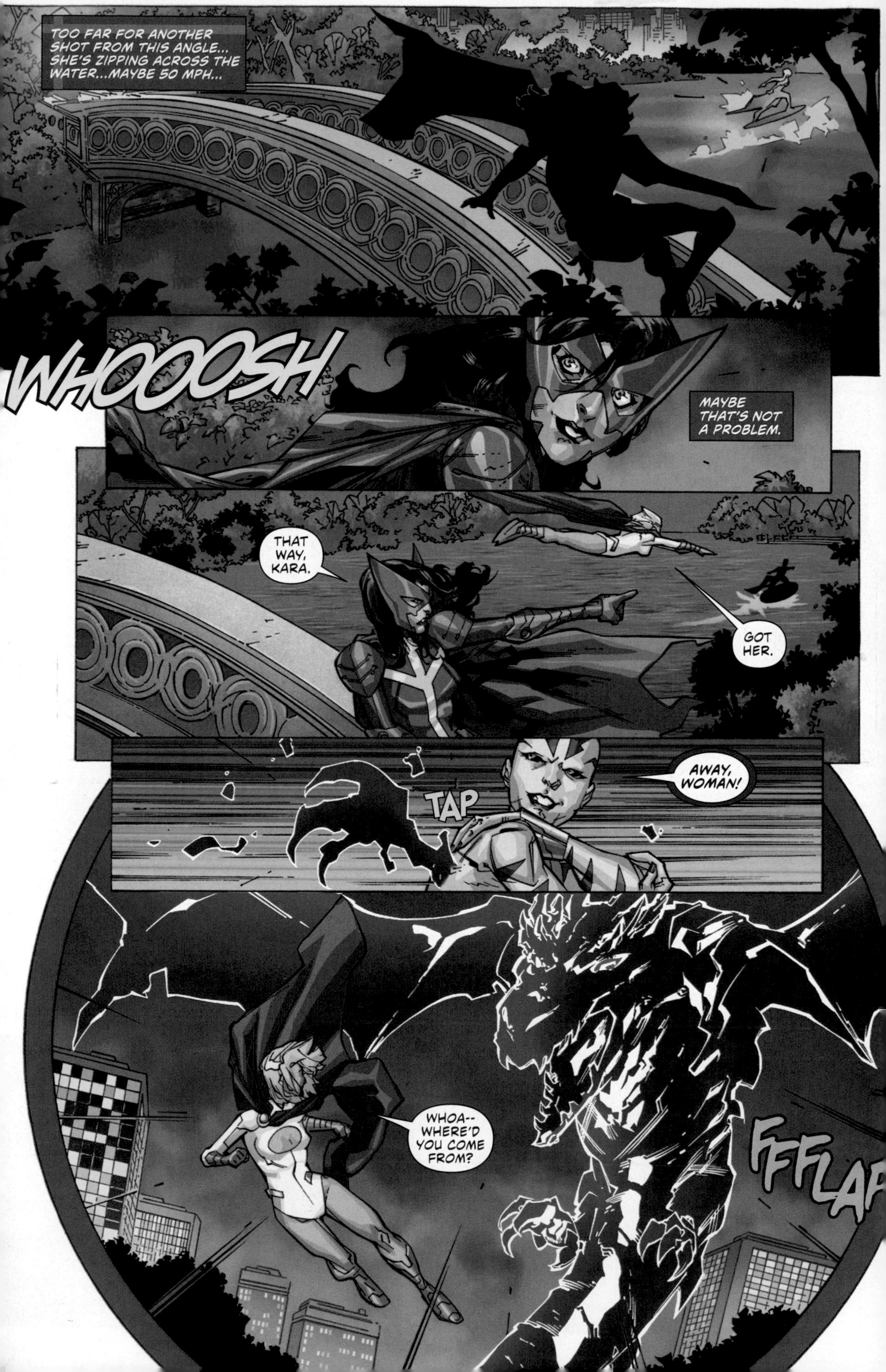
TOO FAR FOR ANOTHER SHOT FROM THIS ANGLE... SHE'S ZIPPING ACROSS THE WATER...MAYBE 50 MPH...
WHOOOSH
MAYBE THAT'S NOT A PROBLEM.
THAT WAY, KARA.
GOT HER.
TAP
AWAY, WOMAN!
WHOA-- WHERE'D YOU COME FROM?
FFFLAP

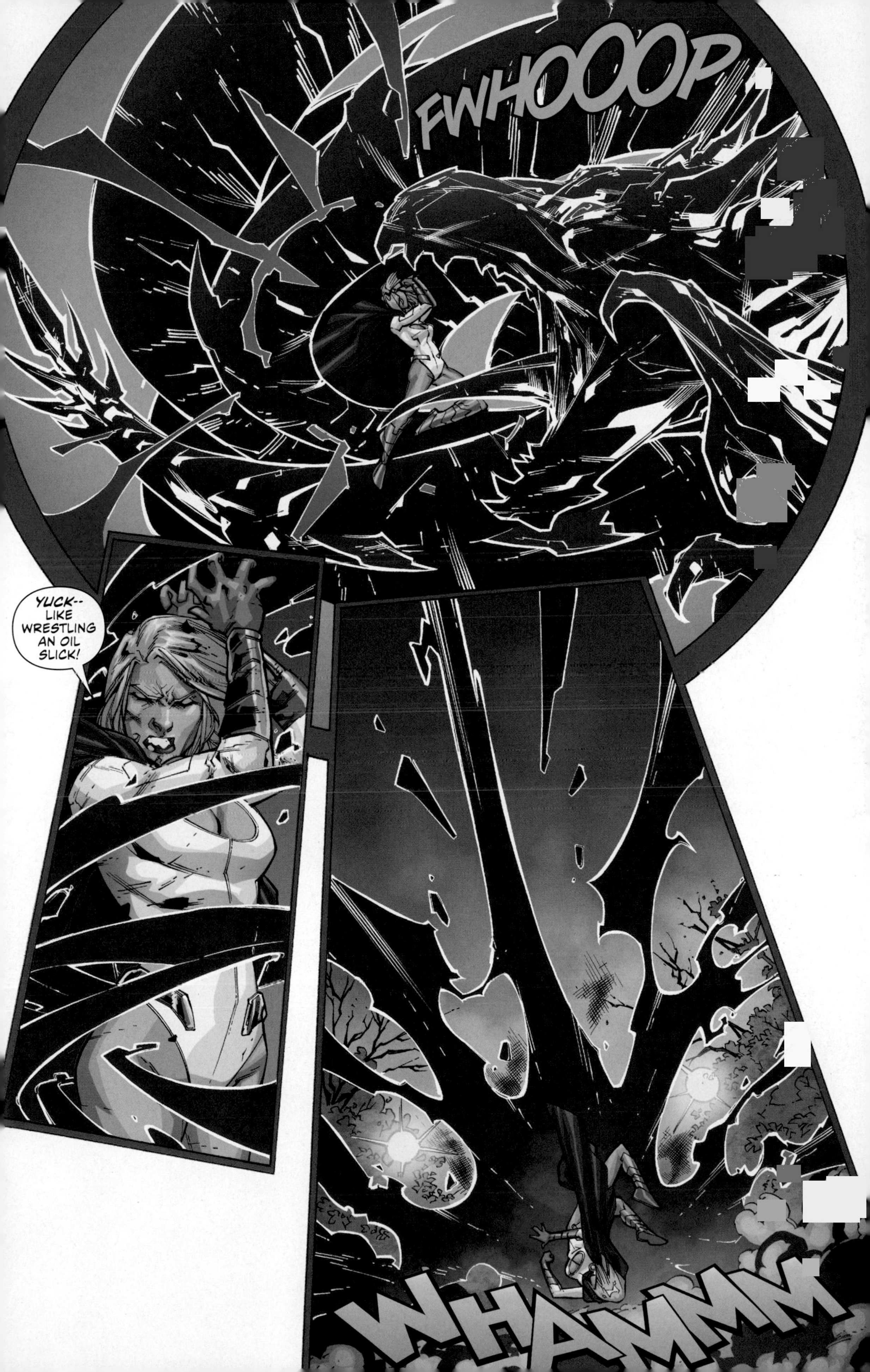

FWHOOOP
YUCK-- LIKE WRESTLING AN OIL SLICK!
WHAMMM

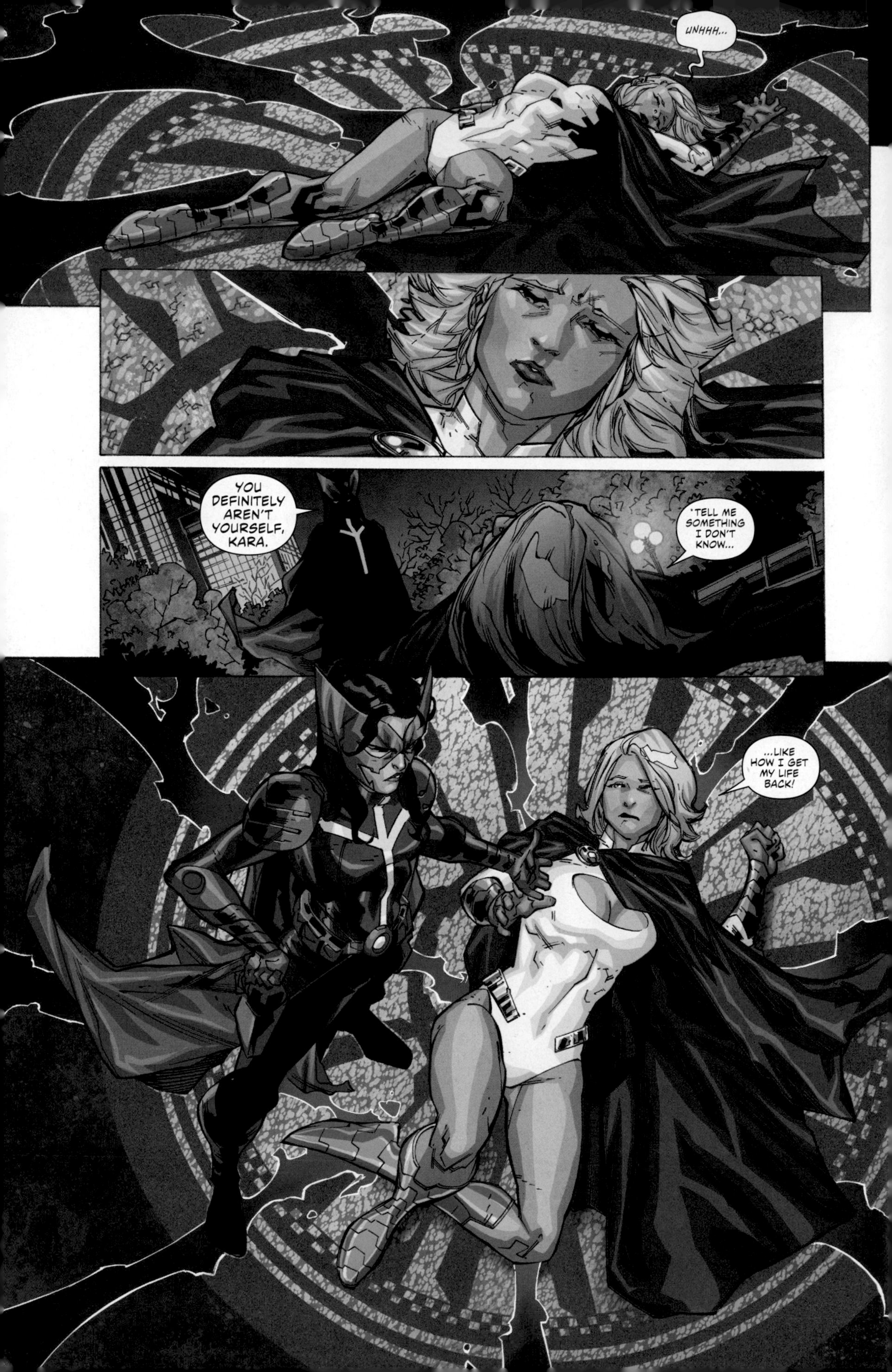
UNHHH...
YOU DEFINITELY AREN'T YOURSELF, KARA.
TELL ME SOMETHING I DON'T KNOW...
...LIKE HOW I GET MY LIFE BACK!

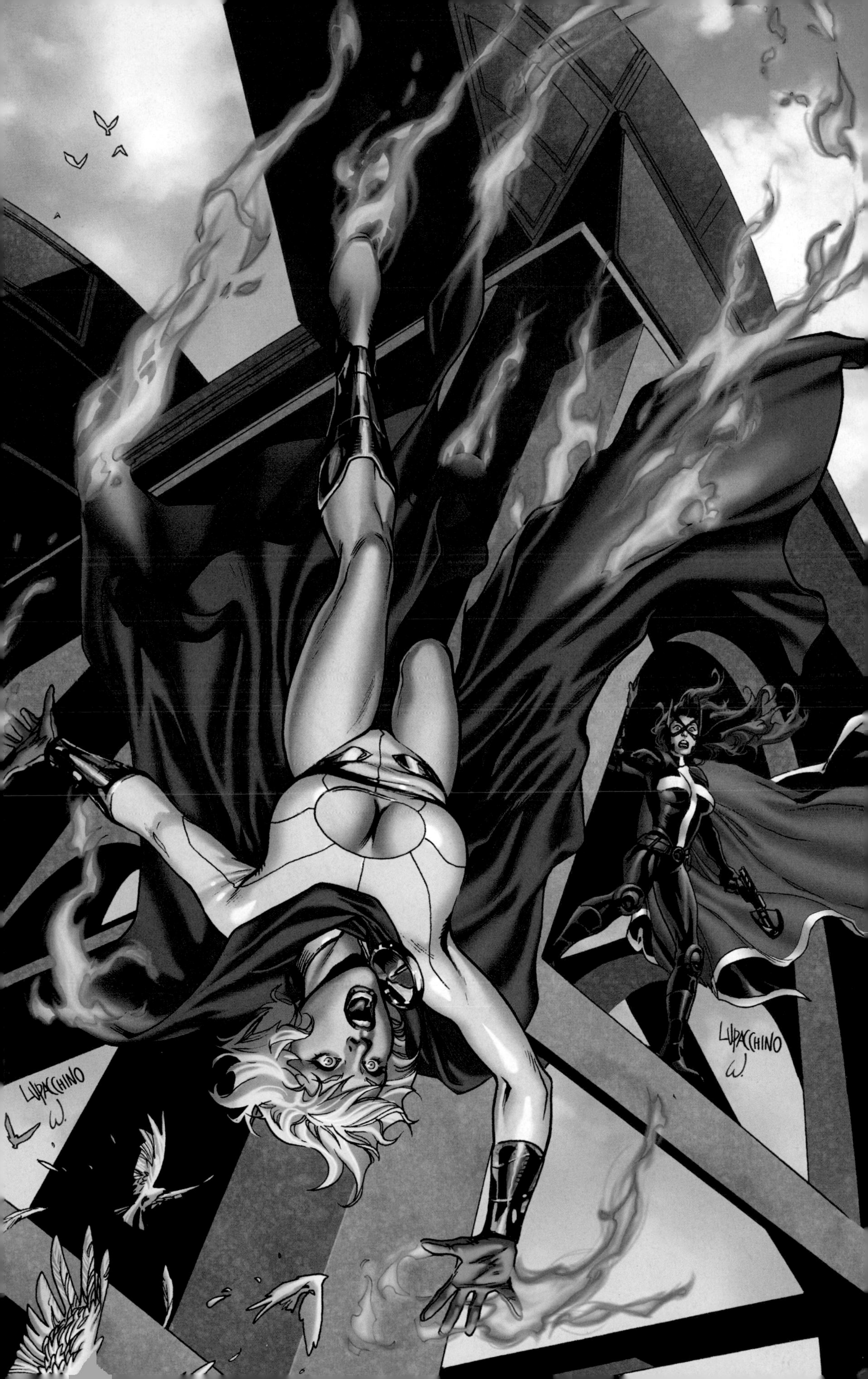
LUPACCHINO
W.
LUPACCHINO
W.

YOUR OWN WORST ENEMY!

SCOTT MCDANIEL breakdowns **R.B. SILVA** penciller **JOE WEEMS with RYAN WINN** inkers
cover art by **EMANUELA LUPACCHINO** with **JASON WRIGHT**

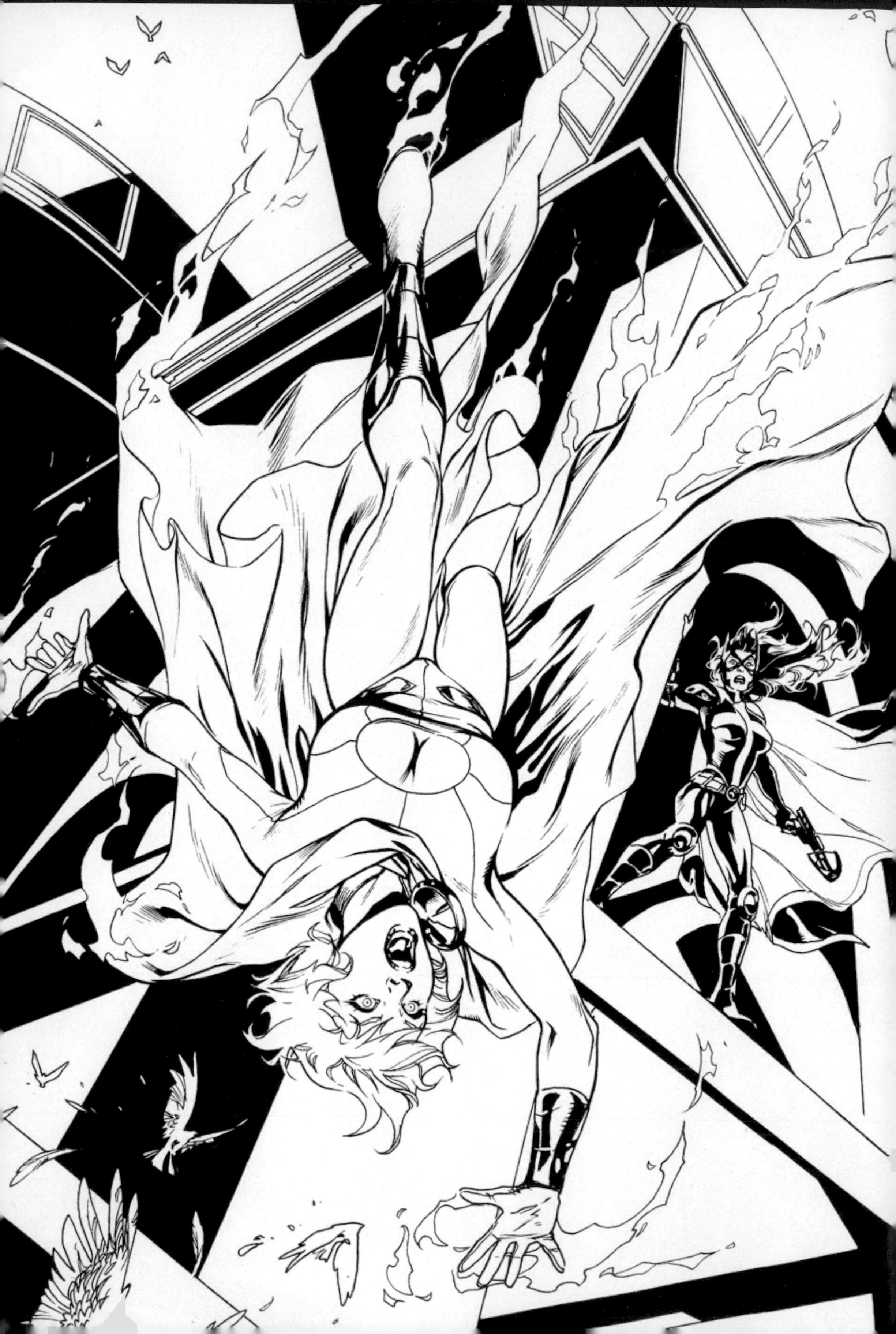

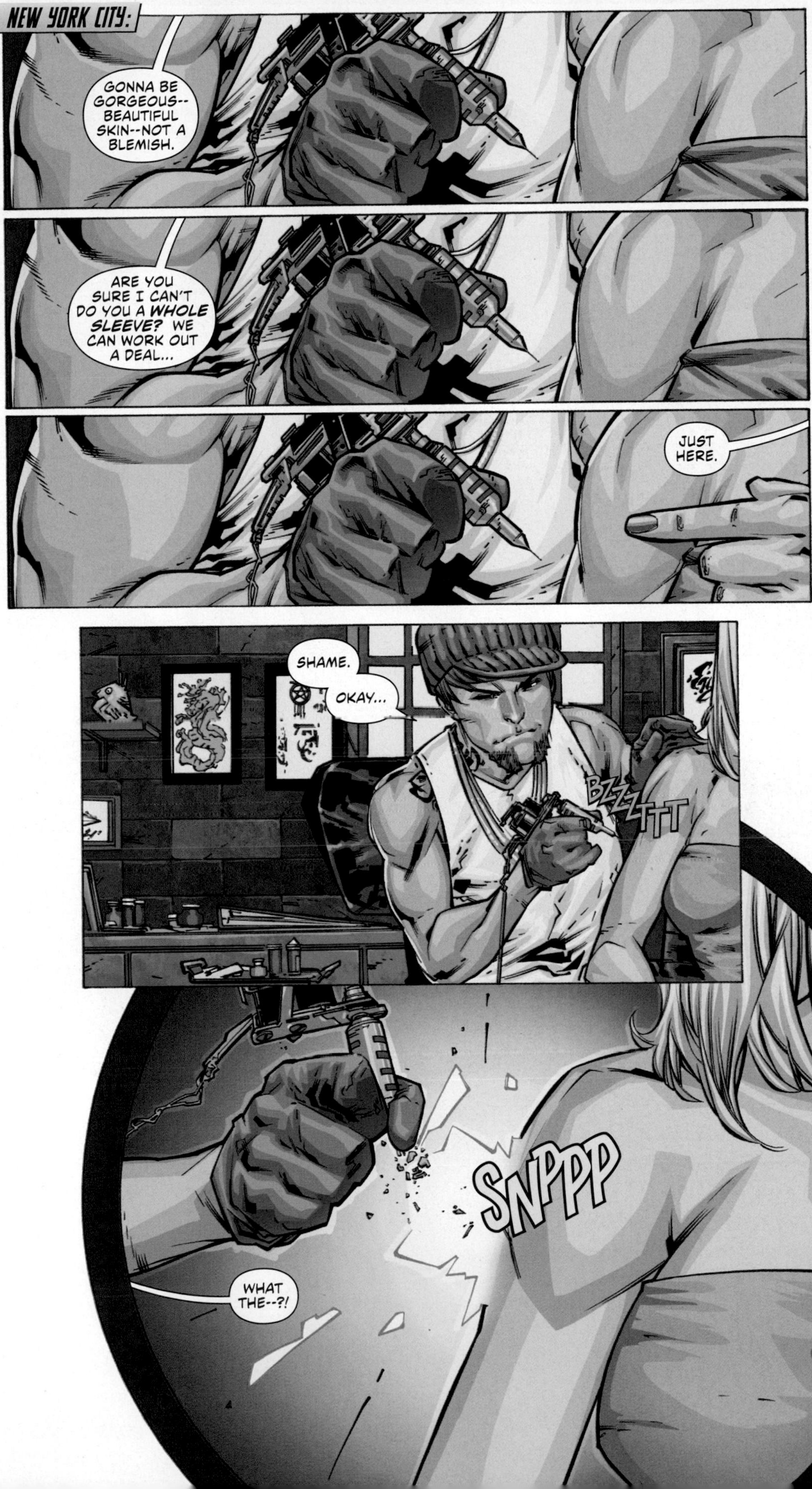
NEW YORK CITY:
GONNA BE GORGEOUS--BEAUTIFUL SKIN--NOT A BLEMISH.
ARE YOU SURE I CAN'T DO YOU A WHOLE SLEEVE? WE CAN WORK OUT A DEAL...
JUST HERE.
SHAME.
OKAY...
BZZZTTT
SNPPP
WHAT THE--?!

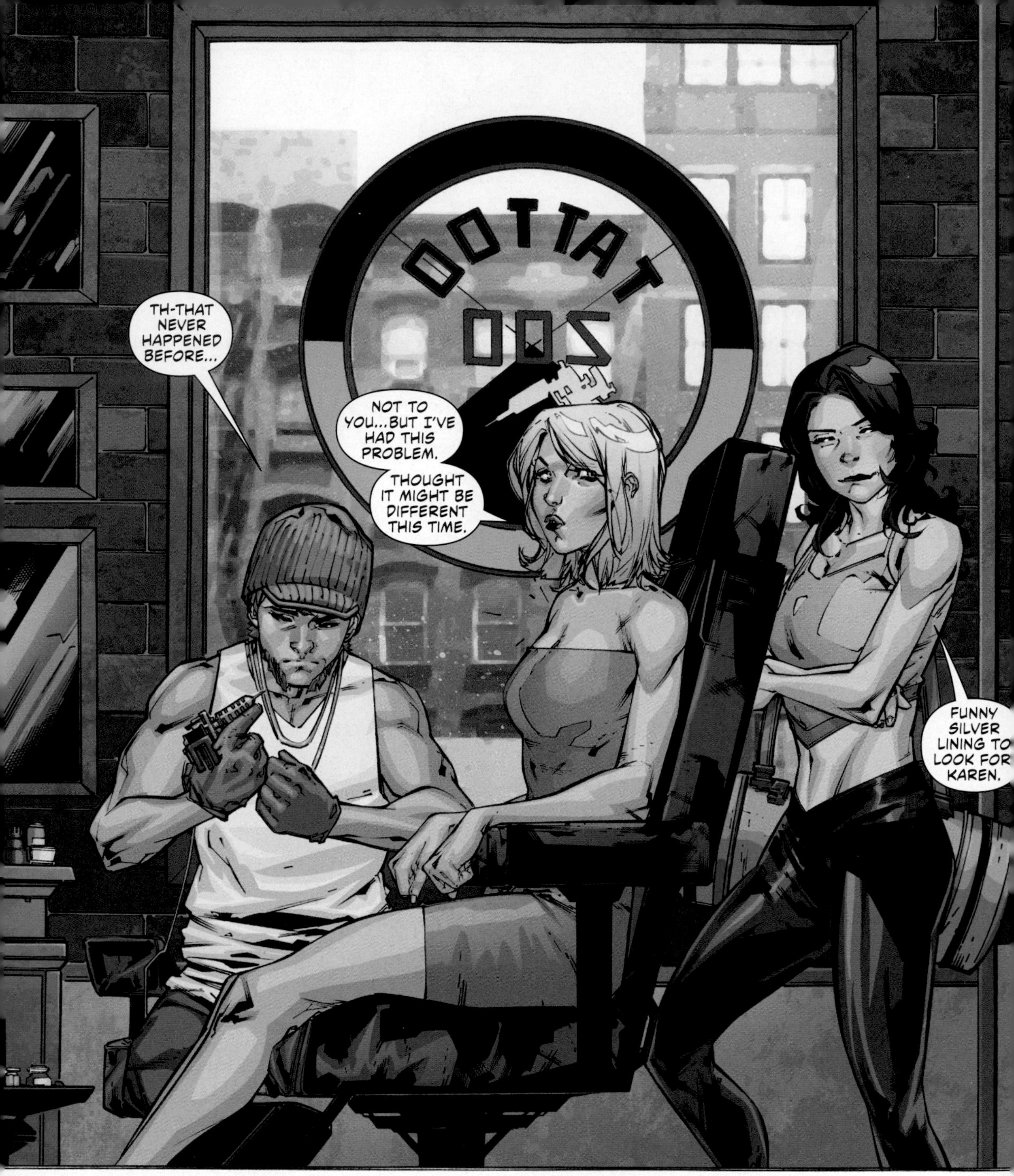
TH-THAT NEVER HAPPENED BEFORE...
NOT TO YOU...BUT I'VE HAD THIS PROBLEM.
THOUGHT IT MIGHT BE DIFFERENT THIS TIME.
FUNNY SILVER LINING TO LOOK FOR KAREN.

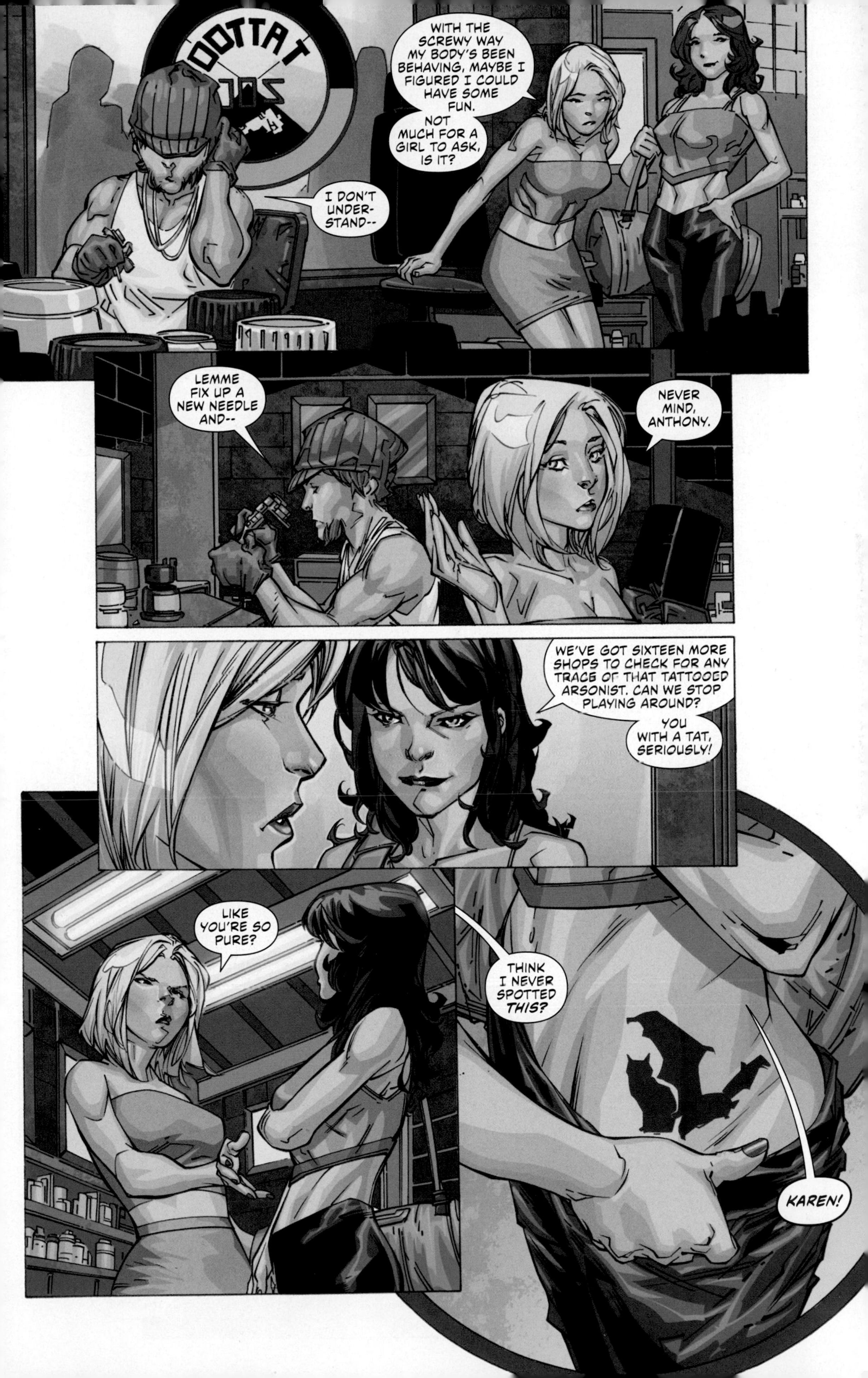
WITH THE SCREWY WAY MY BODY'S BEEN BEHAVING, MAYBE I FIGURED I COULD HAVE SOME FUN.
NOT MUCH FOR A GIRL TO ASK, IS IT?
I DON'T UNDER-STAND--
LEMME FIX UP A NEW NEEDLE AND--
NEVER MIND, ANTHONY.
WE'VE GOT SIXTEEN MORE SHOPS TO CHECK FOR ANY TRACE OF THAT TATTOOED ARSONIST. CAN WE STOP PLAYING AROUND?
YOU WITH A TAT, SERIOUSLY!
LIKE YOU'RE SO PURE?
THINK I NEVER SPOTTED *THIS?*
KAREN!

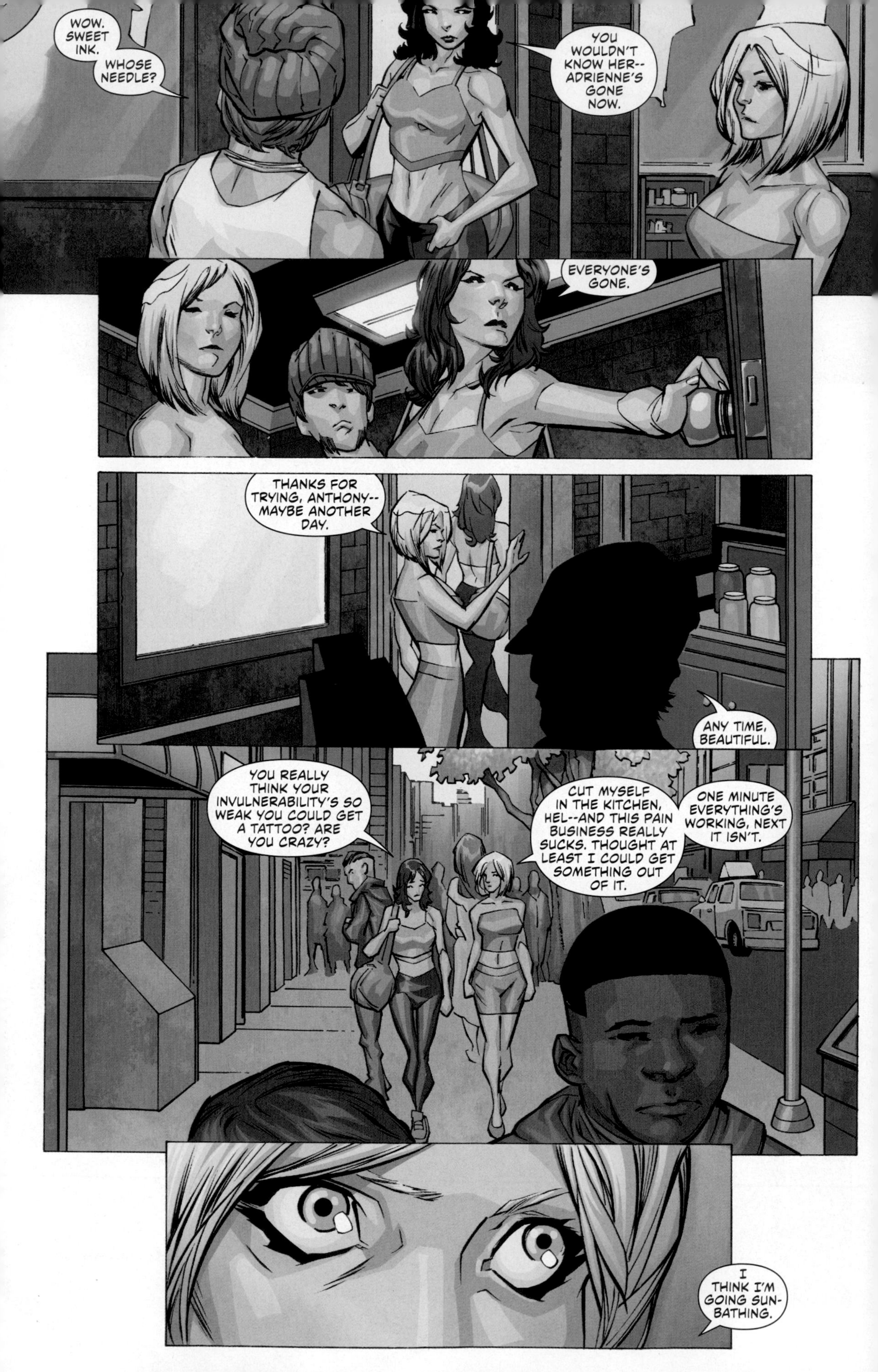
WOW. SWEET INK.
WHOSE NEEDLE?
YOU WOULDN'T KNOW HER--ADRIENNE'S GONE NOW.
EVERYONE'S GONE.
THANKS FOR TRYING, ANTHONY--MAYBE ANOTHER DAY.
ANY TIME, BEAUTIFUL.
YOU REALLY THINK YOUR INVULNERABILITY'S SO WEAK YOU COULD GET A TATTOO? ARE YOU CRAZY?
CUT MYSELF IN THE KITCHEN, HEL--AND THIS PAIN BUSINESS REALLY SUCKS. THOUGHT AT LEAST I COULD GET SOMETHING OUT OF IT.
ONE MINUTE EVERYTHING'S WORKING, NEXT IT ISN'T.
I THINK I'M GOING SUN-BATHING.

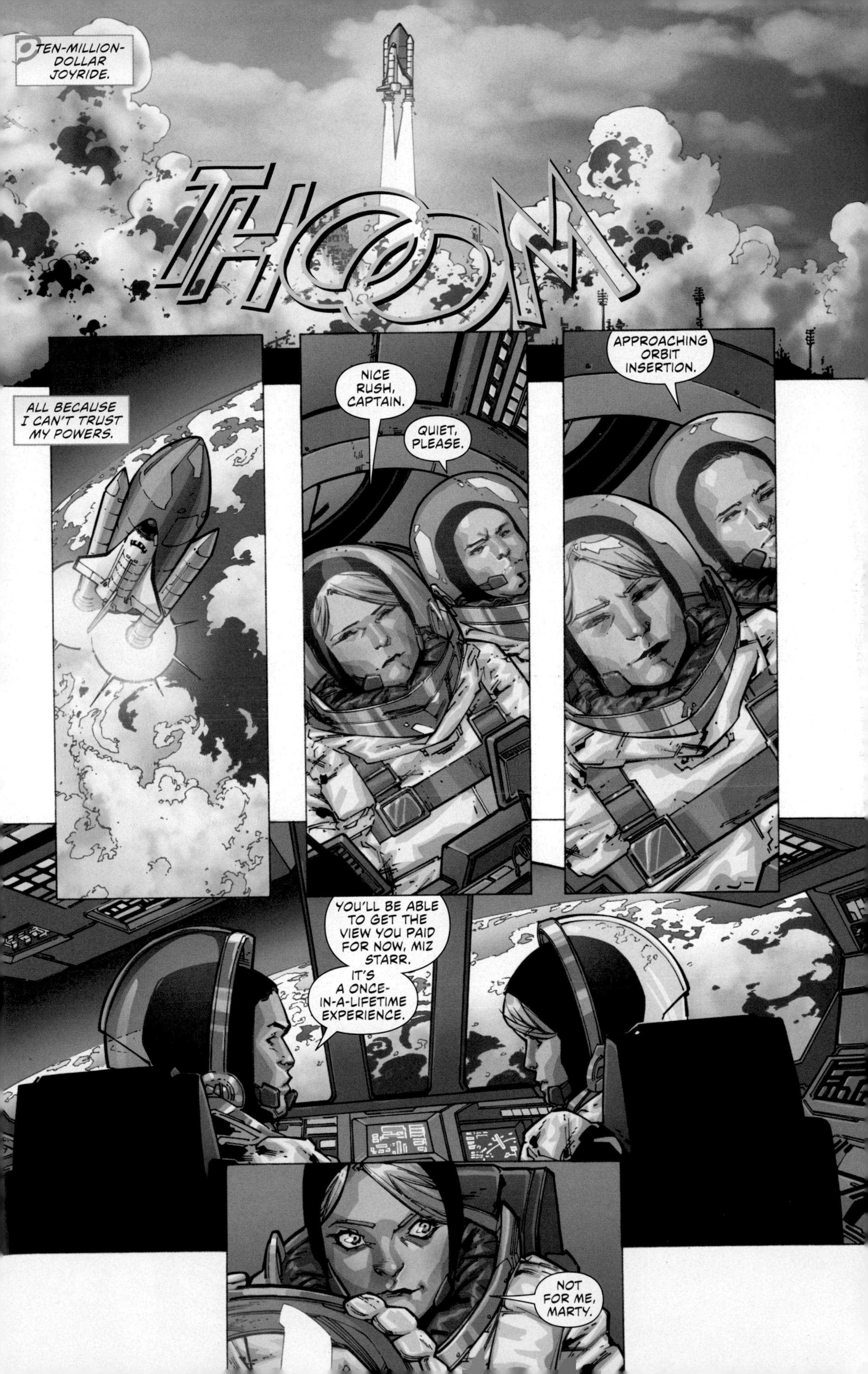
TEN-MILLION-DOLLAR JOYRIDE.
THOOM
ALL BECAUSE I CAN'T TRUST MY POWERS.
NICE RUSH, CAPTAIN.
QUIET, PLEASE.
APPROACHING ORBIT INSERTION.
YOU'LL BE ABLE TO GET THE VIEW YOU PAID FOR NOW, MIZ STARR.
IT'S A ONCE-IN-A-LIFETIME EXPERIENCE.
NOT FOR ME, MARTY.

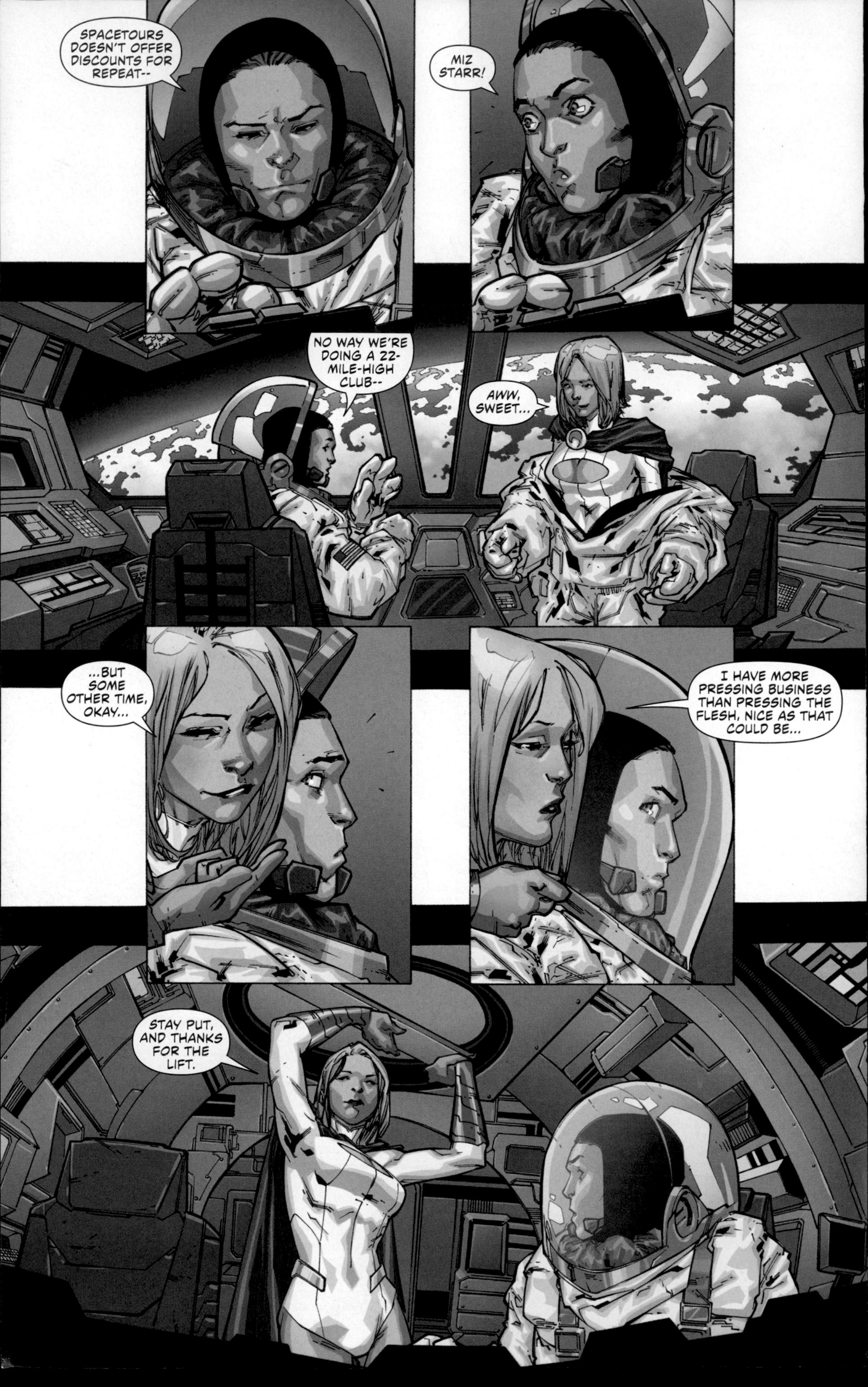
SPACETOURS DOESN'T OFFER DISCOUNTS FOR REPEAT--
MIZ STARR!
NO WAY WE'RE DOING A 22-MILE-HIGH CLUB--
AWW, SWEET...
...BUT SOME OTHER TIME, OKAY...
I HAVE MORE PRESSING BUSINESS THAN PRESSING THE FLESH, NICE AS THAT COULD BE...
STAY PUT, AND THANKS FOR THE LIFT.

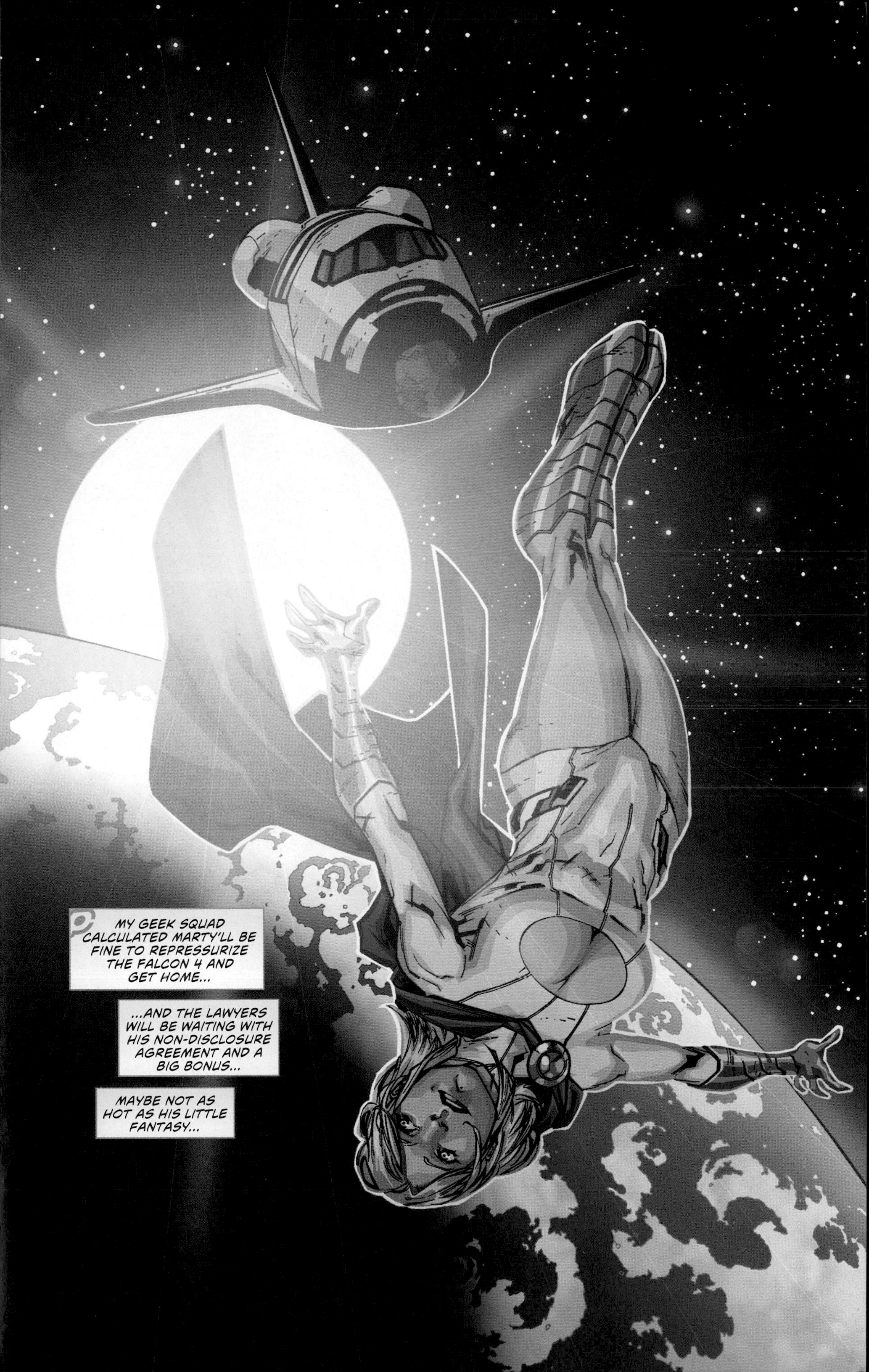
MY GEEK SQUAD CALCULATED MARTY'LL BE FINE TO REPRESSURIZE THE FALCON 4 AND GET HOME...
...AND THE LAWYERS WILL BE WAITING WITH HIS NON-DISCLOSURE AGREEMENT AND A BIG BONUS...
MAYBE NOT AS HOT AS HIS LITTLE FANTASY...

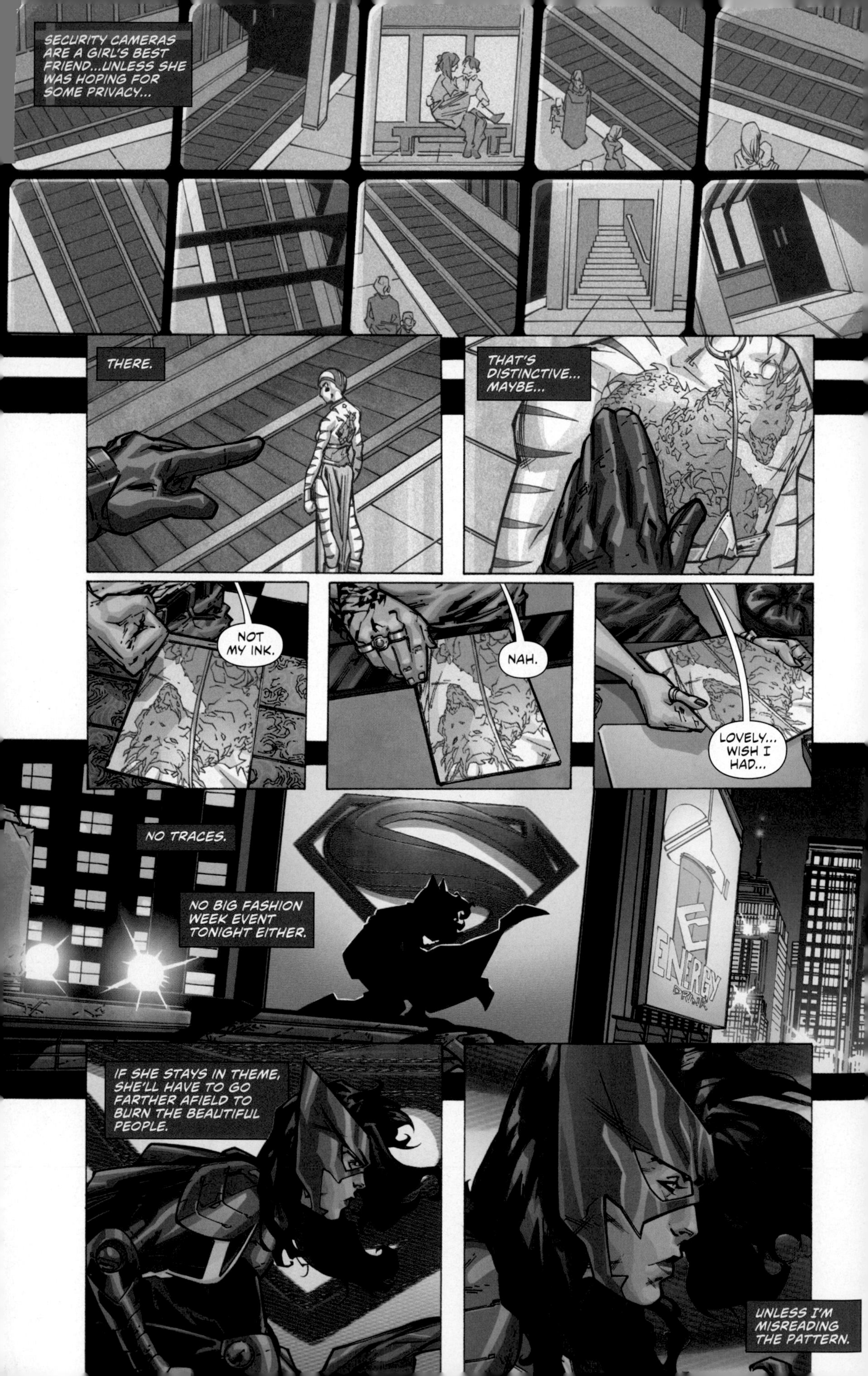
SECURITY CAMERAS ARE A GIRL'S BEST FRIEND...UNLESS SHE WAS HOPING FOR SOME PRIVACY...
THERE.
THAT'S DISTINCTIVE... MAYBE...
NOT MY INK.
NAH.
LOVELY... WISH I HAD...
NO TRACES.
NO BIG FASHION WEEK EVENT TONIGHT EITHER.
ENERGY
IF SHE STAYS IN THEME, SHE'LL HAVE TO GO FARTHER AFIELD TO BURN THE BEAUTIFUL PEOPLE.
UNLESS I'M MISREADING THE PATTERN.

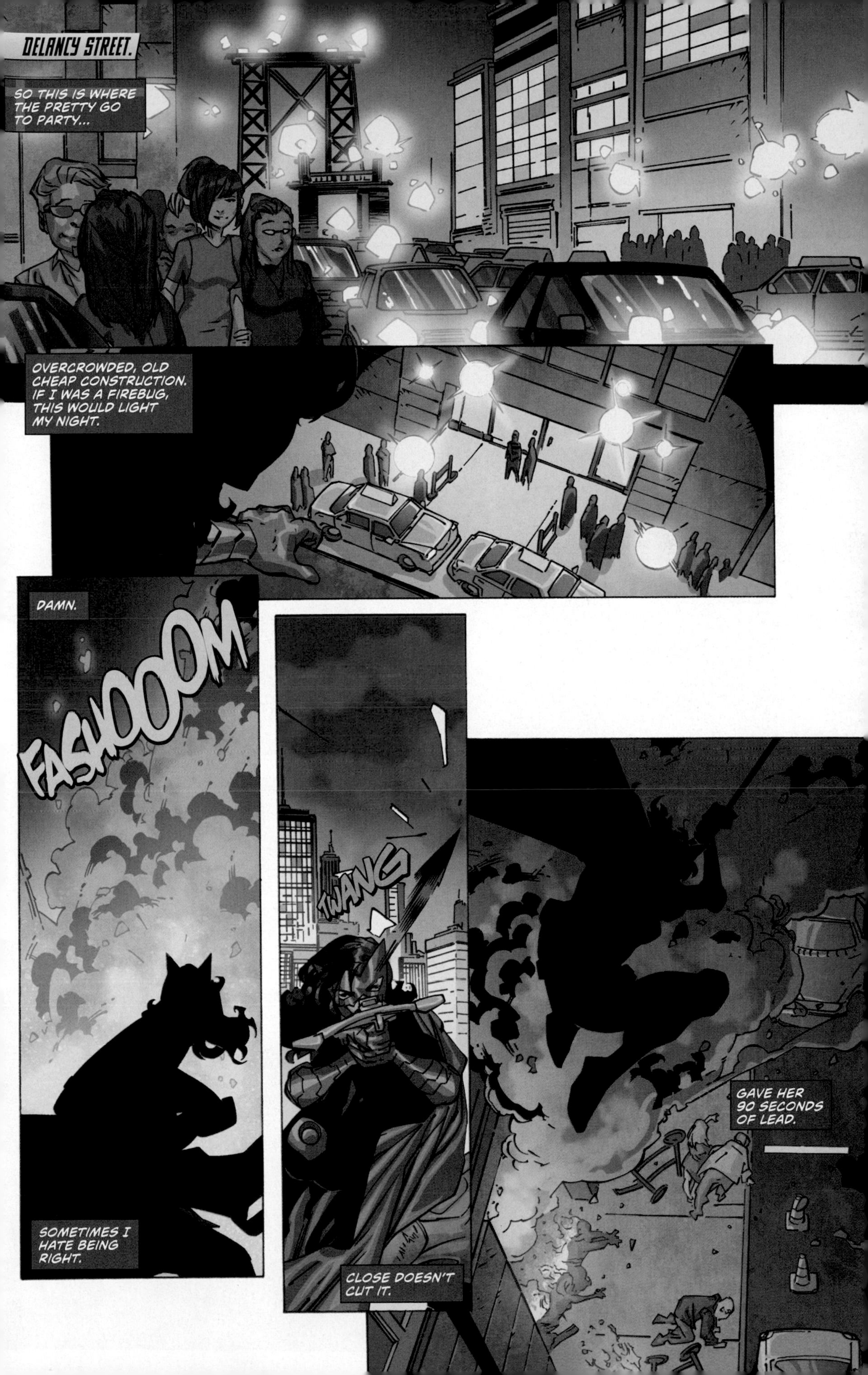

DELANCY STREET.
SO THIS IS WHERE THE PRETTY GO TO PARTY...
OVERCROWDED, OLD CHEAP CONSTRUCTION. IF I WAS A FIREBUG, THIS WOULD LIGHT MY NIGHT.
DAMN.
FASHOOOOM
SOMETIMES I HATE BEING RIGHT.
TWANG
CLOSE DOESN'T CUT IT.
GAVE HER 90 SECONDS OF LEAD.

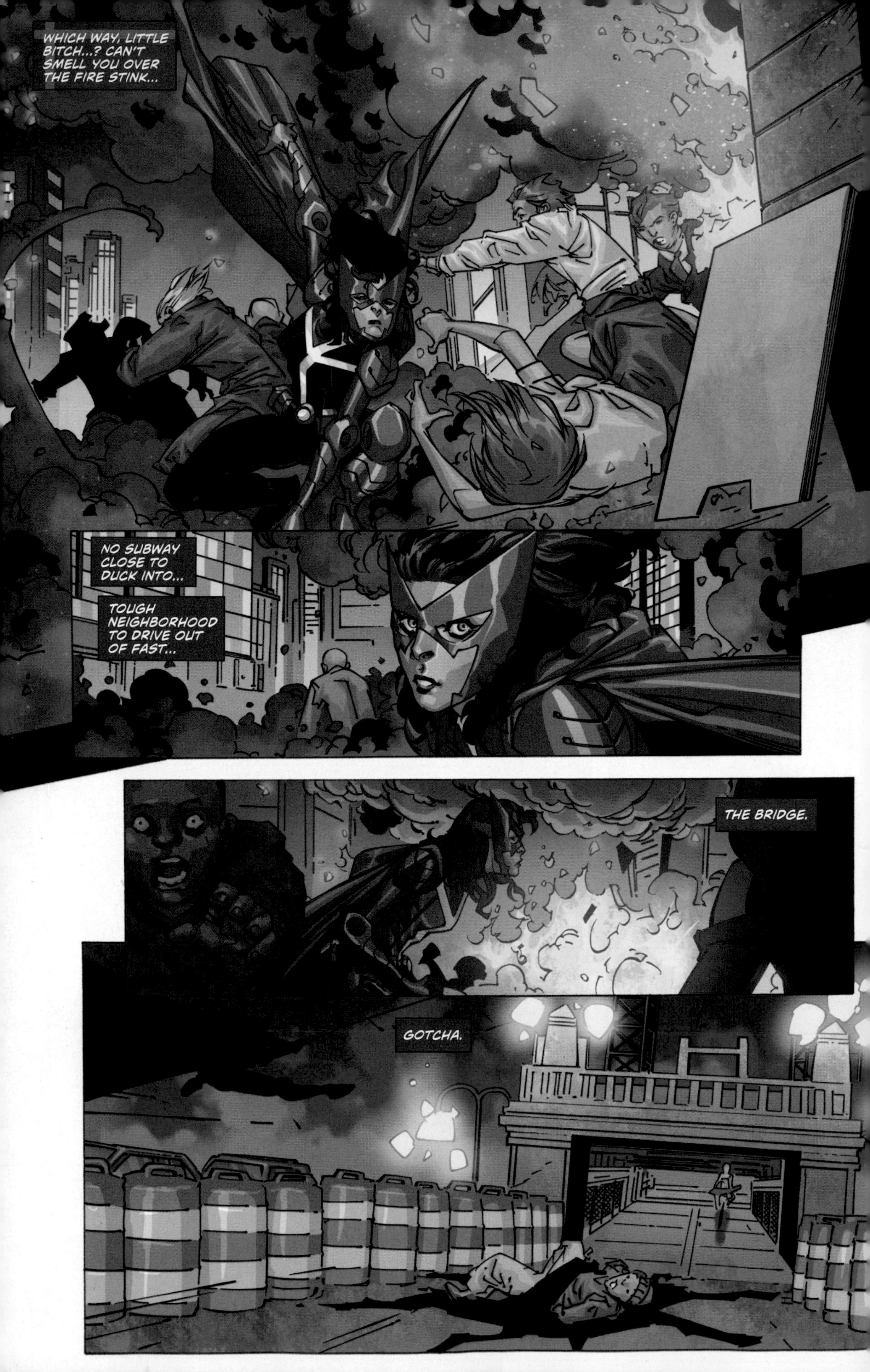
WHICH WAY, LITTLE BITCH...? CAN'T SMELL YOU OVER THE FIRE STINK...
NO SUBWAY CLOSE TO DUCK INTO...
TOUGH NEIGHBORHOOD TO DRIVE OUT OF FAST...
THE BRIDGE.
GOTCHA.

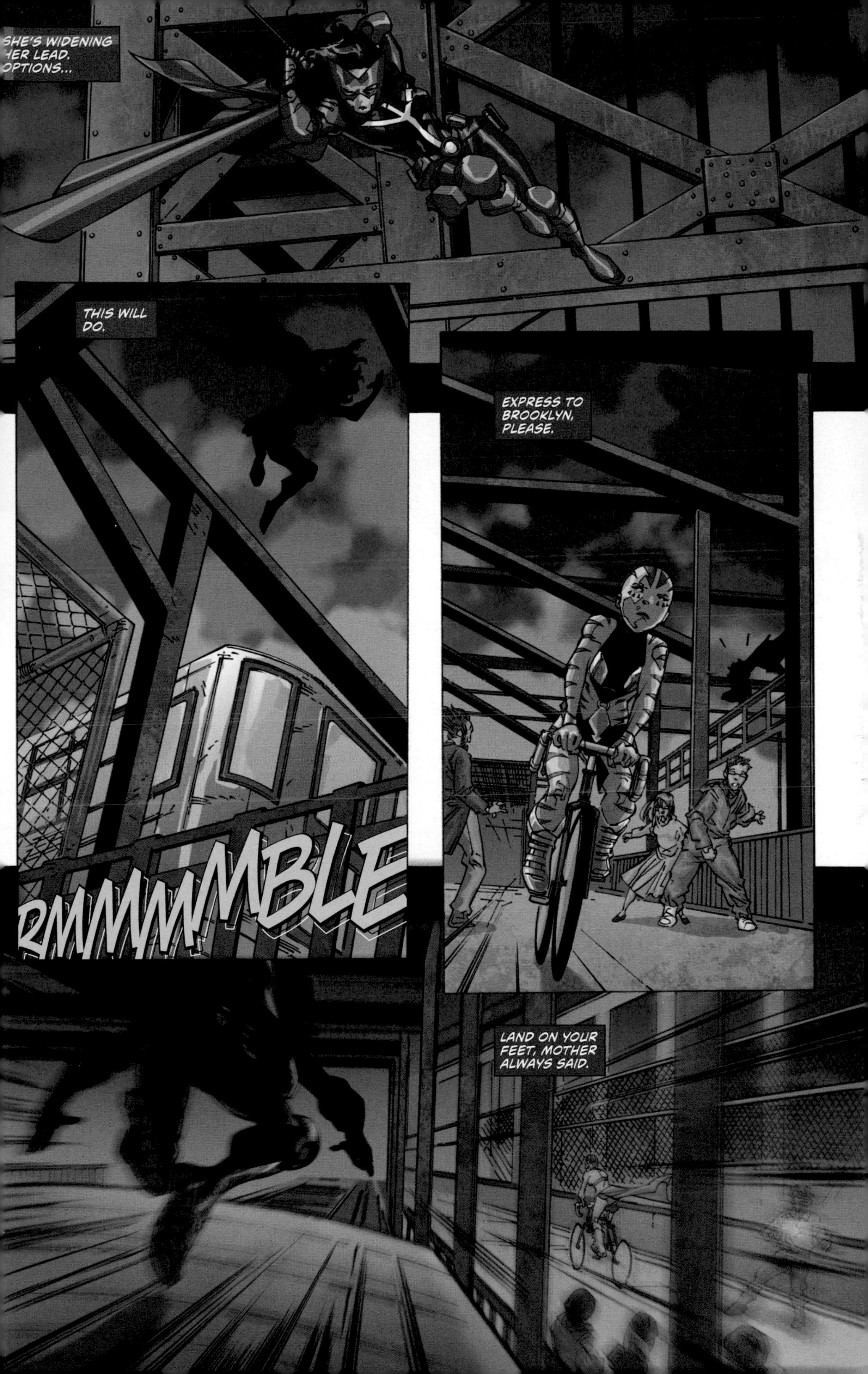
SHE'S WIDENING
HER LEAD.
OPTIONS...
THIS WILL
DO.
RMMMMBLE
EXPRESS TO
BROOKLYN,
PLEASE.
LAND ON YOUR
FEET, MOTHER
ALWAYS SAID.

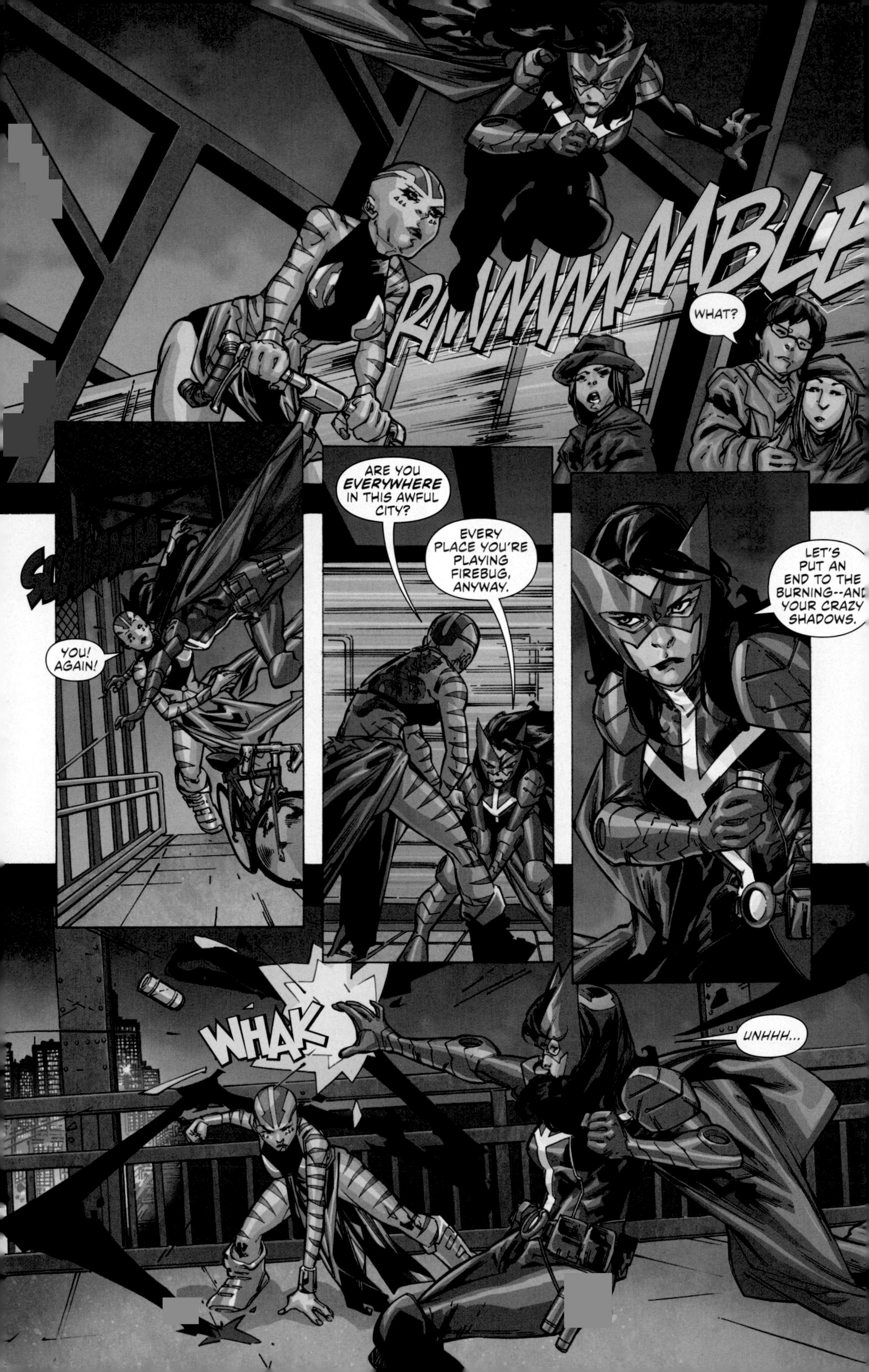
RMMMMMBLE
WHAT?
YOU! AGAIN!
ARE YOU EVERYWHERE IN THIS AWFUL CITY?
EVERY PLACE YOU'RE PLAYING FIREBUG, ANYWAY.
LET'S PUT AN END TO THE BURNING--AND YOUR CRAZY SHADOWS.
WHAK
UNHHH...

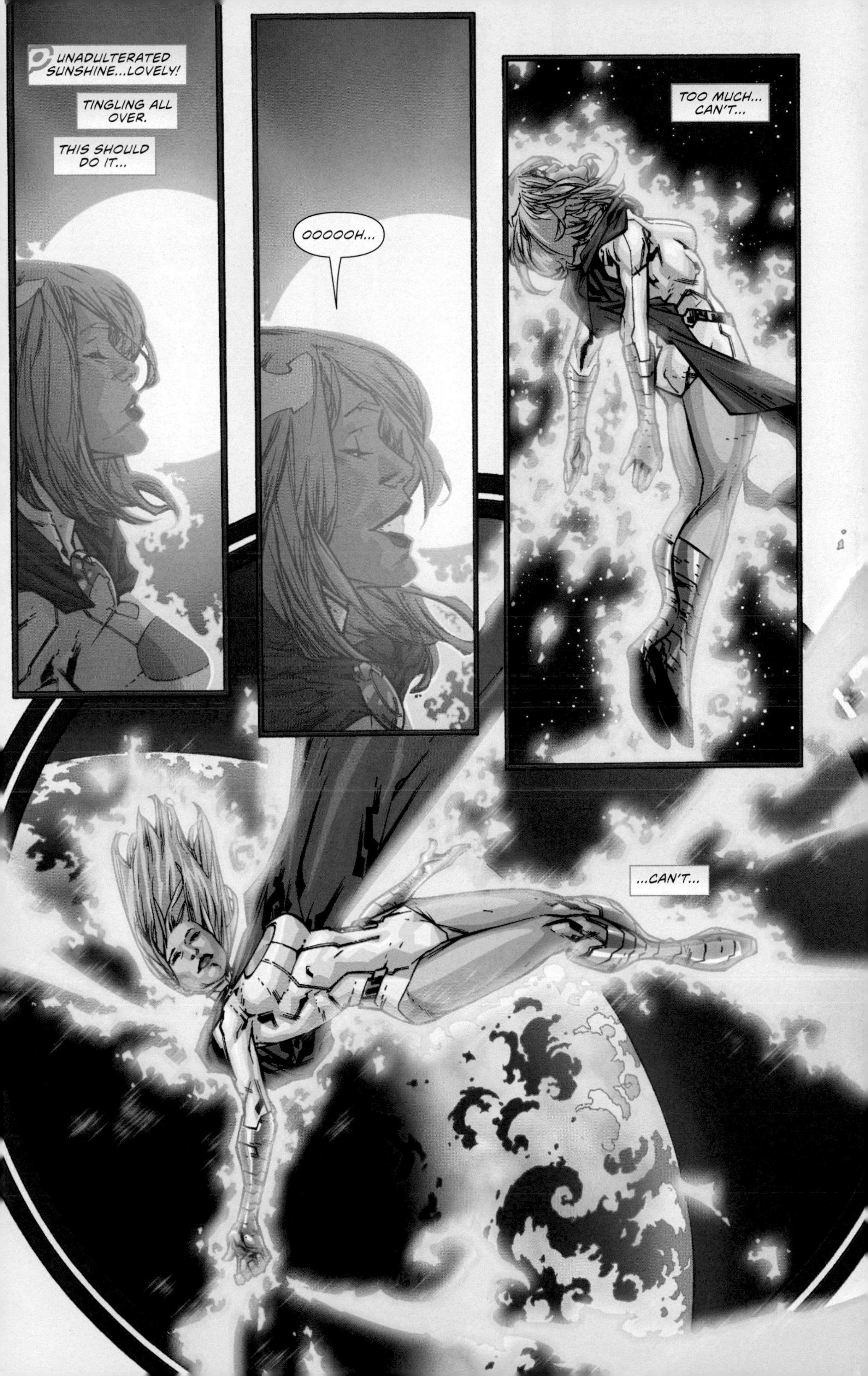
UNADULTERATED SUNSHINE...LOVELY!
TINGLING ALL OVER.
THIS SHOULD DO IT...
OOOOOH...
TOO MUCH... CAN'T...
...CAN'T...

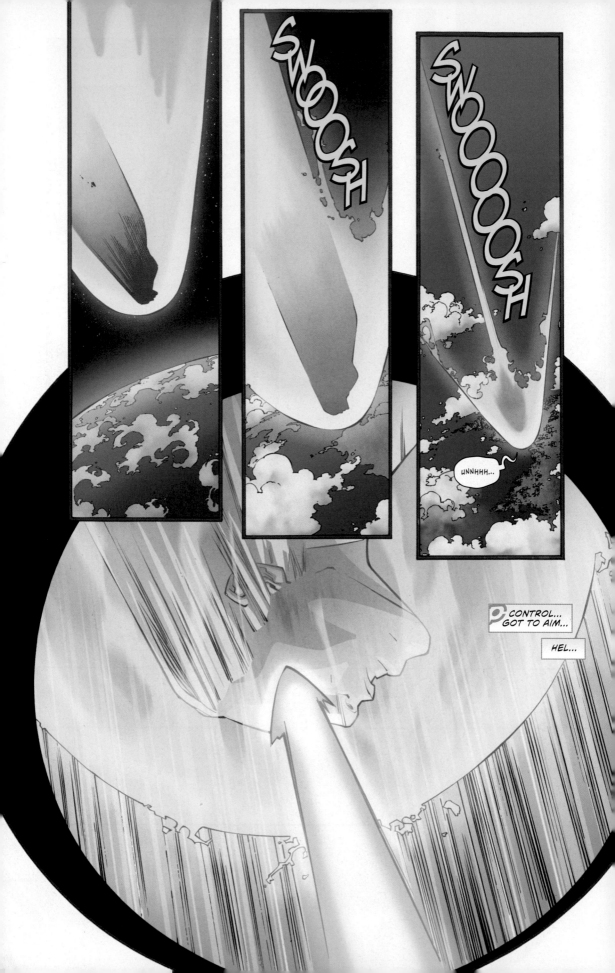

SNOOOSH

SNOOOOSH

UNNHHH...

CONTROL...
GOT TO AIM...

HEL...

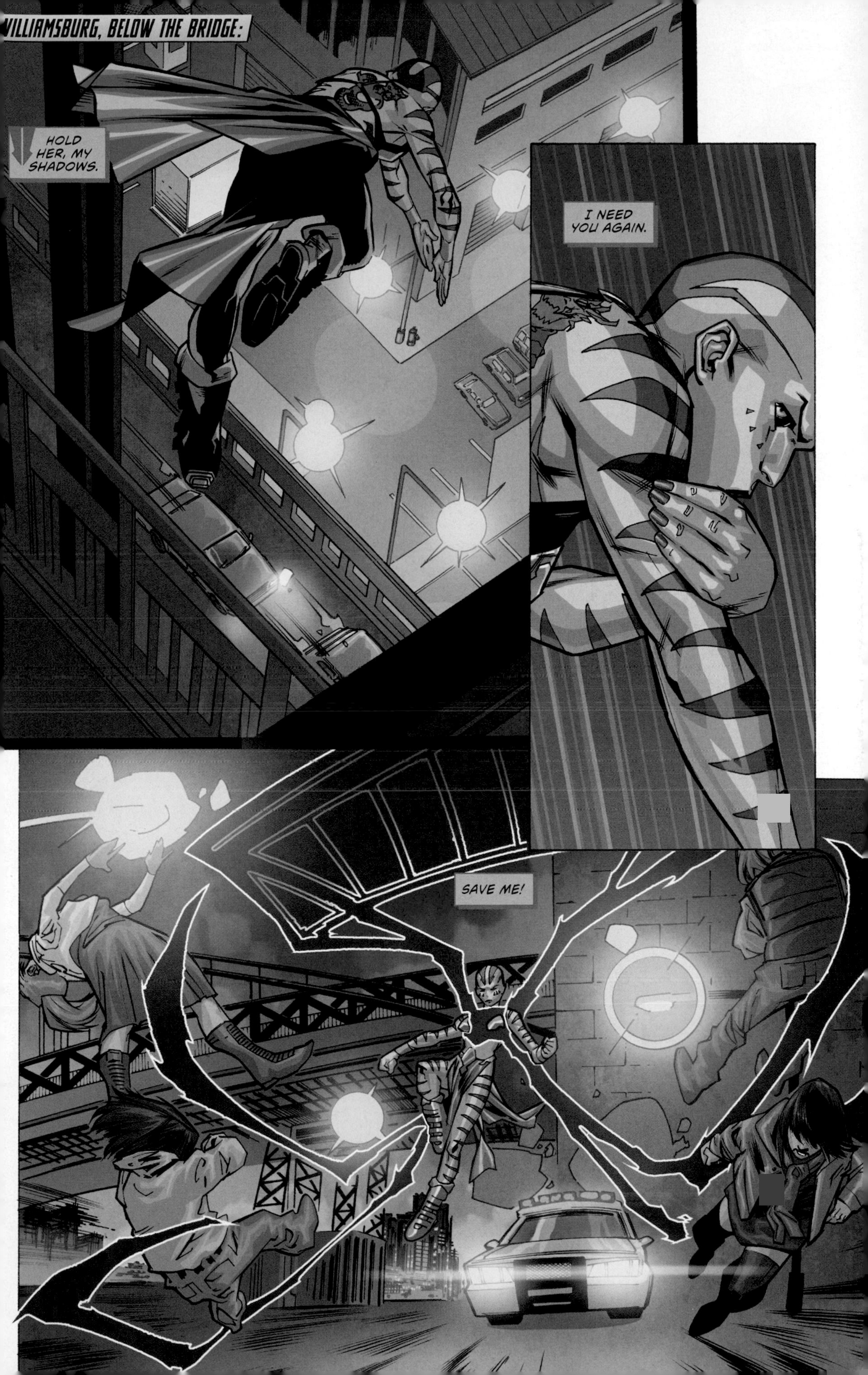
WILLIAMSBURG, BELOW THE BRIDGE:
HOLD HER, MY SHADOWS.
I NEED YOU AGAIN.
SAVE ME!

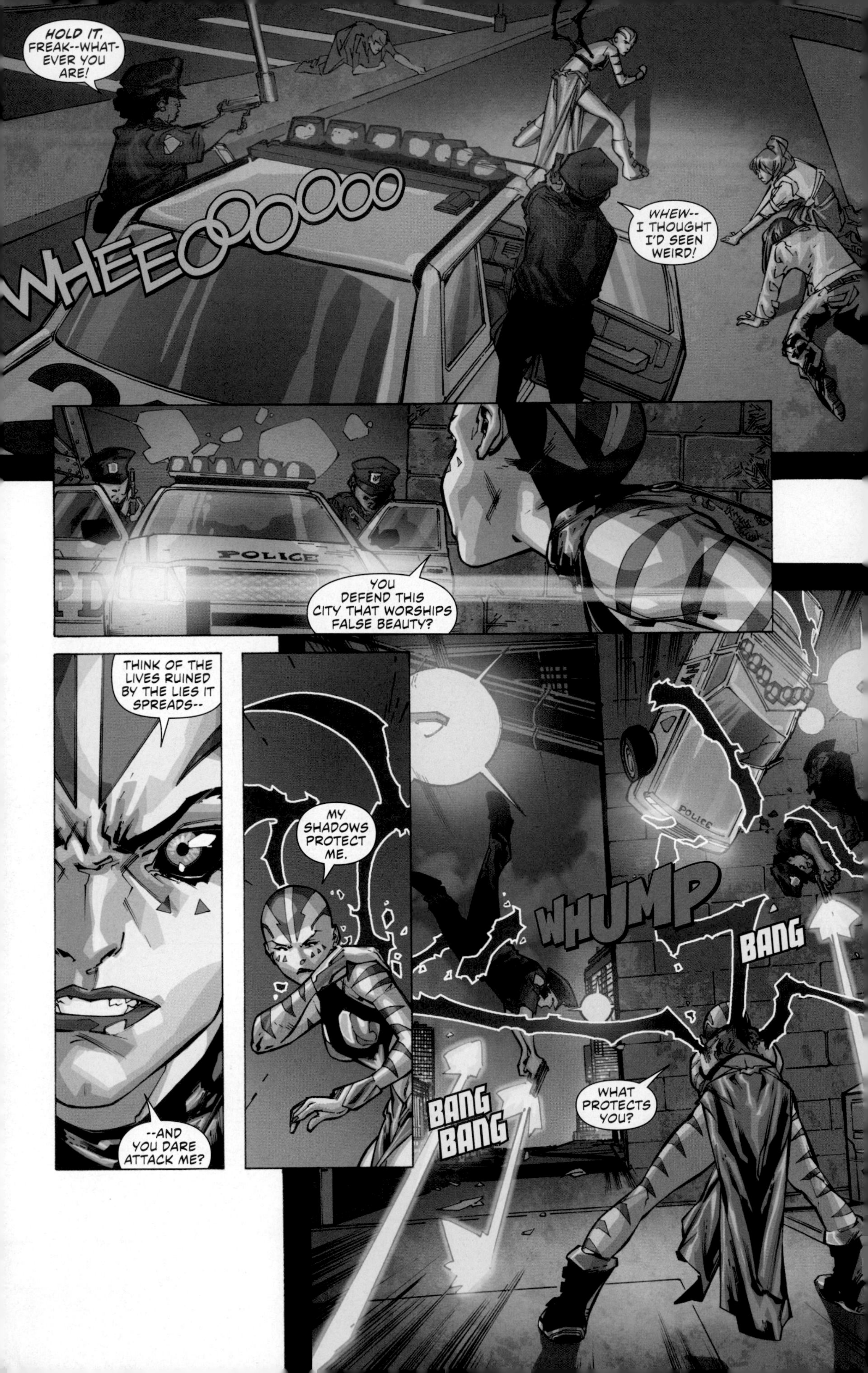
HOLD IT, FREAK--WHATEVER YOU ARE!
WHEEOOOOOOO
WHEW--I THOUGHT I'D SEEN WEIRD!
POLICE
YOU DEFEND THIS CITY THAT WORSHIPS FALSE BEAUTY?
THINK OF THE LIVES RUINED BY THE LIES IT SPREADS--
--AND YOU DARE ATTACK ME?
MY SHADOWS PROTECT ME.
POLICE
WHUMP
BANG
BANG BANG
WHAT PROTECTS YOU?

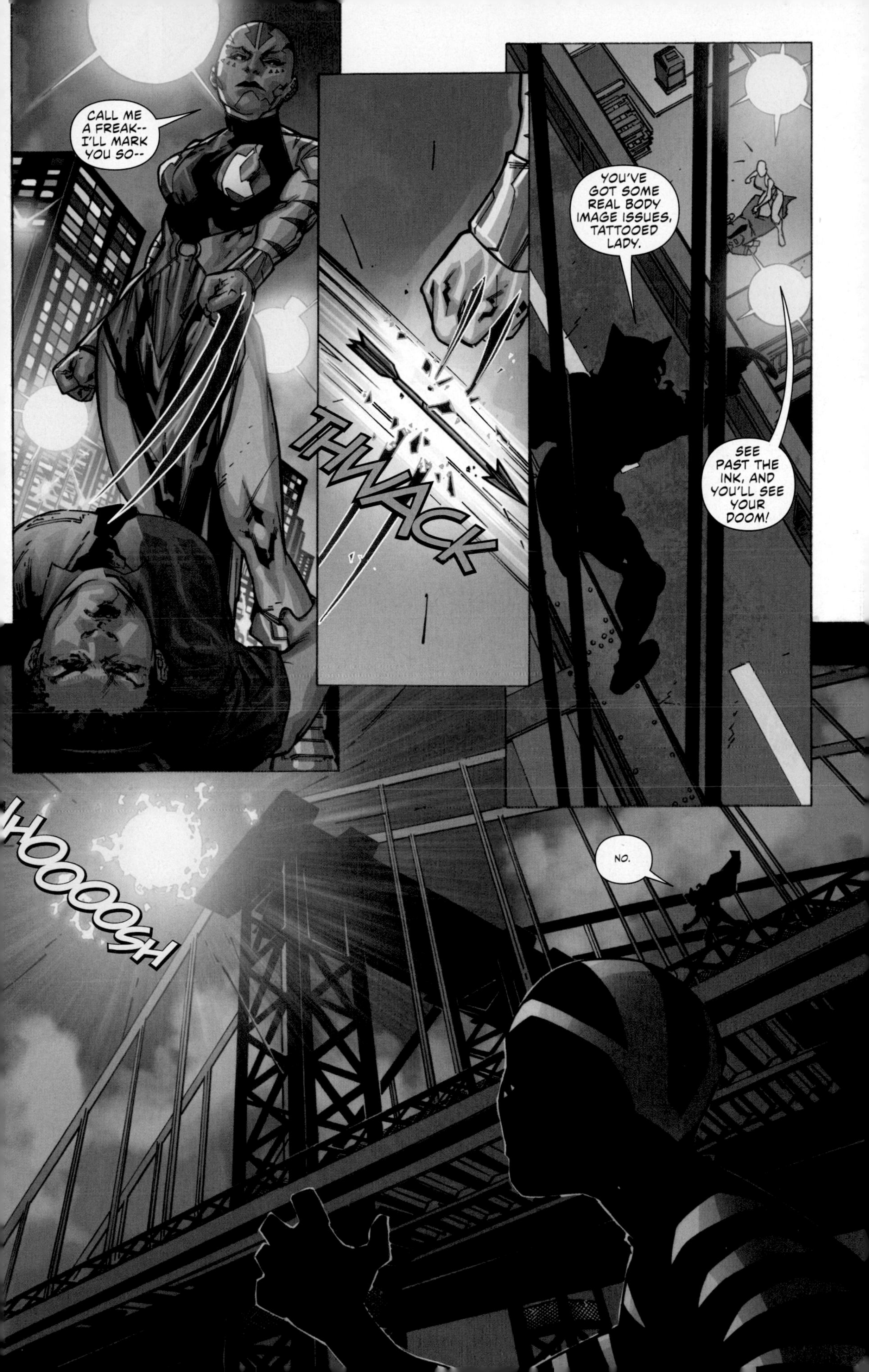
CALL ME A FREAK-- I'LL MARK YOU SO--
THWACK
YOU'VE GOT SOME REAL BODY IMAGE ISSUES, TATTOOED LADY.
SEE PAST THE INK, AND YOU'LL SEE YOUR DOOM!
HOOOOSH
NO.

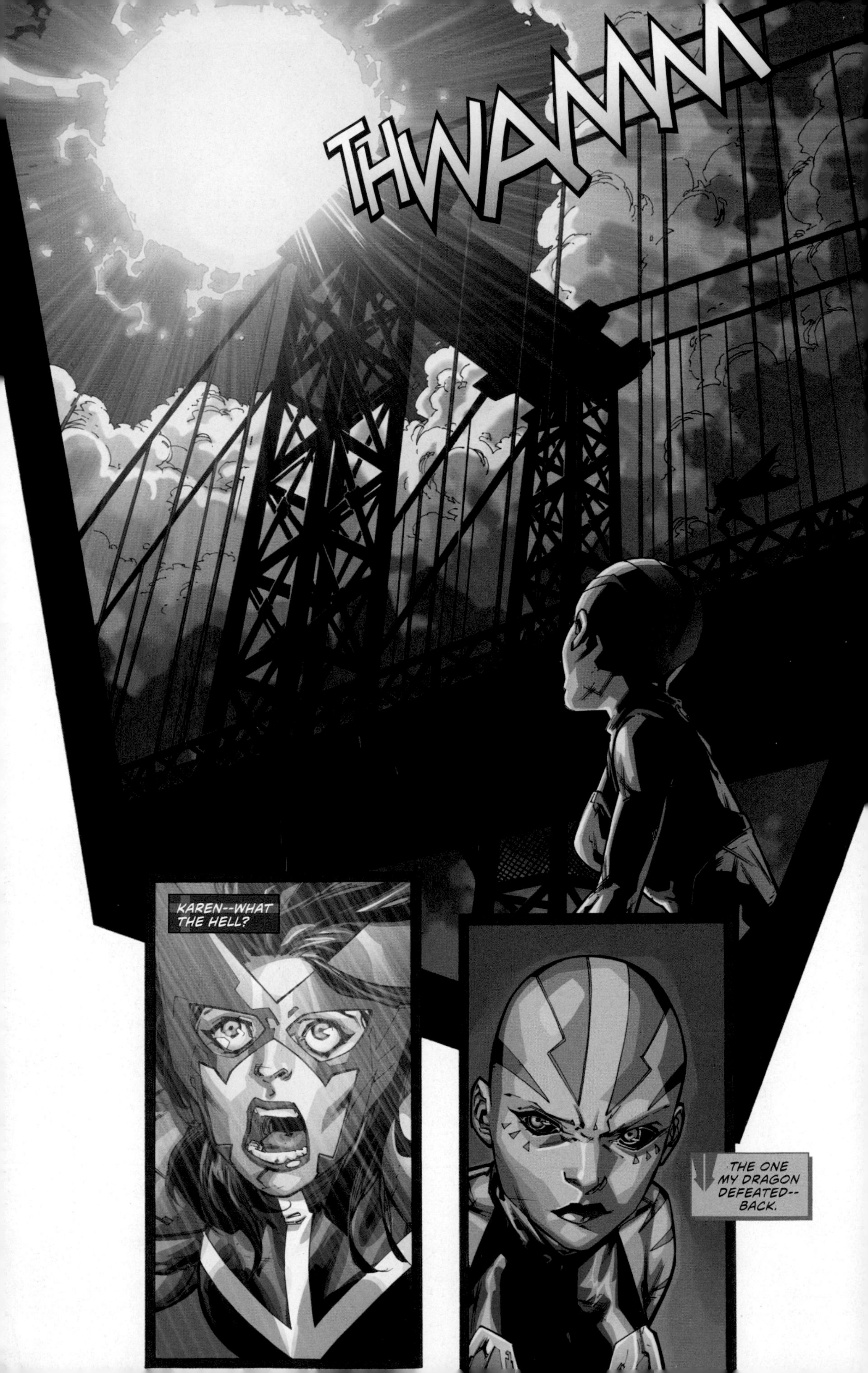
THWAMM
KAREN--WHAT THE HELL?
THE ONE MY DRAGON DEFEATED-- BACK.

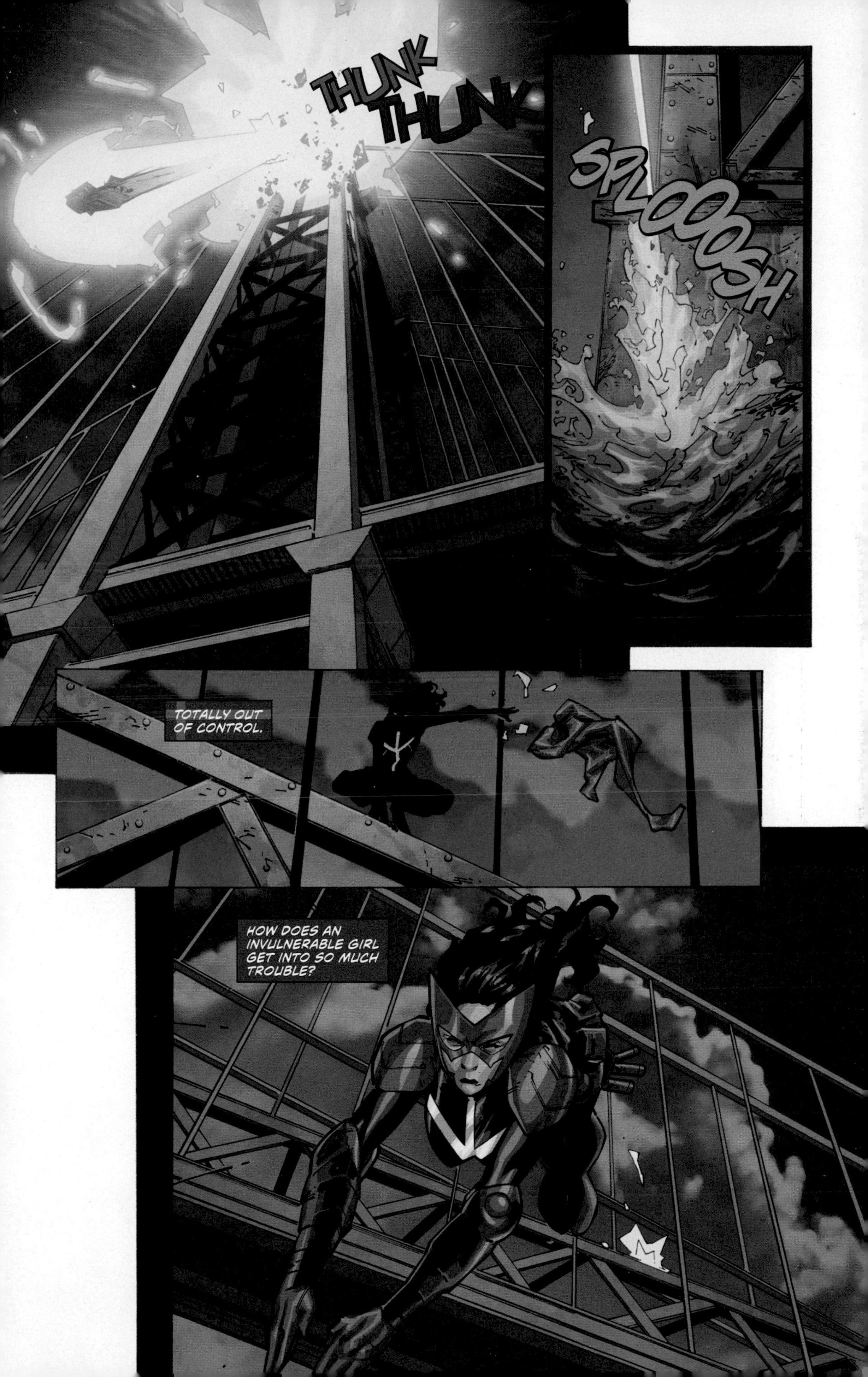
THUNK
THUNK
SPLOOOOSH
TOTALLY OUT OF CONTROL.
HOW DOES AN INVULNERABLE GIRL GET INTO SO MUCH TROUBLE?

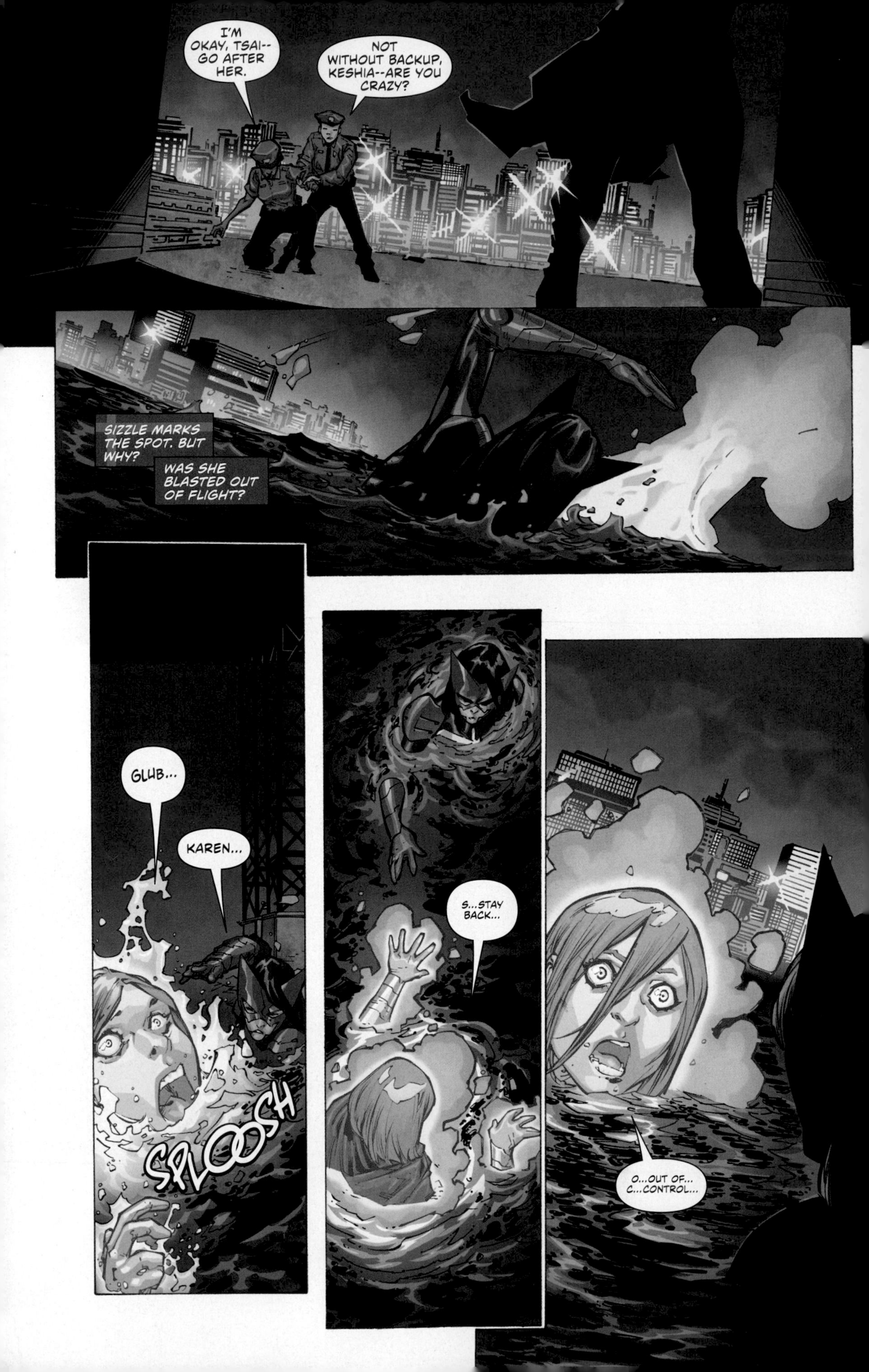
I'M OKAY, TSAI-- GO AFTER HER.
NOT WITHOUT BACKUP, KESHIA--ARE YOU CRAZY?
SIZZLE MARKS THE SPOT. BUT WHY?
WAS SHE BLASTED OUT OF FLIGHT?
GLUB...
KAREN...
SPLOOSH
S...STAY BACK...
O...OUT OF... C...CONTROL...

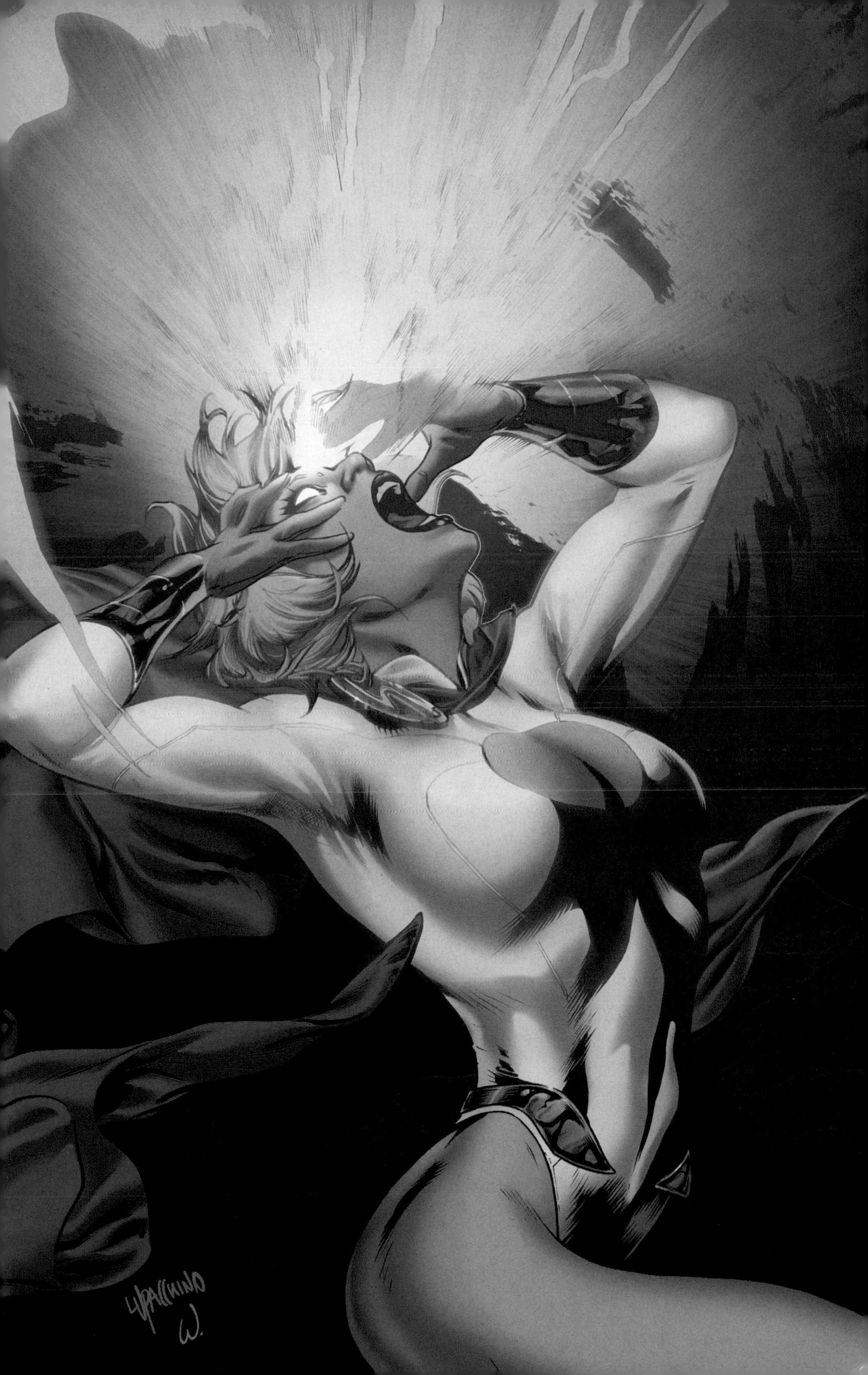
LUPACCHINO
W.

CONTROL ISSUES

SCOTT MCDANIEL breakdowns **R.B. SILVA** penciller **JOE WEEMS** inker

cover art by **EMANUELA LUPACCHINO** with **JASON WRIGHT**

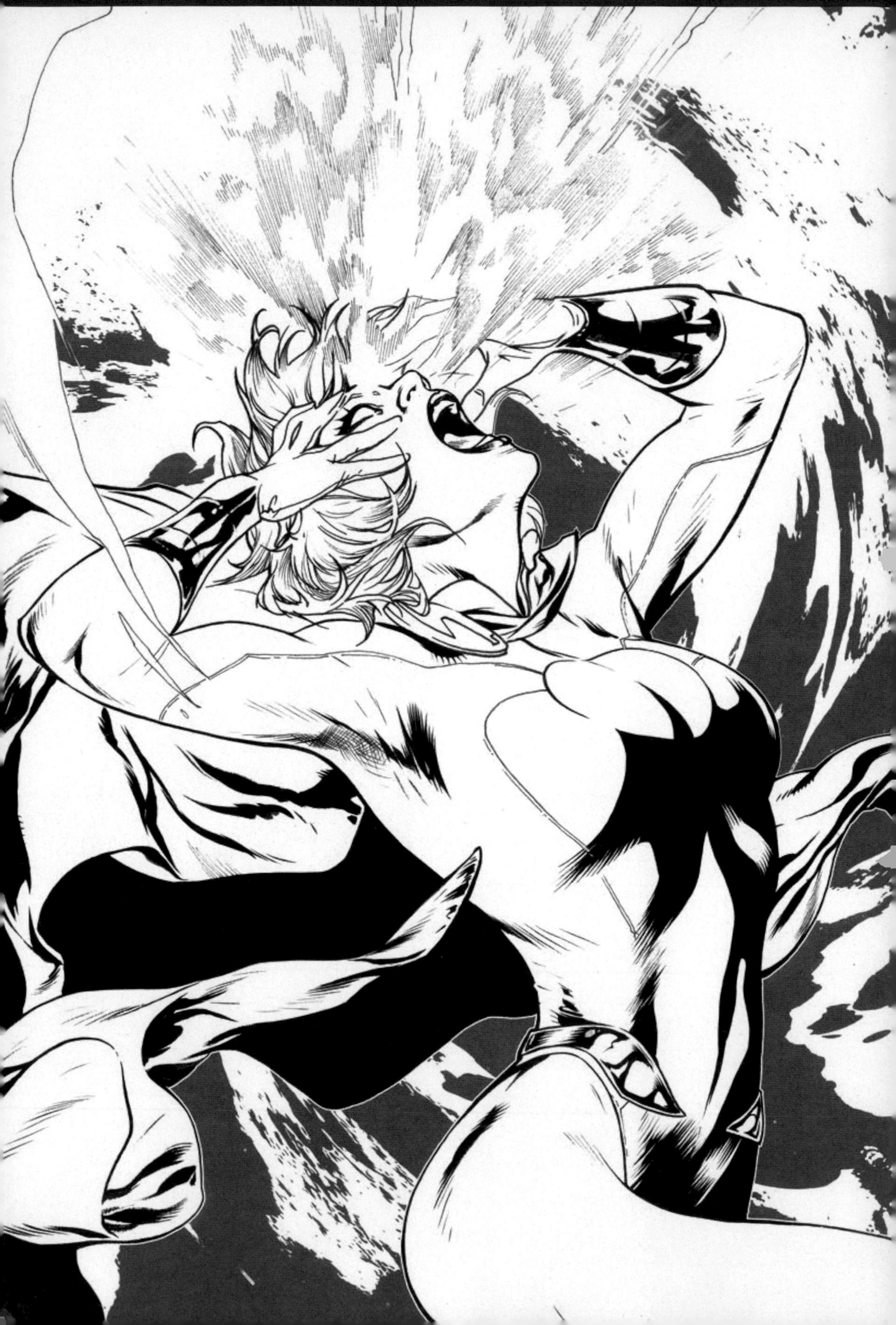

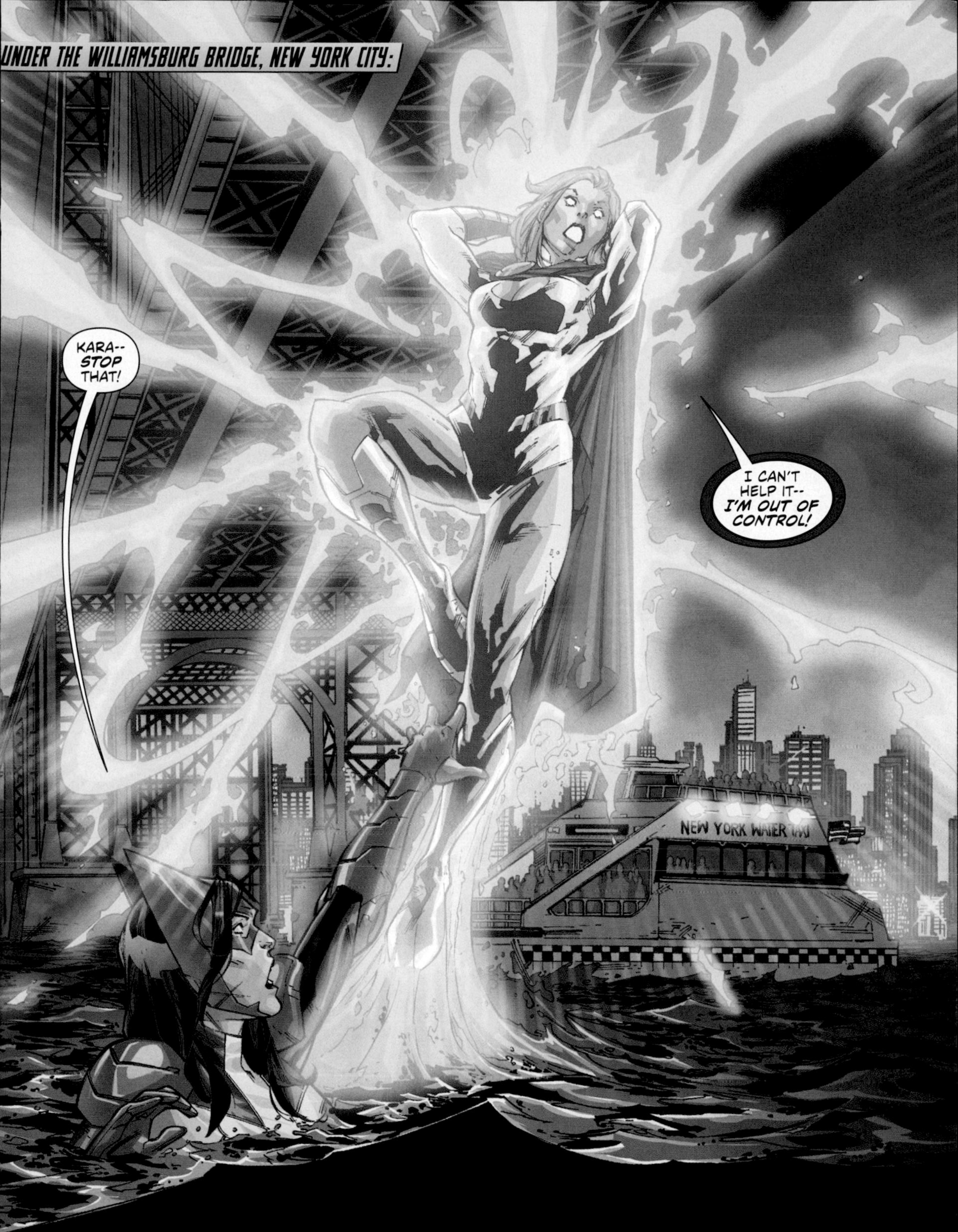
UNDER THE WILLIAMSBURG BRIDGE, NEW YORK CITY:
KARA-- STOP THAT!
I CAN'T HELP IT-- I'M OUT OF CONTROL!
NEW YORK WATER TAXI

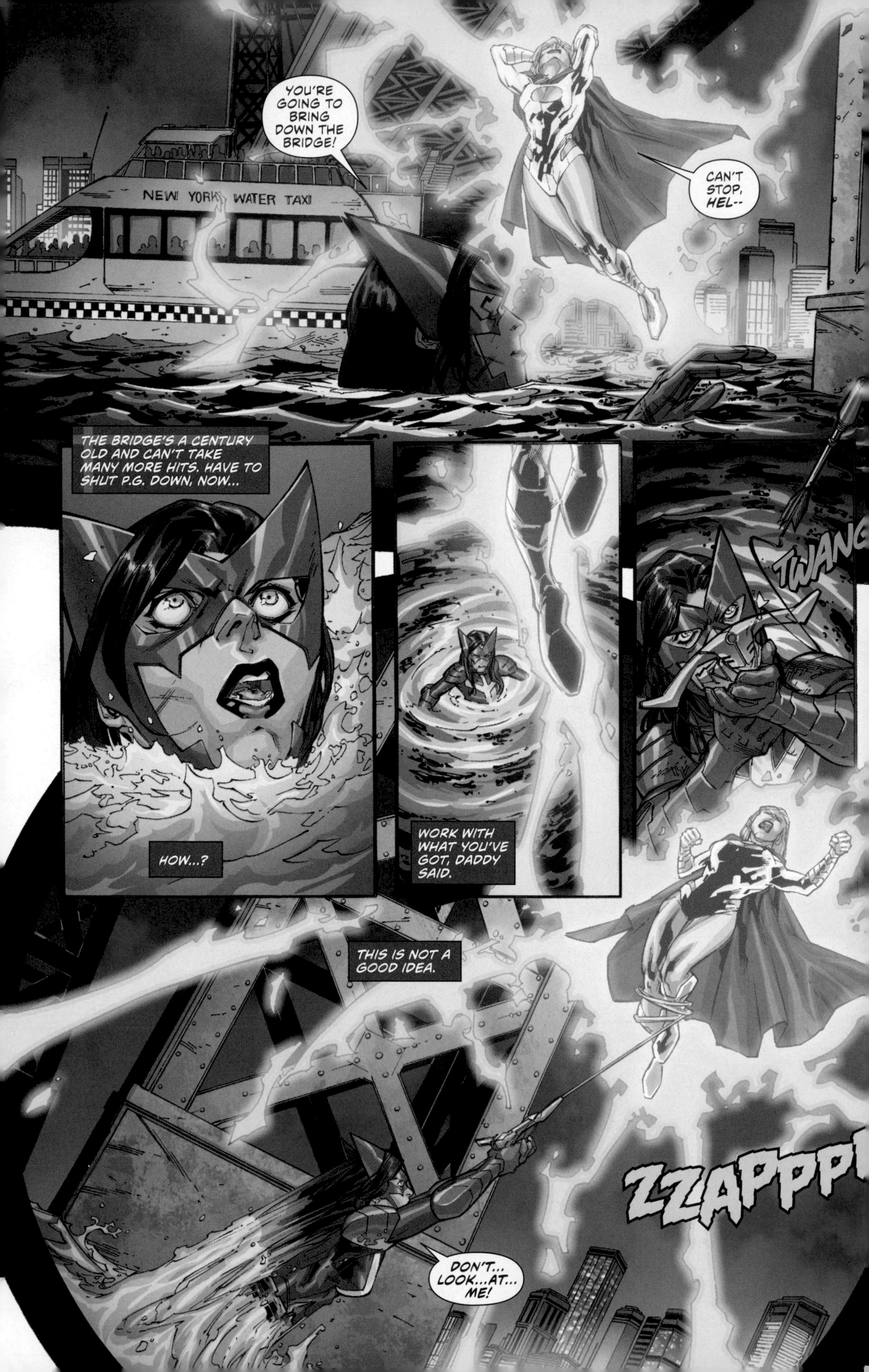
YOU'RE GOING TO BRING DOWN THE BRIDGE!
NEW YORK WATER TAXI
CAN'T STOP, HEL--
THE BRIDGE'S A CENTURY OLD AND CAN'T TAKE MANY MORE HITS. HAVE TO SHUT P.G. DOWN, NOW...
HOW...?
WORK WITH WHAT YOU'VE GOT, DADDY SAID.
TWANG
THIS IS NOT A GOOD IDEA.
ZZAPPP
DON'T... LOOK...AT... ME!

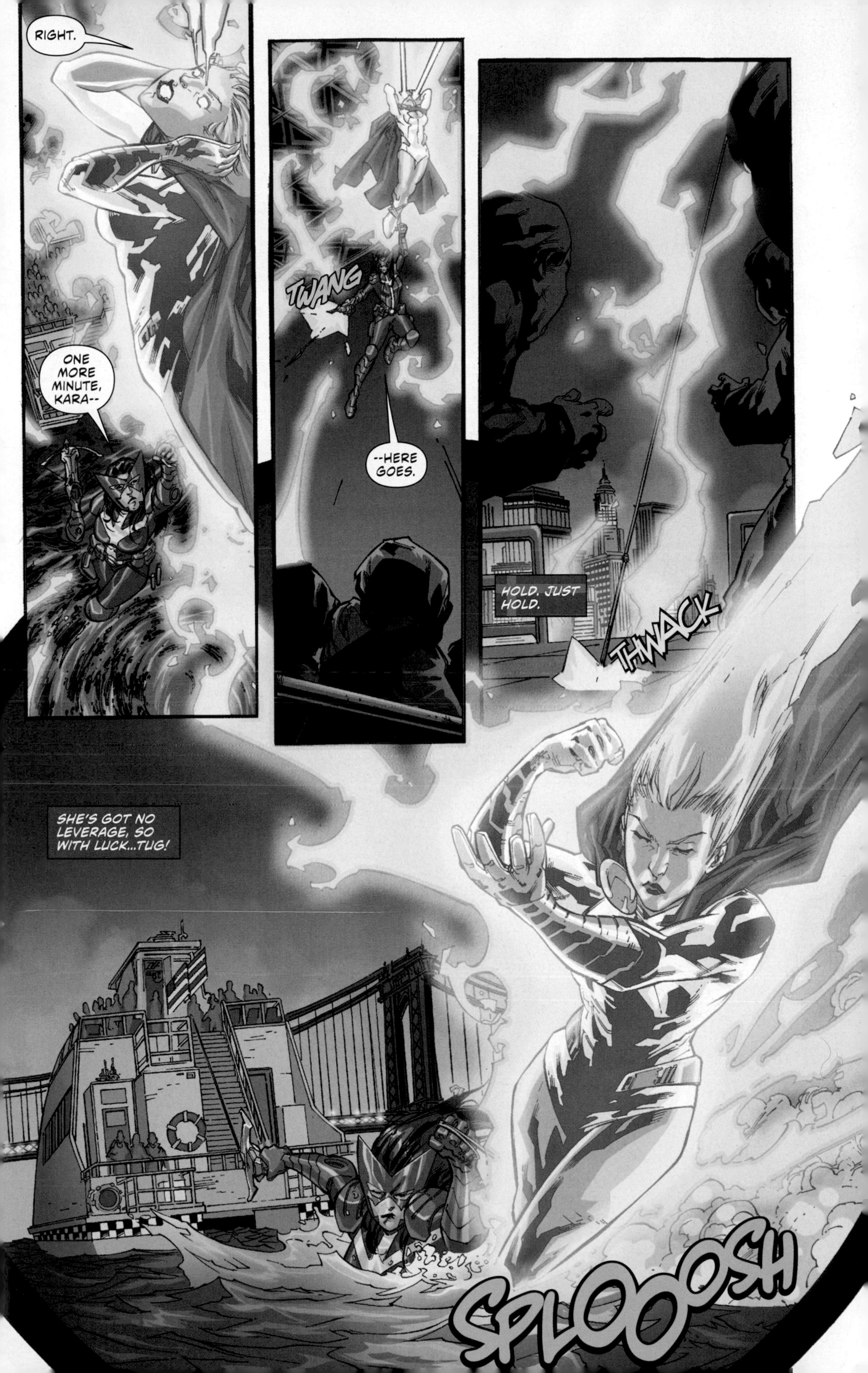
RIGHT.
ONE MORE MINUTE, KARA--
TWANG
--HERE GOES.
HOLD. JUST HOLD.
THWACK
SHE'S GOT NO LEVERAGE, SO WITH LUCK...TUG!
SPLOOOSH

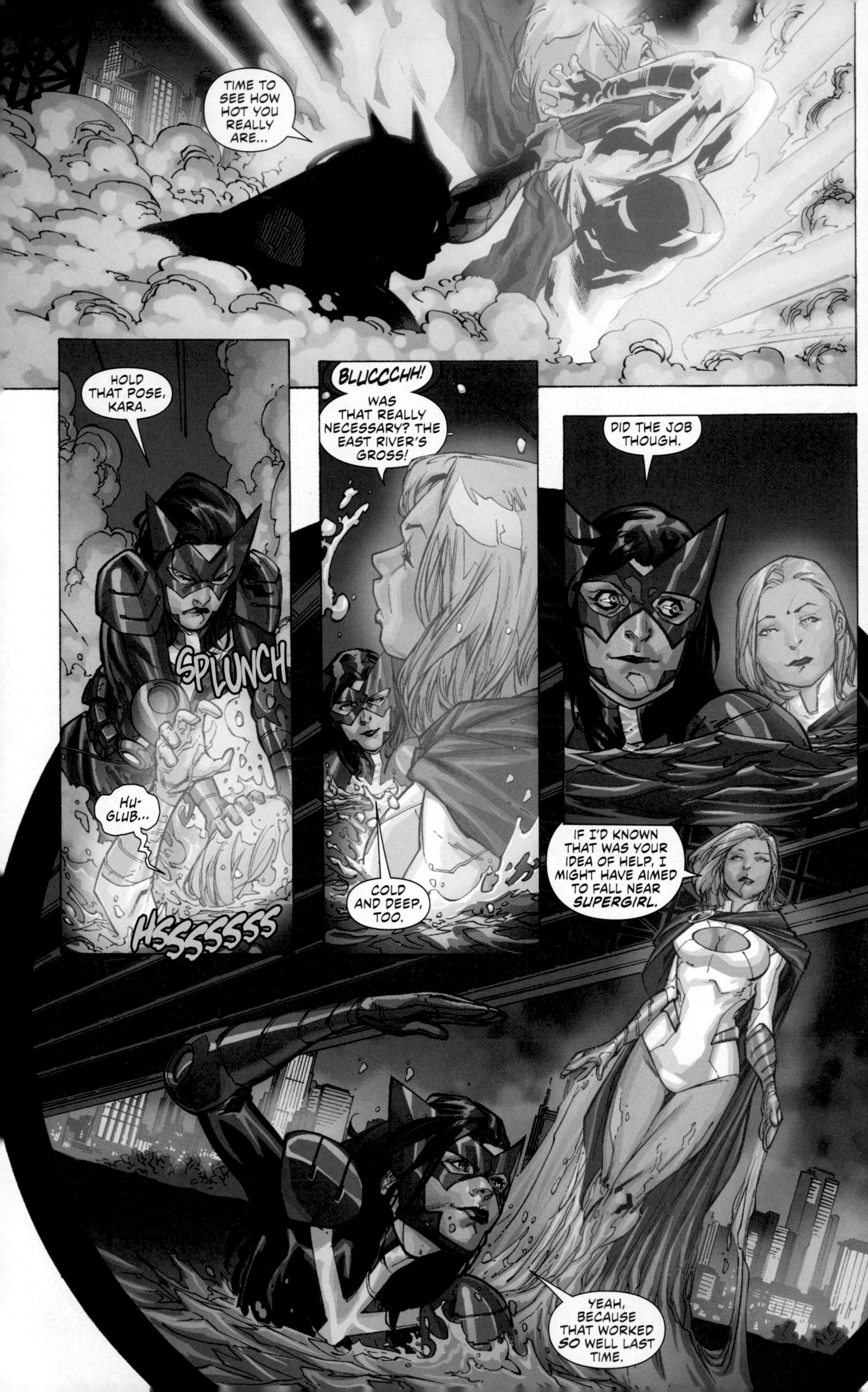
TIME TO SEE HOW HOT YOU REALLY ARE...
HOLD THAT POSE, KARA.
SPLUNCH
HU-GLUB...
HSSSSSSS
BLUCCCHH!
WAS THAT REALLY NECESSARY? THE EAST RIVER'S GROSS!
COLD AND DEEP, TOO.
DID THE JOB THOUGH.
IF I'D KNOWN THAT WAS YOUR IDEA OF HELP, I MIGHT HAVE AIMED TO FALL NEAR SUPERGIRL.
YEAH, BECAUSE THAT WORKED SO WELL LAST TIME.

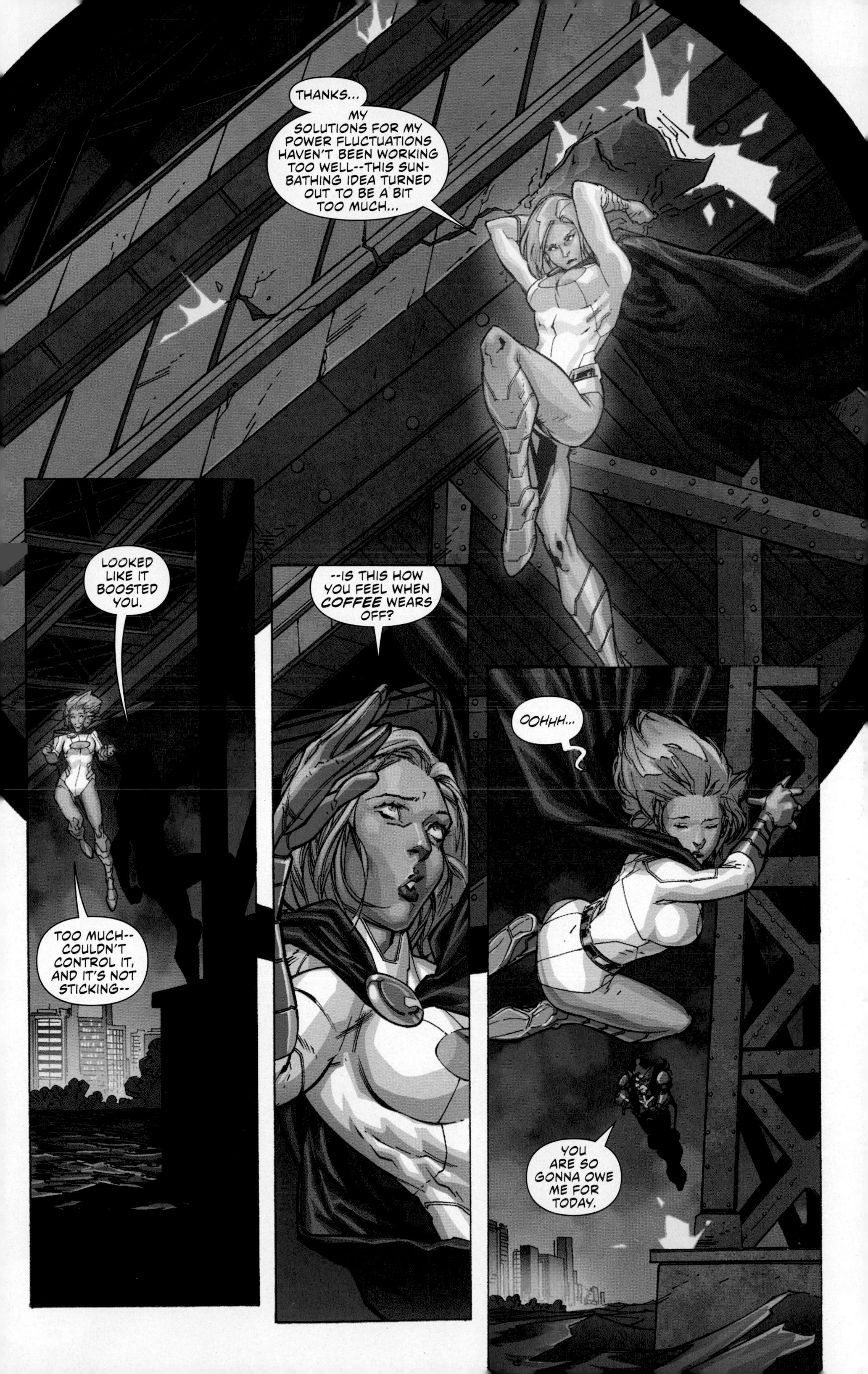
THANKS... MY SOLUTIONS FOR MY POWER FLUCTUATIONS HAVEN'T BEEN WORKING TOO WELL--THIS SUN-BATHING IDEA TURNED OUT TO BE A BIT TOO MUCH...
LOOKED LIKE IT BOOSTED YOU.
TOO MUCH--COULDN'T CONTROL IT, AND IT'S NOT STICKING--
--IS THIS HOW YOU FEEL WHEN COFFEE WEARS OFF?
OOHHH...
YOU ARE SO GONNA OWE ME FOR TODAY.

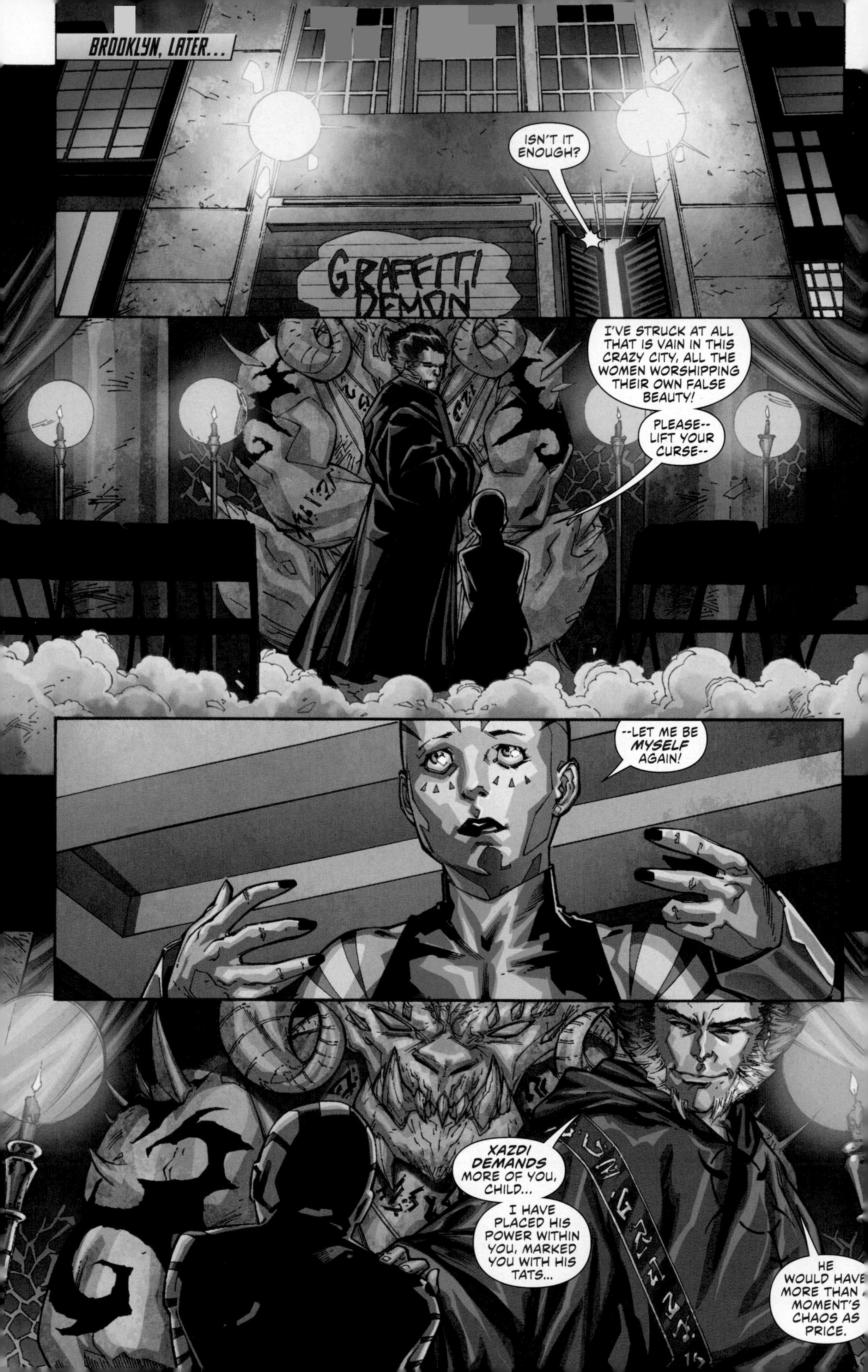
BROOKLYN, LATER...
ISN'T IT ENOUGH?
GRAFFITI DEMON
I'VE STRUCK AT ALL THAT IS VAIN IN THIS CRAZY CITY, ALL THE WOMEN WORSHIPPING THEIR OWN FALSE BEAUTY!
PLEASE-- LIFT YOUR CURSE--
--LET ME BE MYSELF AGAIN!
XAZDI DEMANDS MORE OF YOU, CHILD...
I HAVE PLACED HIS POWER WITHIN YOU, MARKED YOU WITH HIS TATS...
HE WOULD HAVE MORE THAN MOMENT'S CHAOS AS PRICE.

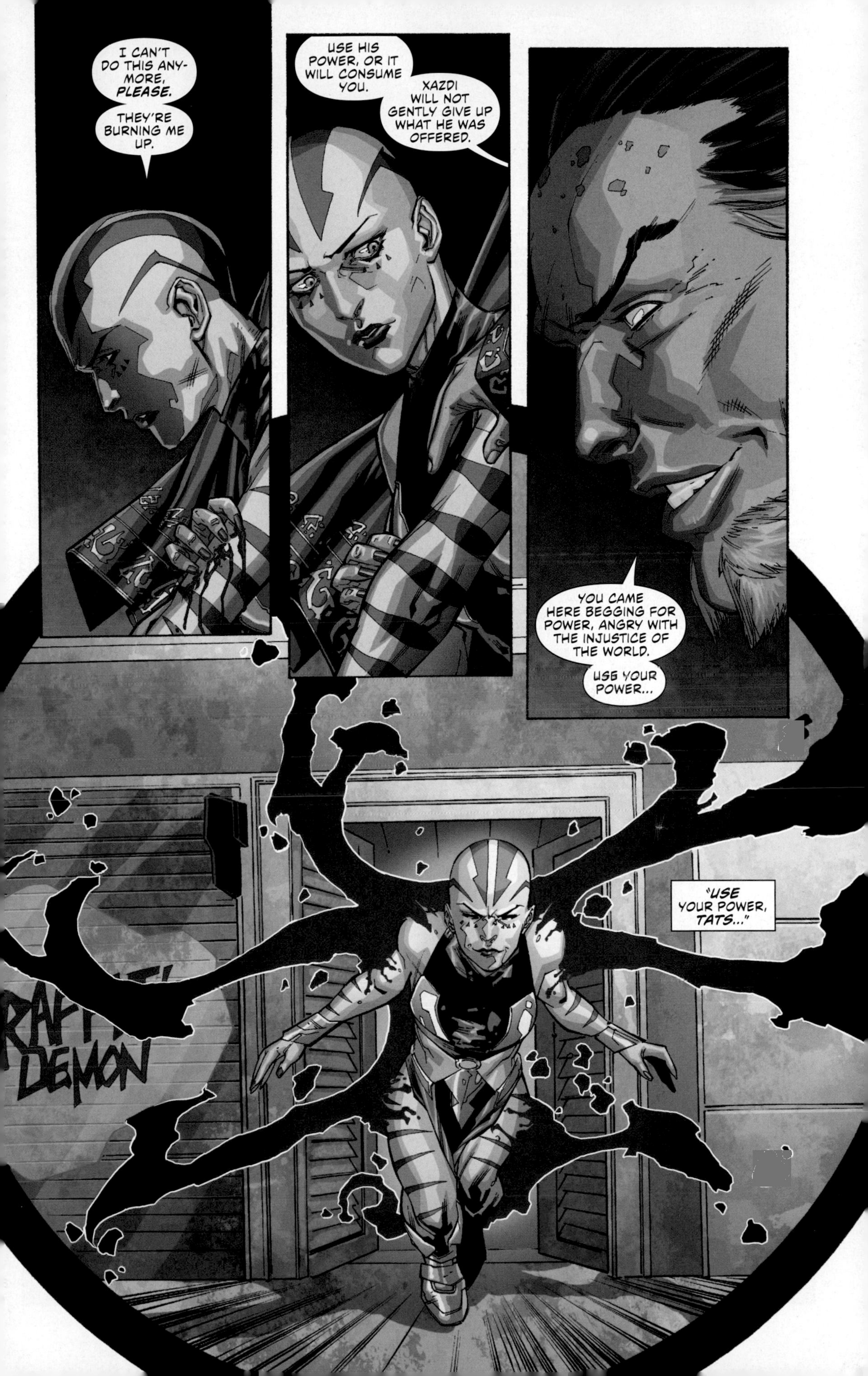
I CAN'T DO THIS ANY-MORE, PLEASE.
THEY'RE BURNING ME UP.
USE HIS POWER, OR IT WILL CONSUME YOU.
XAZDI WILL NOT GENTLY GIVE UP WHAT HE WAS OFFERED.
YOU CAME HERE BEGGING FOR POWER, ANGRY WITH THE INJUSTICE OF THE WORLD.
USE YOUR POWER...
"USE YOUR POWER, TATS..."
DEMON

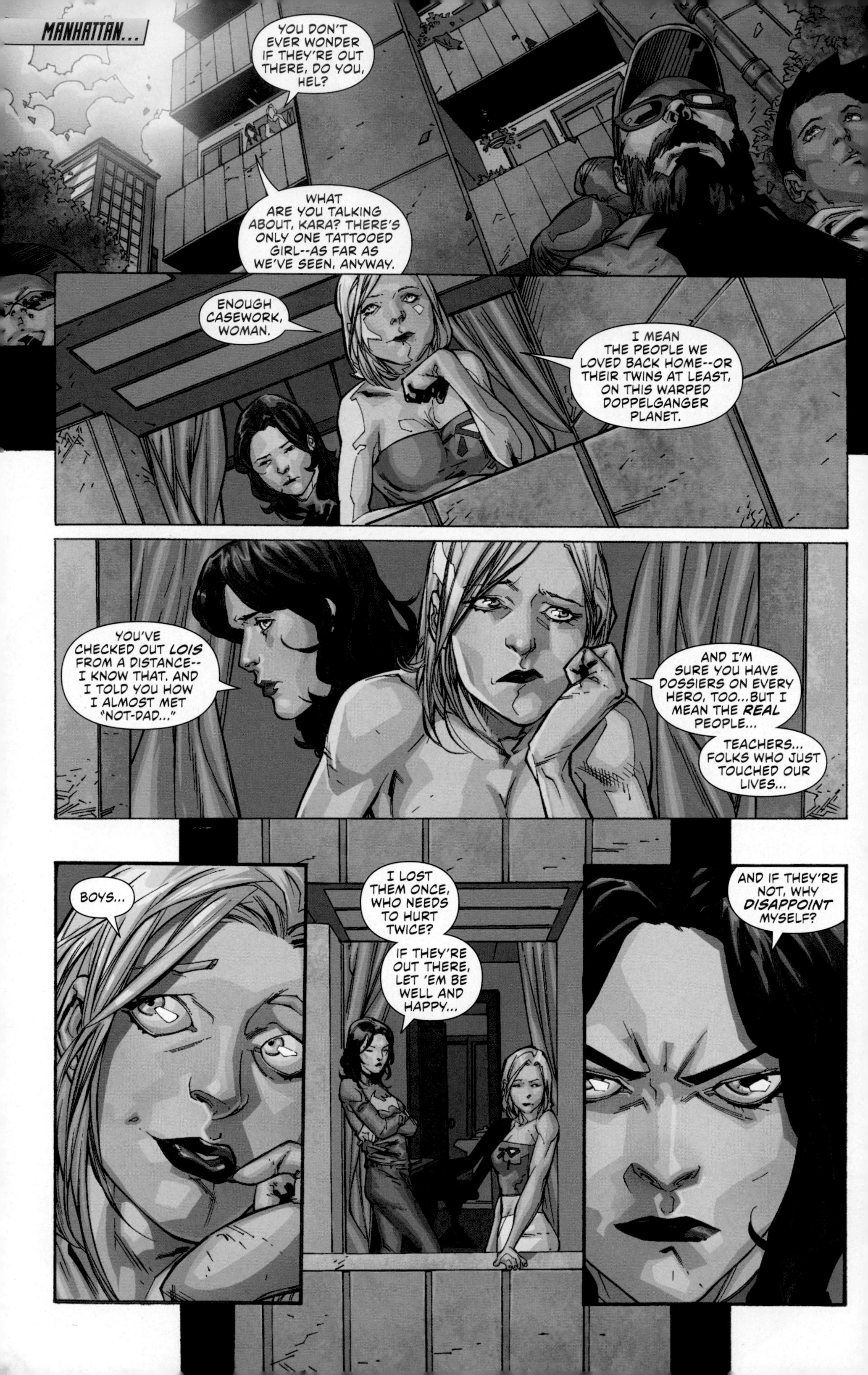
MANHATTAN...
YOU DON'T EVER WONDER IF THEY'RE OUT THERE, DO YOU, HEL?
WHAT ARE YOU TALKING ABOUT, KARA? THERE'S ONLY ONE TATTOOED GIRL--AS FAR AS WE'VE SEEN, ANYWAY.
ENOUGH CASEWORK, WOMAN.
I MEAN THE PEOPLE WE LOVED BACK HOME--OR THEIR TWINS AT LEAST, ON THIS WARPED DOPPELGANGER PLANET.
YOU'VE CHECKED OUT LOIS FROM A DISTANCE-- I KNOW THAT. AND I TOLD YOU HOW I ALMOST MET "NOT-DAD..."
AND I'M SURE YOU HAVE DOSSIERS ON EVERY HERO, TOO...BUT I MEAN THE REAL PEOPLE...
TEACHERS... FOLKS WHO JUST TOUCHED OUR LIVES...
BOYS...
I LOST THEM ONCE, WHO NEEDS TO HURT TWICE?
IF THEY'RE OUT THERE, LET 'EM BE WELL AND HAPPY...
AND IF THEY'RE NOT, WHY DISAPPOINT MYSELF?

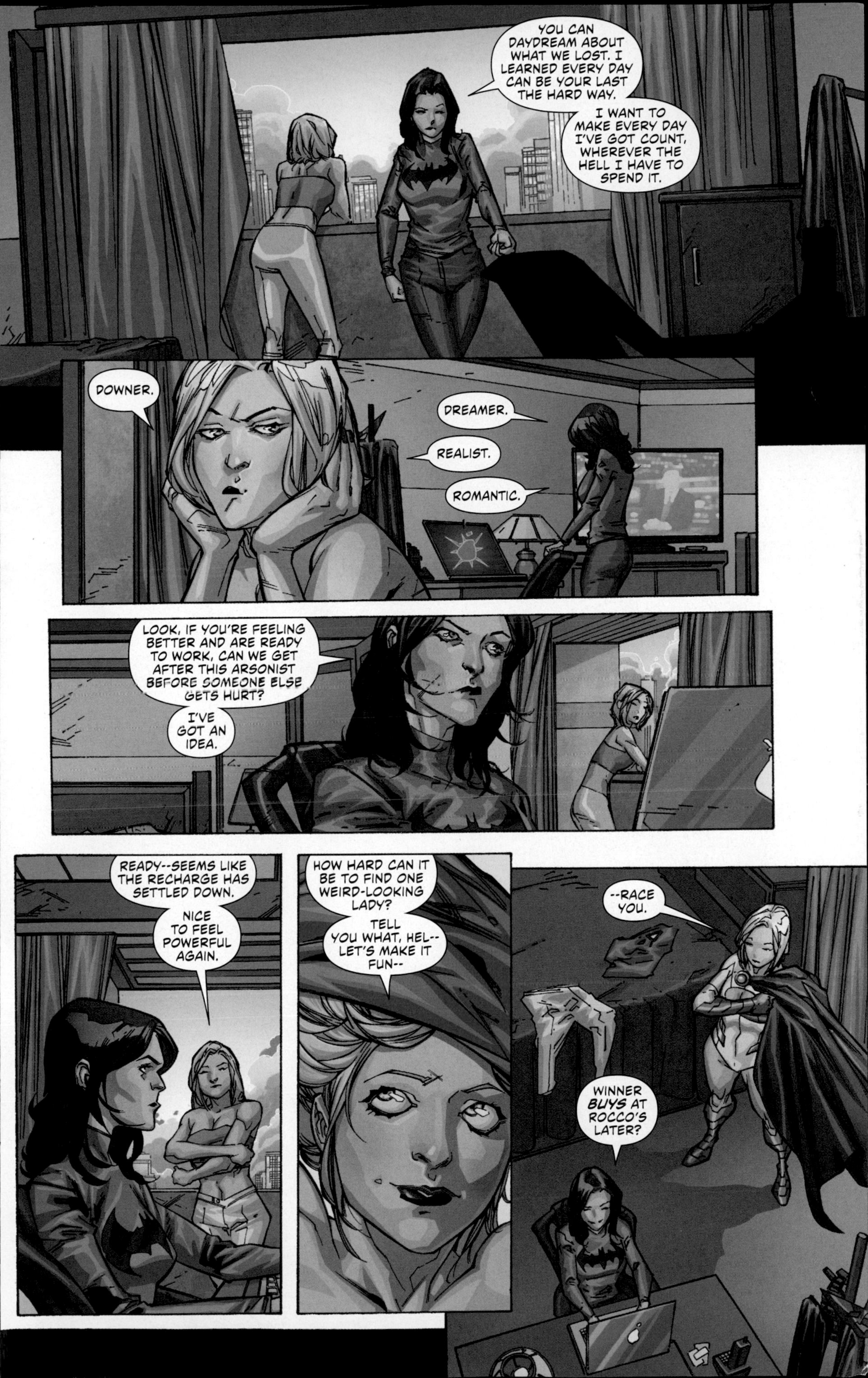
YOU CAN DAYDREAM ABOUT WHAT WE LOST. I LEARNED EVERY DAY CAN BE YOUR LAST THE HARD WAY.
I WANT TO MAKE EVERY DAY I'VE GOT COUNT, WHEREVER THE HELL I HAVE TO SPEND IT.
DOWNER.
DREAMER.
REALIST.
ROMANTIC.
LOOK, IF YOU'RE FEELING BETTER AND ARE READY TO WORK, CAN WE GET AFTER THIS ARSONIST BEFORE SOMEONE ELSE GETS HURT?
I'VE GOT AN IDEA.
READY--SEEMS LIKE THE RECHARGE HAS SETTLED DOWN.
NICE TO FEEL POWERFUL AGAIN.
HOW HARD CAN IT BE TO FIND ONE WEIRD-LOOKING LADY?
TELL YOU WHAT, HEL--LET'S MAKE IT FUN--
--RACE YOU.
WINNER BUYS AT ROCCO'S LATER?

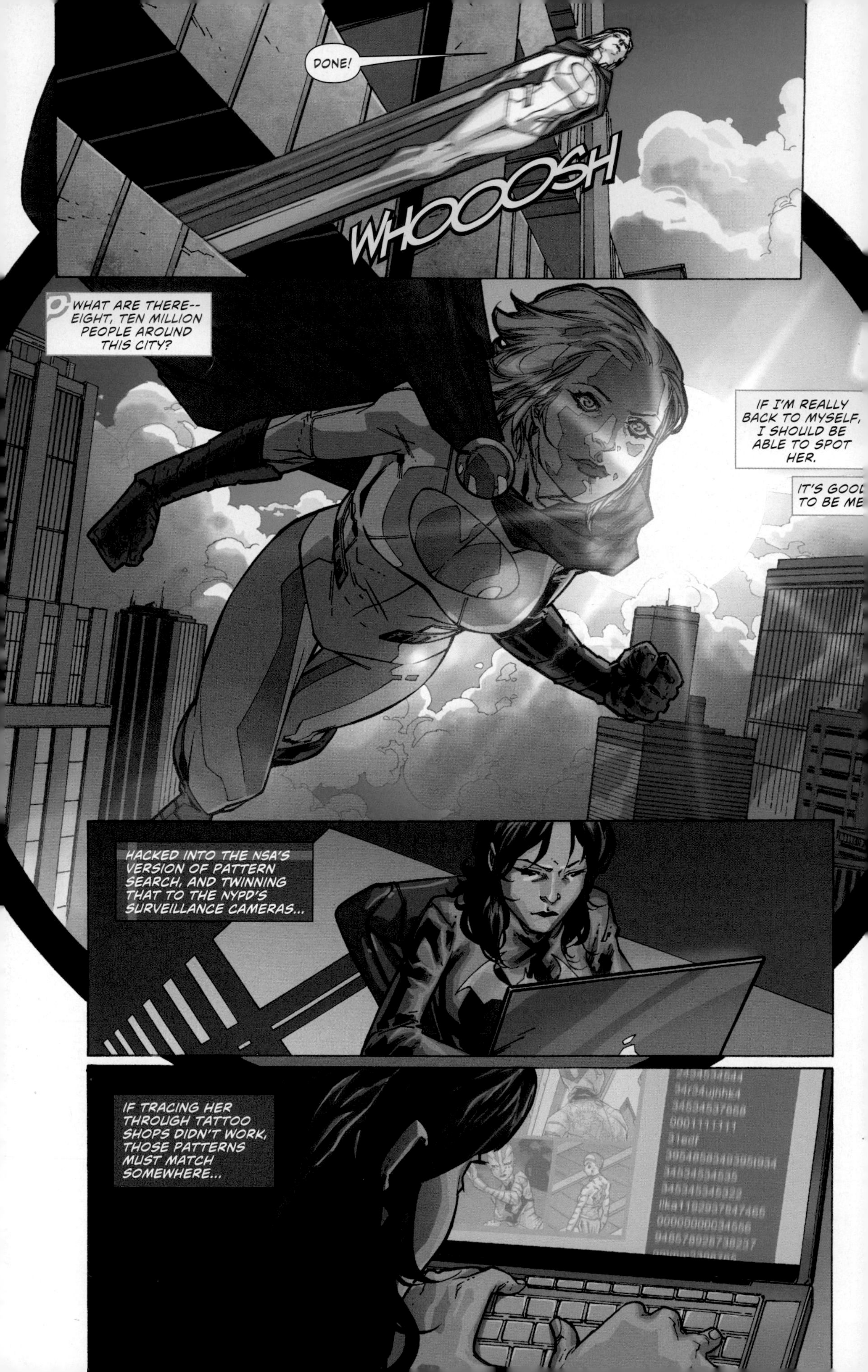
DONE!
WHOOOOSH
WHAT ARE THERE-- EIGHT, TEN MILLION PEOPLE AROUND THIS CITY?
IF I'M REALLY BACK TO MYSELF, I SHOULD BE ABLE TO SPOT HER.
IT'S GOOD TO BE ME
HACKED INTO THE NSA'S VERSION OF PATTERN SEARCH, AND TWINNING THAT TO THE NYPD'S SURVEILLANCE CAMERAS...
IF TRACING HER THROUGH TATTOO SHOPS DIDN'T WORK, THOSE PATTERNS MUST MATCH SOMEWHERE...

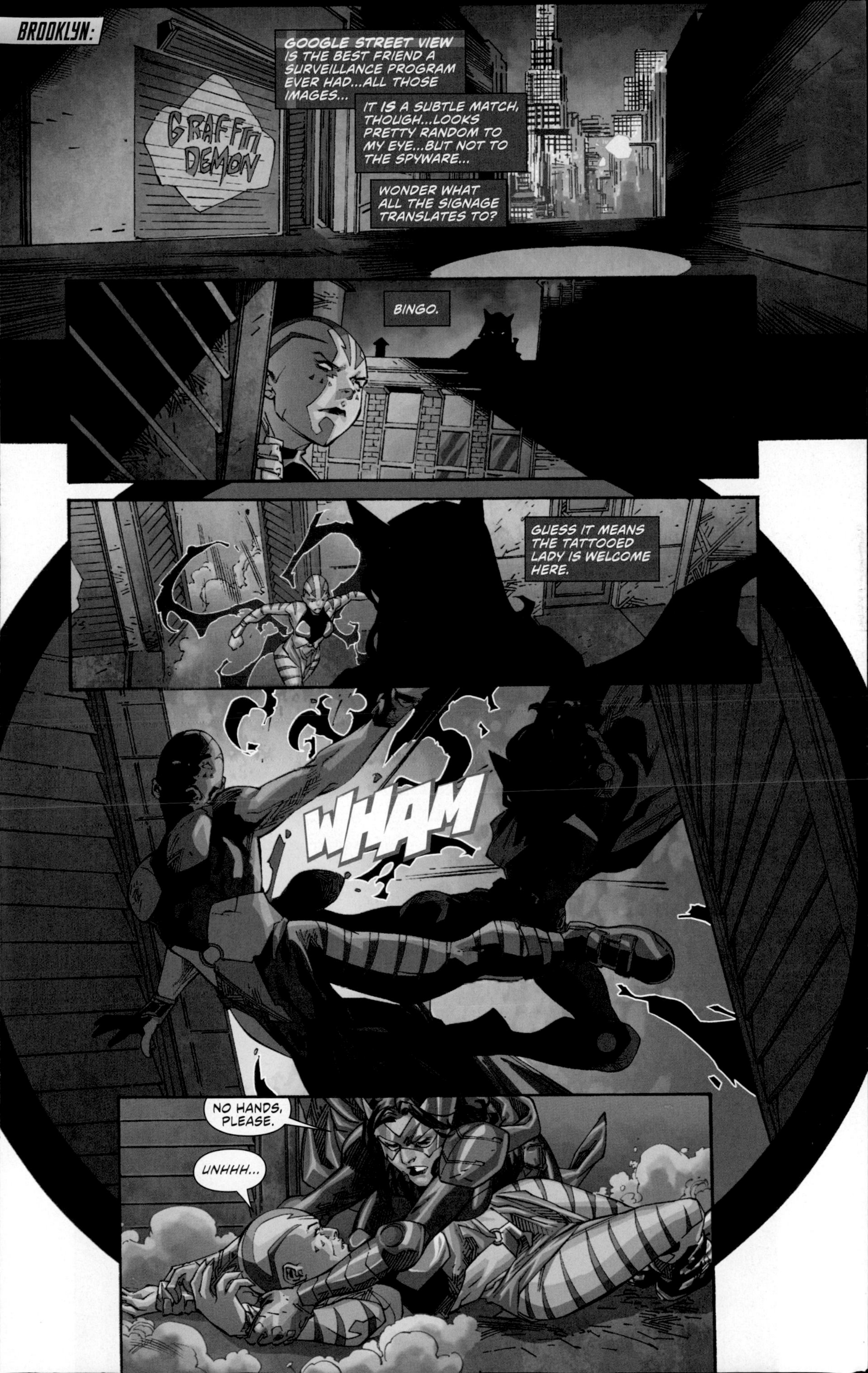
BROOKLYN:
GOOGLE STREET VIEW IS THE BEST FRIEND A SURVEILLANCE PROGRAM EVER HAD...ALL THOSE IMAGES...
IT IS A SUBTLE MATCH, THOUGH...LOOKS PRETTY RANDOM TO MY EYE...BUT NOT TO THE SPYWARE...
GRAFFITI DEMON
WONDER WHAT ALL THE SIGNAGE TRANSLATES TO?
BINGO.
GUESS IT MEANS THE TATTOOED LADY IS WELCOME HERE.
WHAM
NO HANDS, PLEASE.
UNHHH...

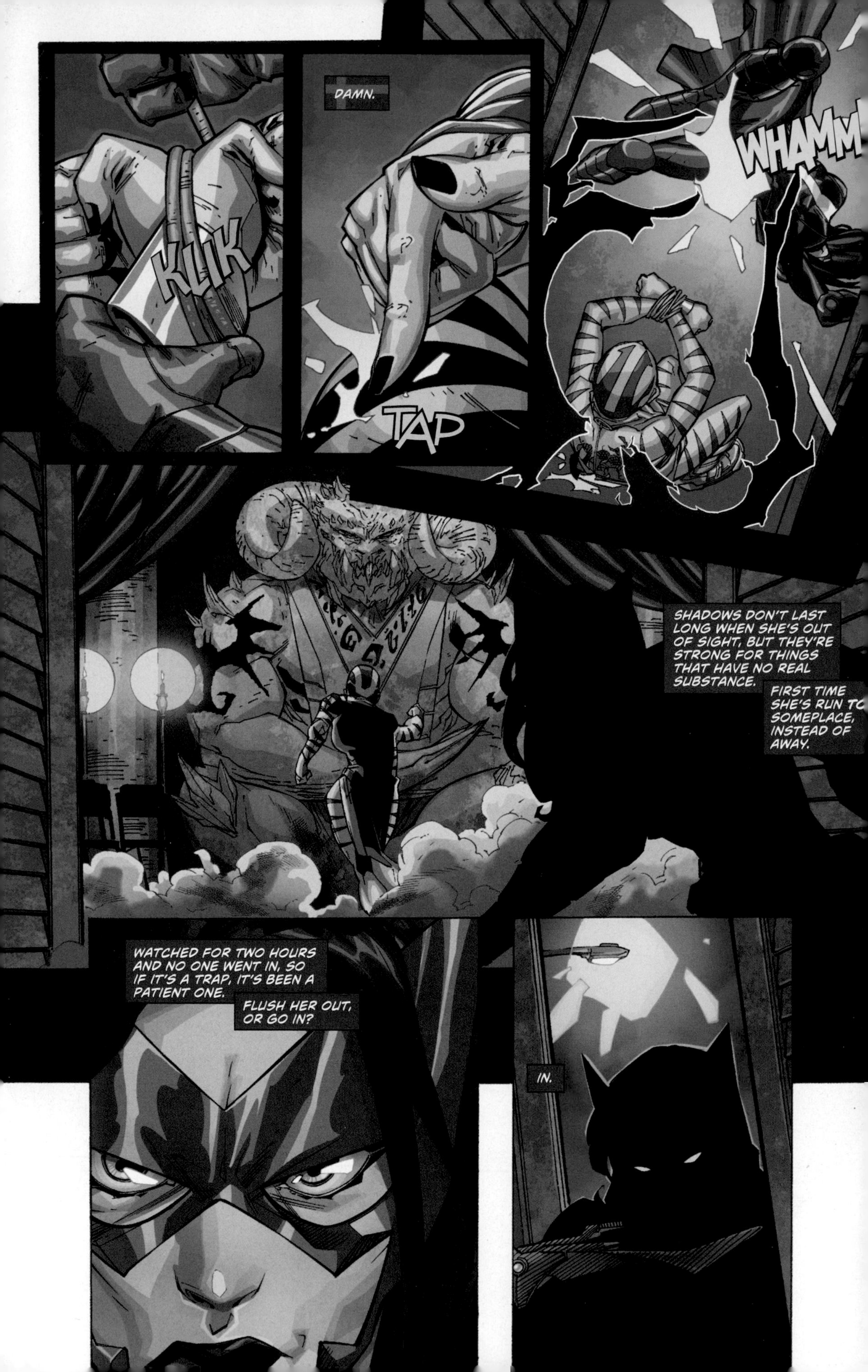
KLIK
DAMN.
TAP
WHAMM
SHADOWS DON'T LAST LONG WHEN SHE'S OUT OF SIGHT, BUT THEY'RE STRONG FOR THINGS THAT HAVE NO REAL SUBSTANCE.
FIRST TIME SHE'S RUN TO SOMEPLACE, INSTEAD OF AWAY.
WATCHED FOR TWO HOURS AND NO ONE WENT IN, SO IF IT'S A TRAP, IT'S BEEN A PATIENT ONE.
FLUSH HER OUT, OR GO IN?
IN.

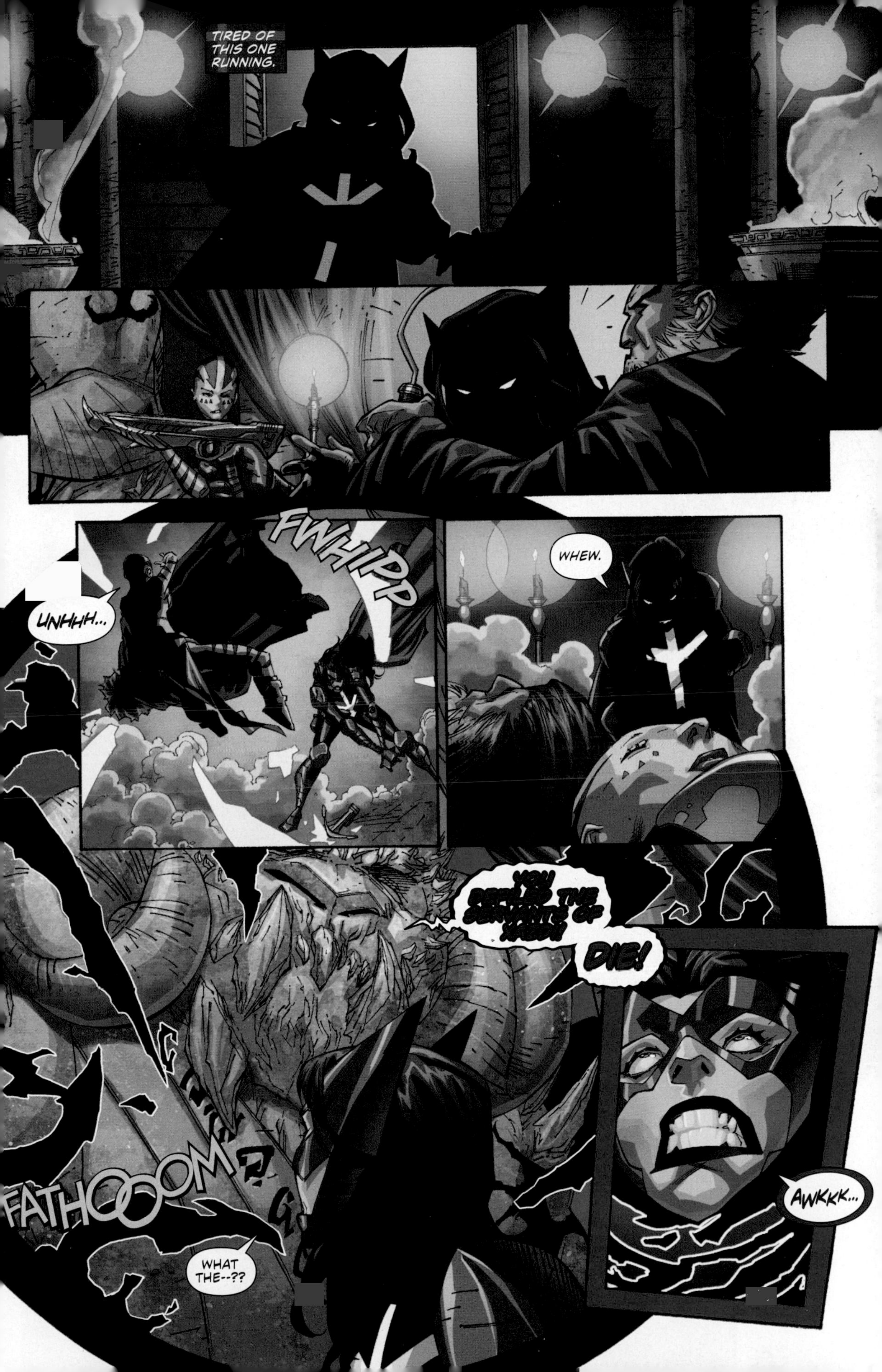
TIRED OF THIS ONE RUNNING.
UNHHH...
FWHIPP
WHEW.
YOU DEFILED THE SERVANTS OF
DIE!
FATHOOOOM
WHAT THE--??
AWKKK...

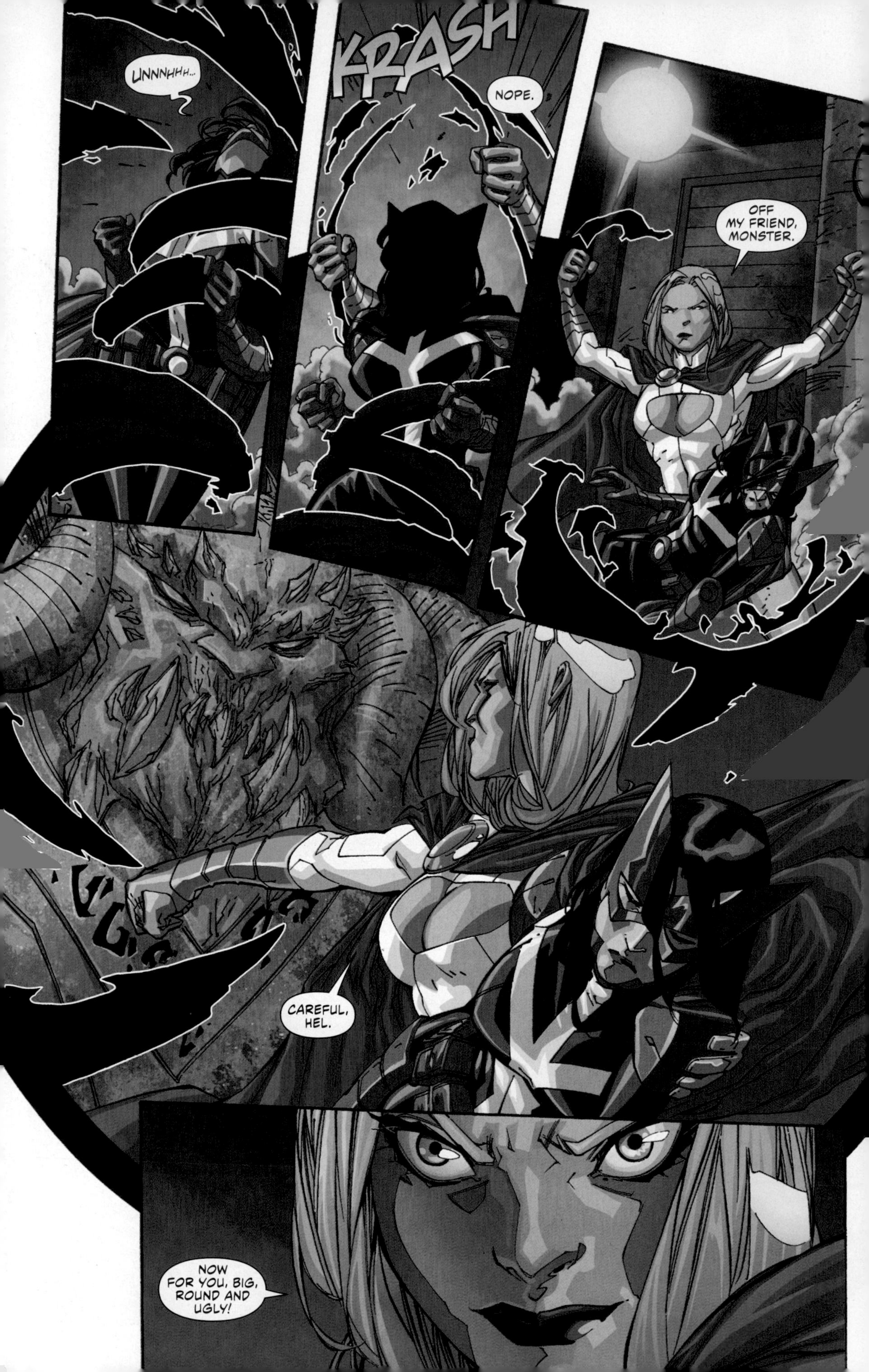
UNNNHHH...
KRASH
NOPE.
OFF MY FRIEND, MONSTER.
CAREFUL, HEL.
NOW FOR YOU, BIG, ROUND AND UGLY!

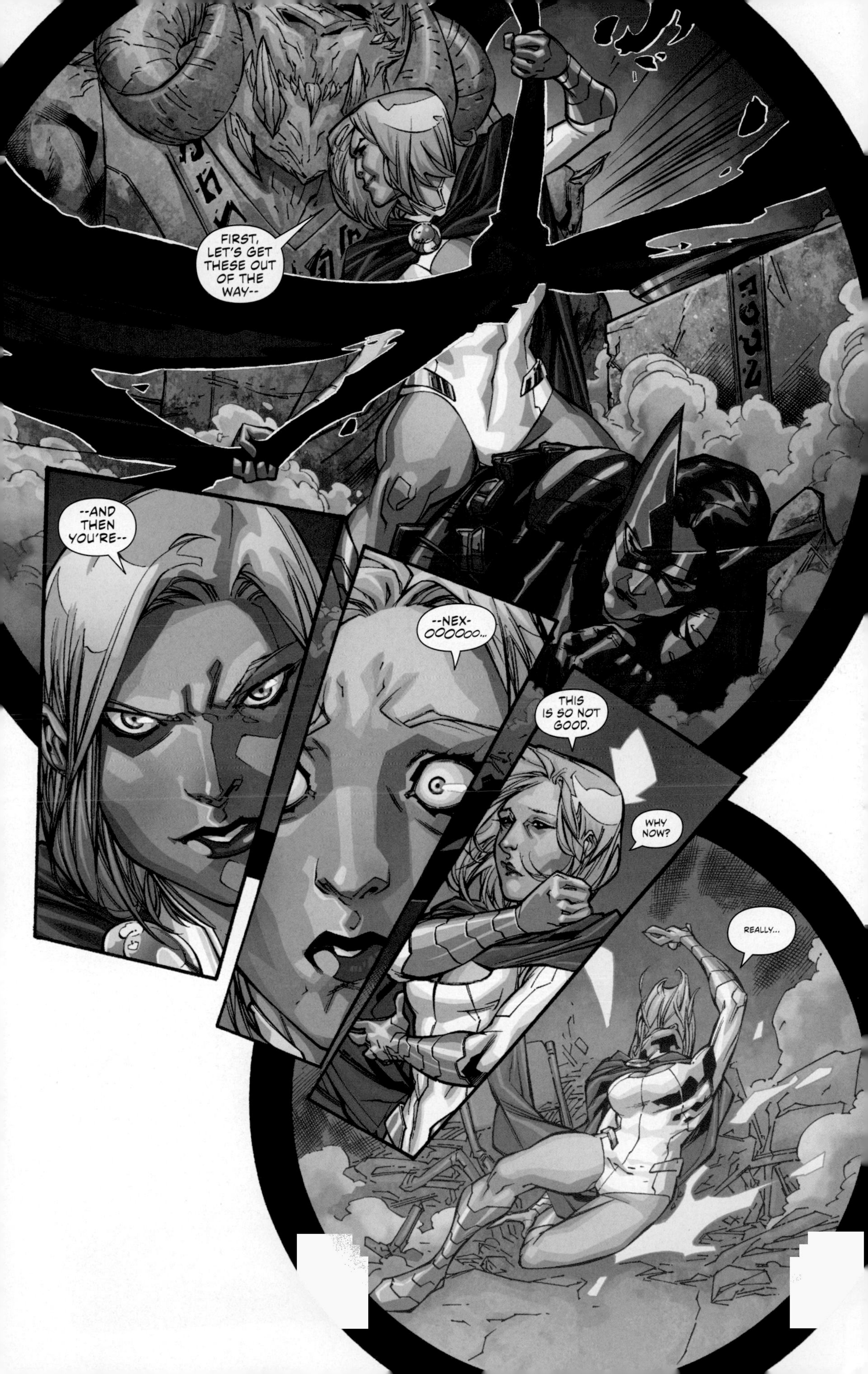
FIRST, LET'S GET THESE OUT OF THE WAY--
--AND THEN YOU'RE--
--NEX-OOOOOO...
THIS IS SO NOT GOOD.
WHY NOW?
REALLY...

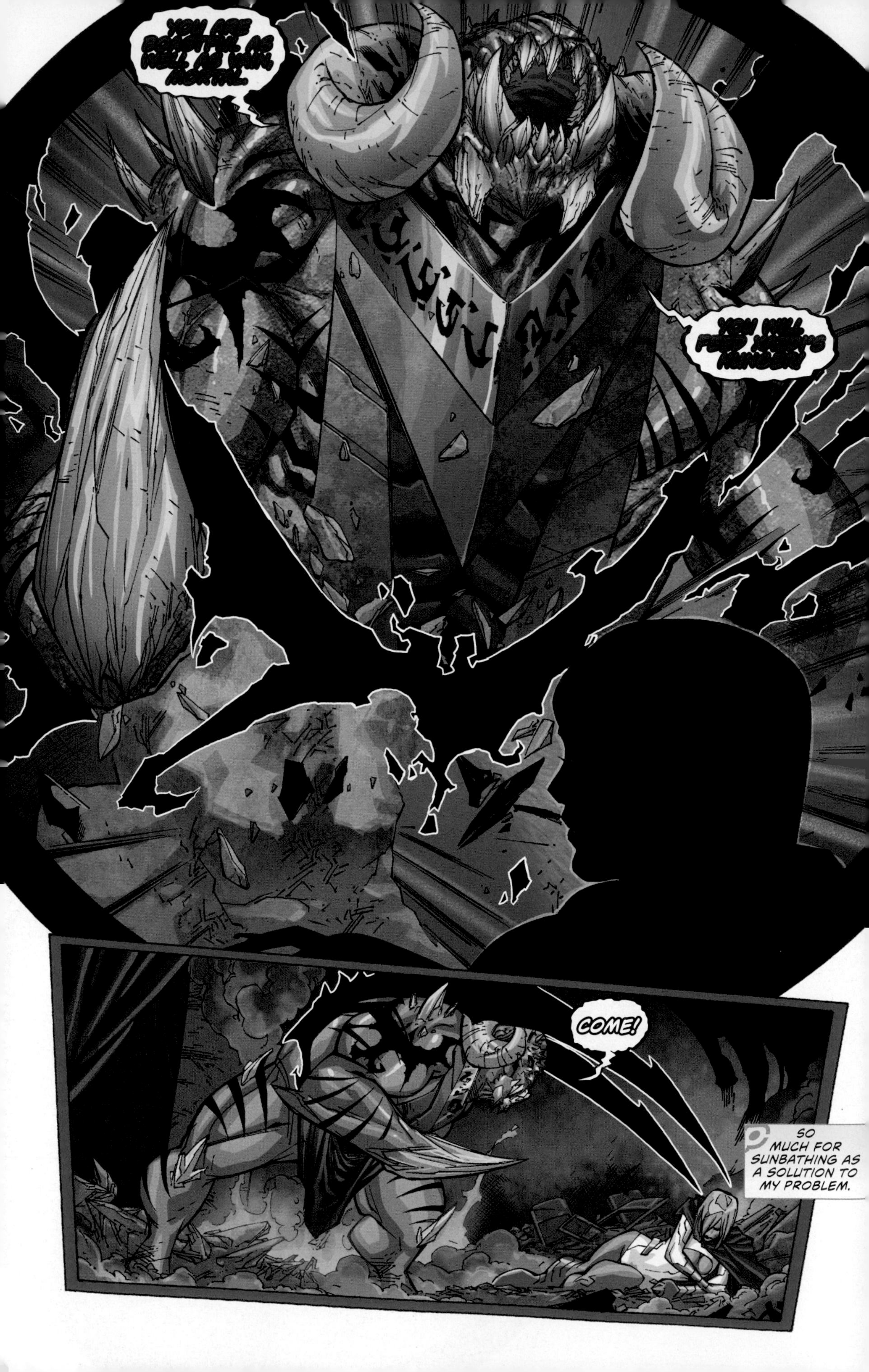
YOU ARE BOASTFUL AS WELL AS VAIN, MORTAL.
COME!
SO MUCH FOR SUNBATHING AS A SOLUTION TO MY PROBLEM.

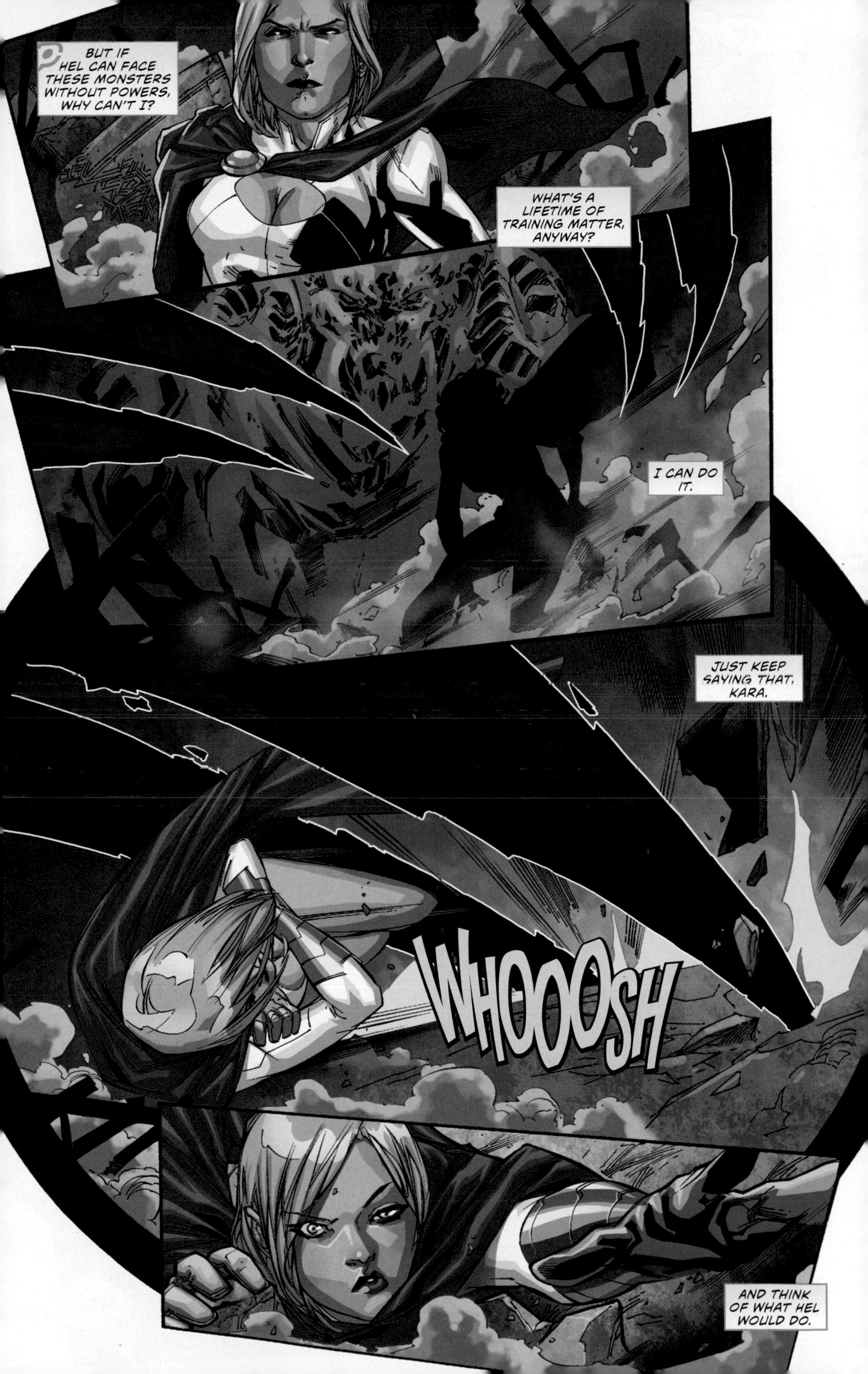
BUT IF HEL CAN FACE THESE MONSTERS WITHOUT POWERS, WHY CAN'T I?
WHAT'S A LIFETIME OF TRAINING MATTER, ANYWAY?
I CAN DO IT.
JUST KEEP SAYING THAT, KARA.
WHOOOSH
AND THINK OF WHAT HEL WOULD DO.

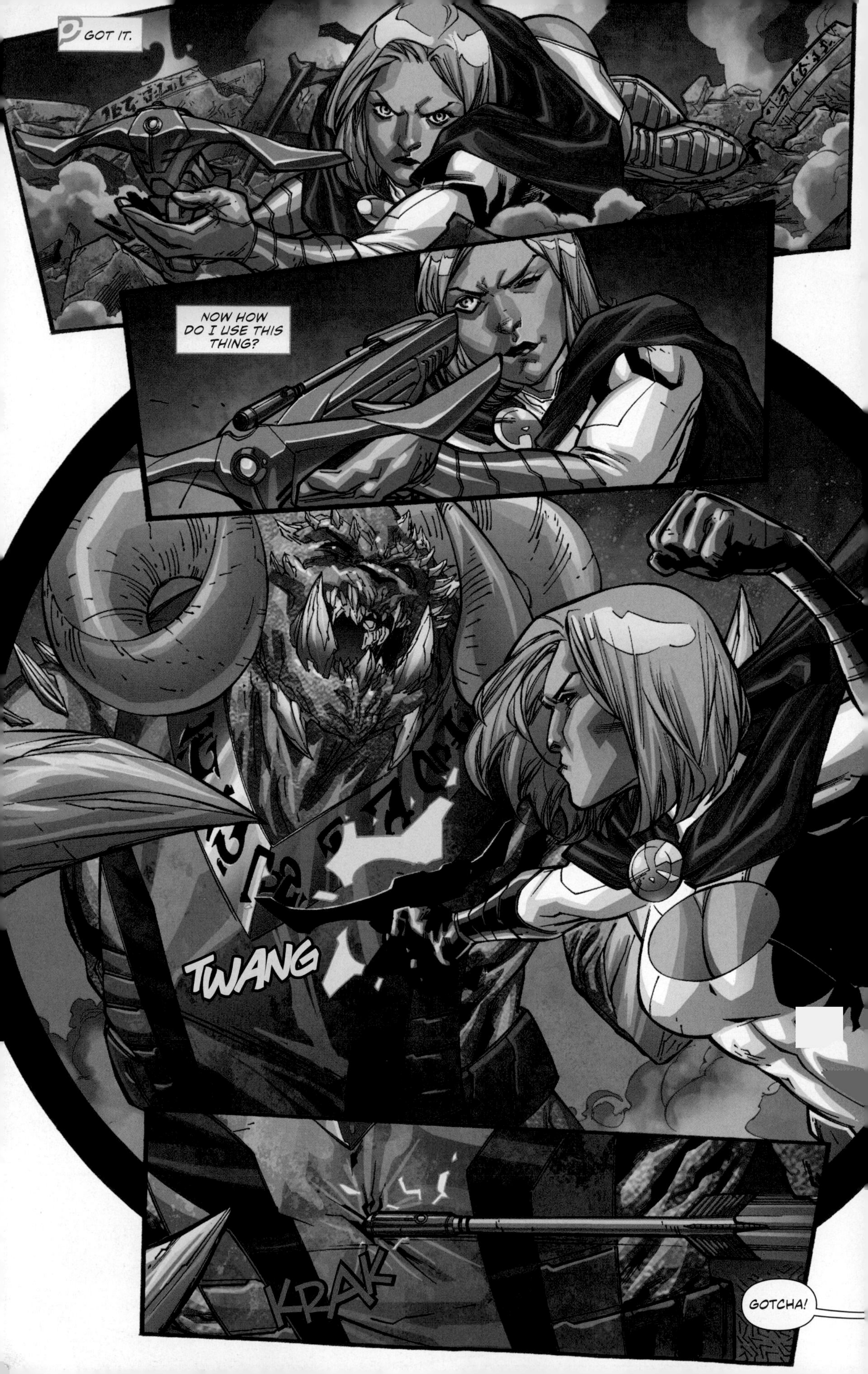
GOT IT.
NOW HOW DO I USE THIS THING?
TWANG
KRAK
GOTCHA!

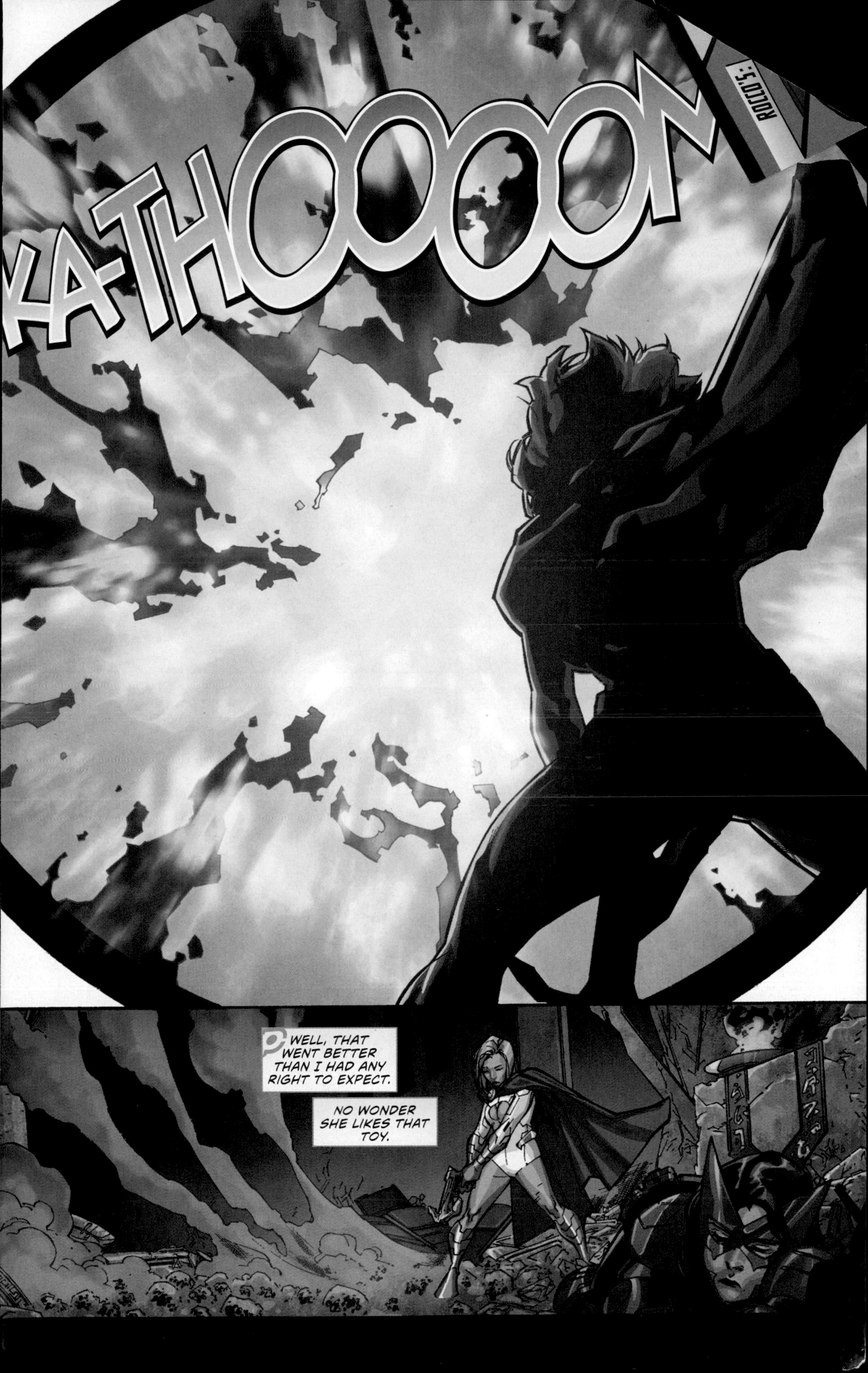
KA-THOOOOM
ROCCO'S:
WELL, THAT WENT BETTER THAN I HAD ANY RIGHT TO EXPECT.
NO WONDER SHE LIKES THAT TOY.

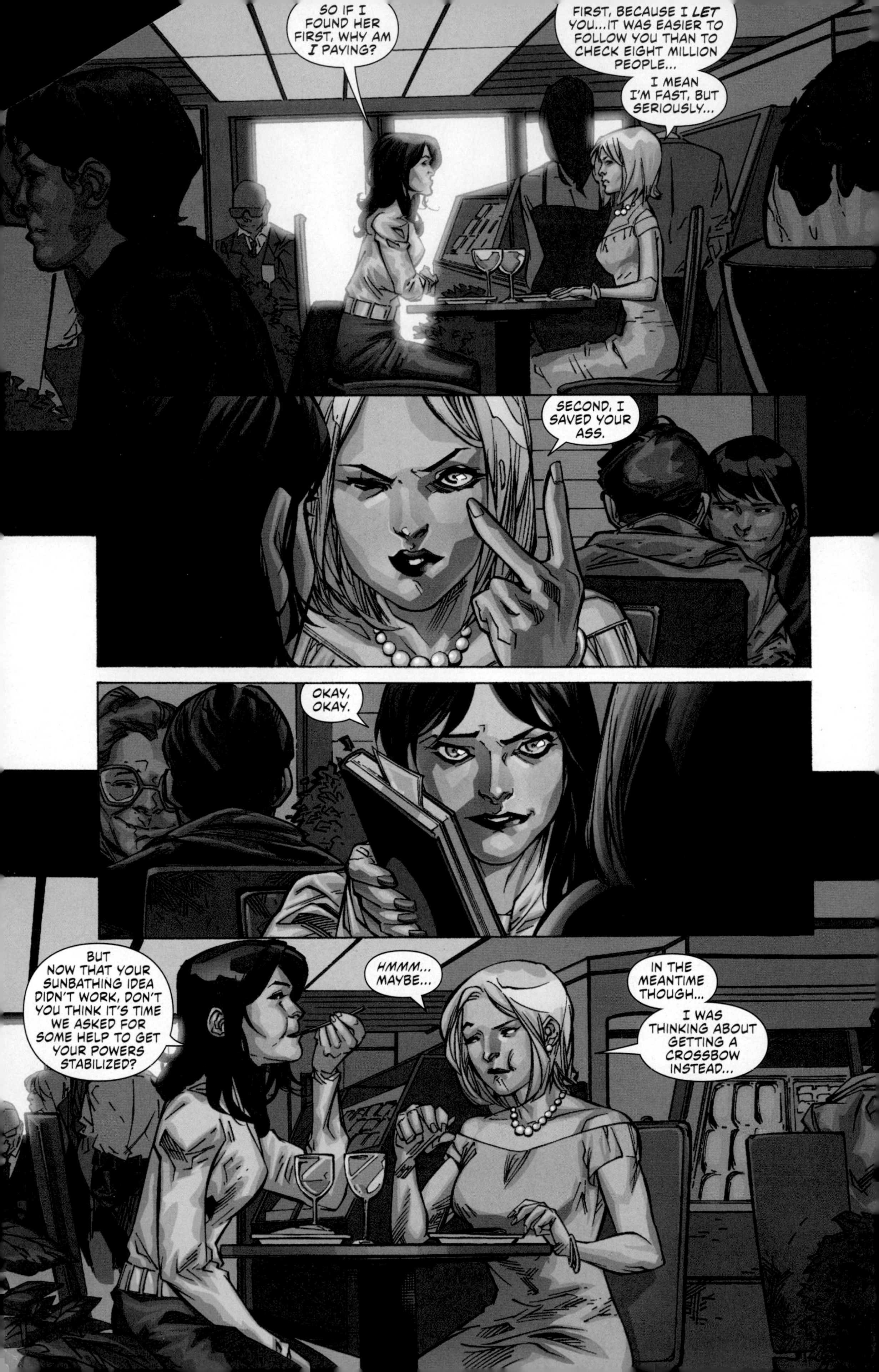

SO IF I FOUND HER FIRST, WHY AM I PAYING?
FIRST, BECAUSE I LET YOU...IT WAS EASIER TO FOLLOW YOU THAN TO CHECK EIGHT MILLION PEOPLE...
I MEAN I'M FAST, BUT SERIOUSLY...
SECOND, I SAVED YOUR ASS.
OKAY, OKAY.
BUT NOW THAT YOUR SUNBATHING IDEA DIDN'T WORK, DON'T YOU THINK IT'S TIME WE ASKED FOR SOME HELP TO GET YOUR POWERS STABILIZED?
HMMM... MAYBE...
IN THE MEANTIME THOUGH...
I WAS THINKING ABOUT GETTING A CROSSBOW INSTEAD...

WORLDS' FINEST

TAT CHARACTER DESIGN BY R.B. SILVA

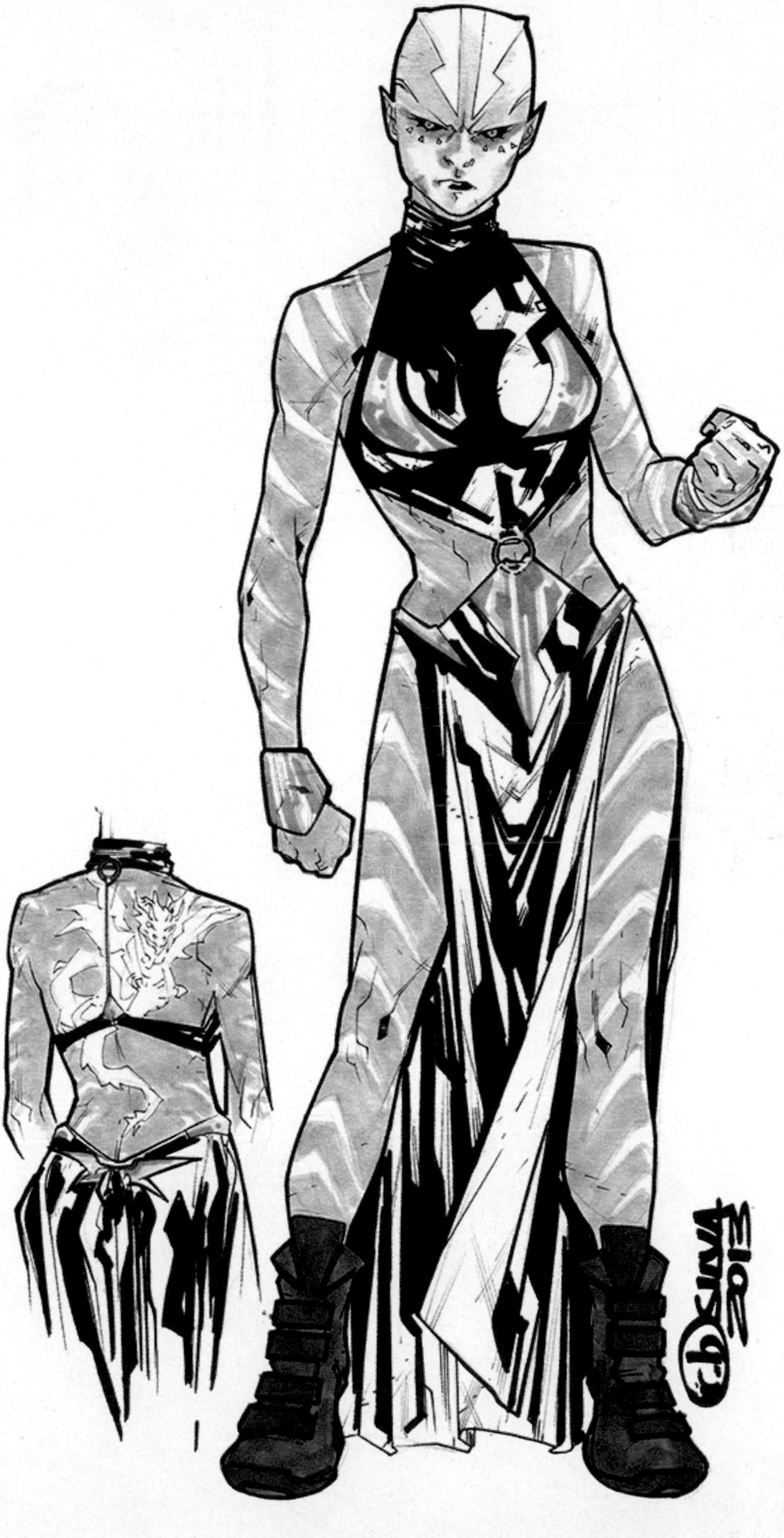

SILVA
2013

WORLDS' FINEST #14

PENCILS BY ROBSON ROCHA

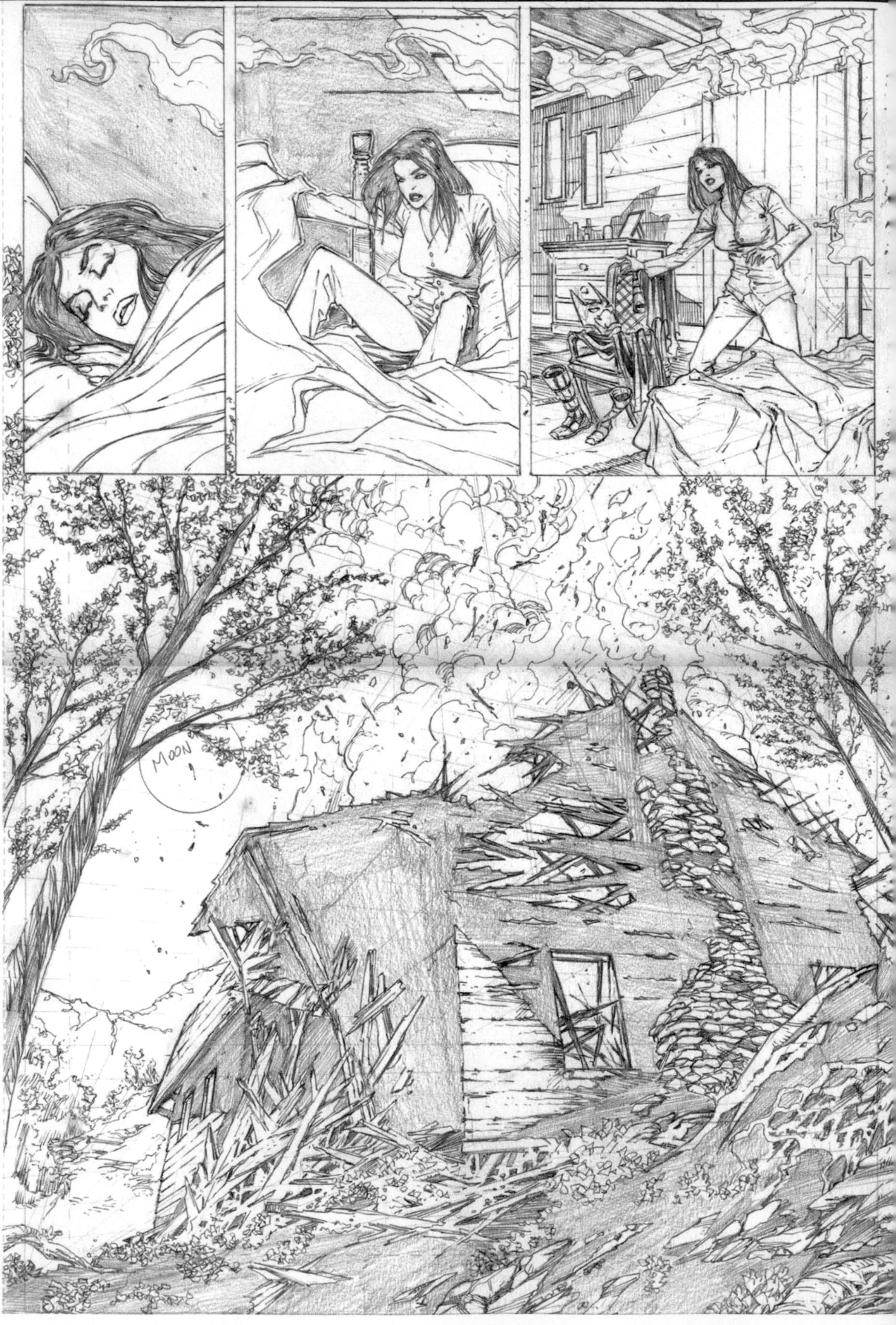
MOON

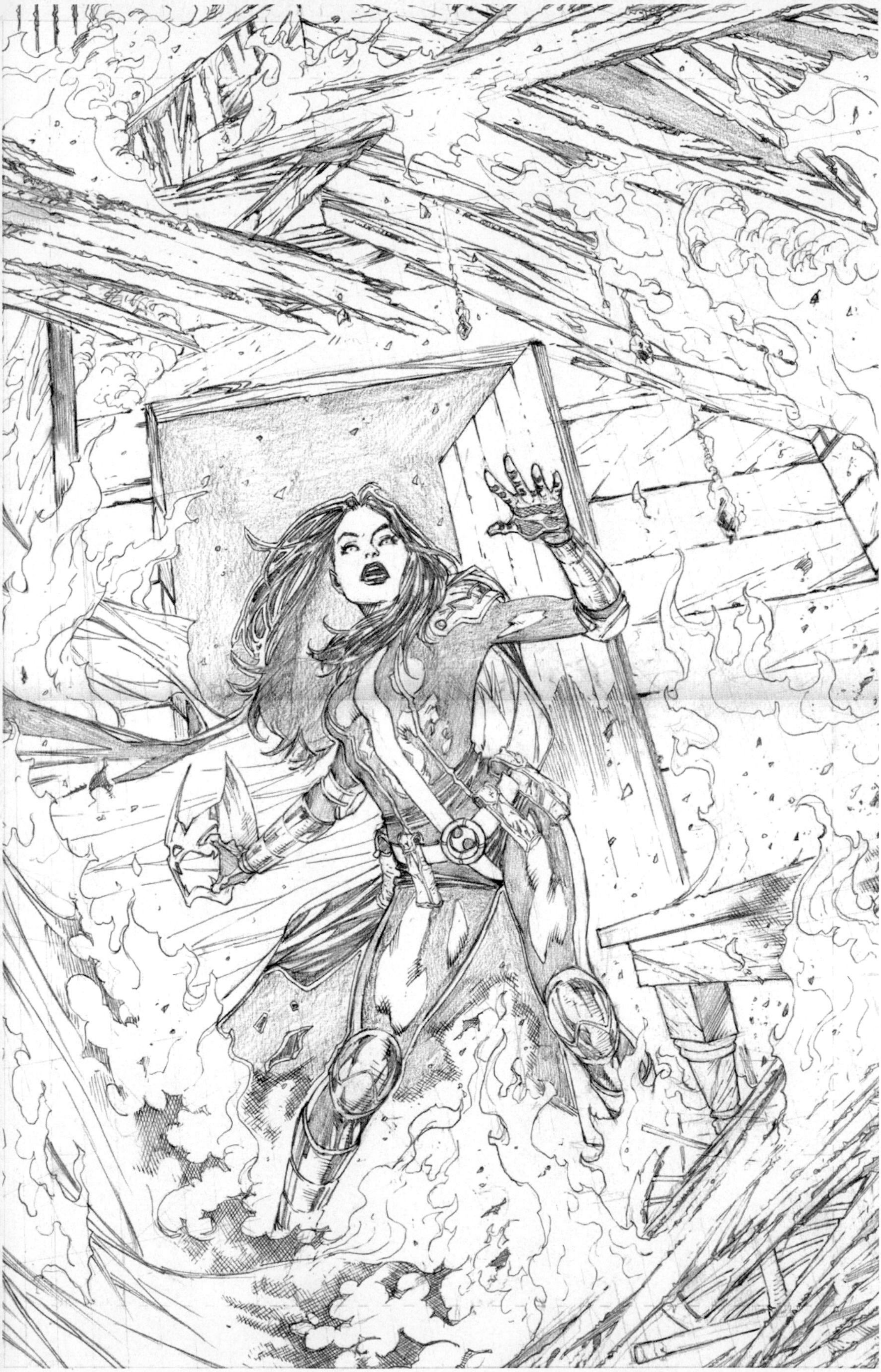

WORLDS' FINEST #15
LAYOUTS AND PENCILS BY EMANUELA LUPACCHINO

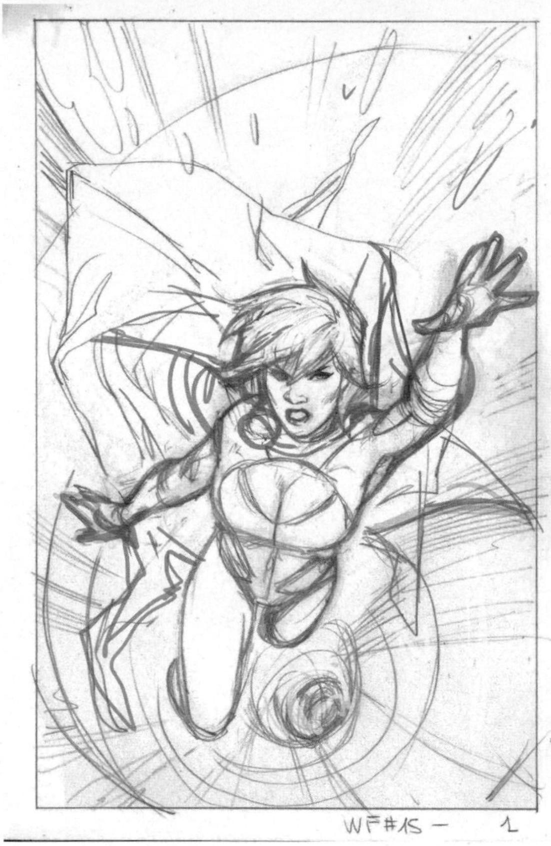
WF#15 — 1

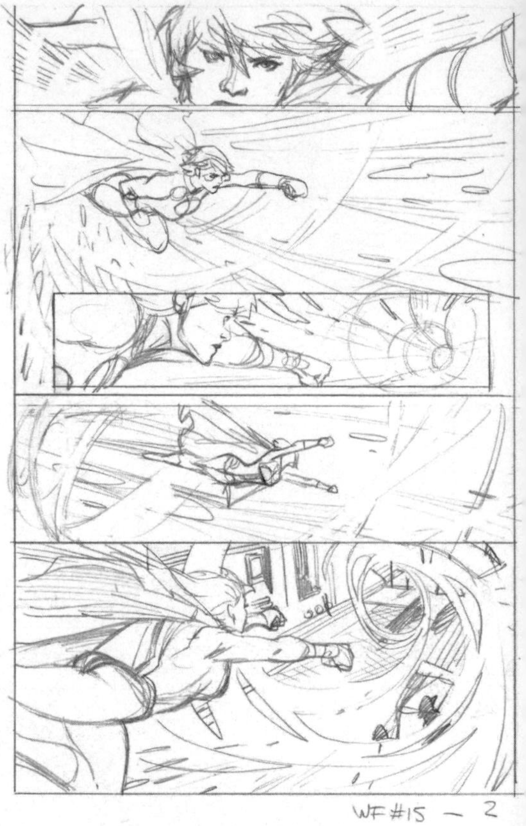
WF#15 — 2

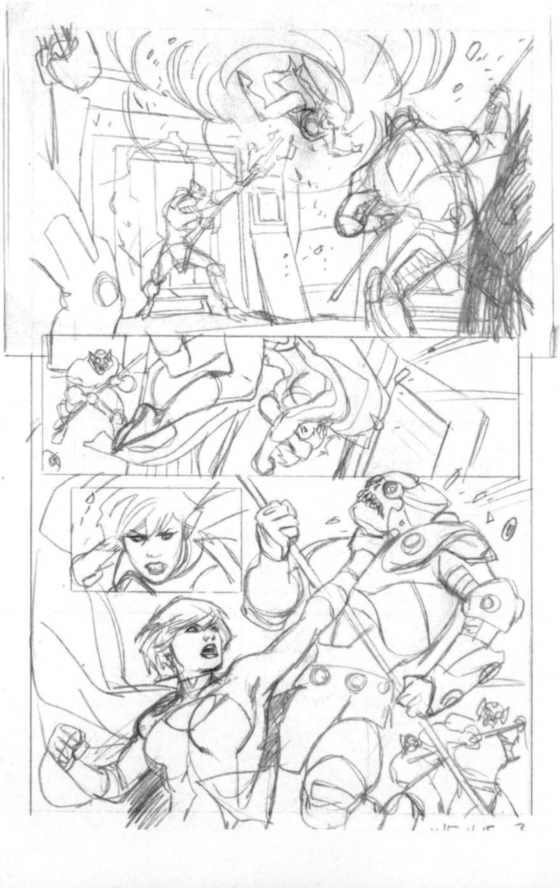

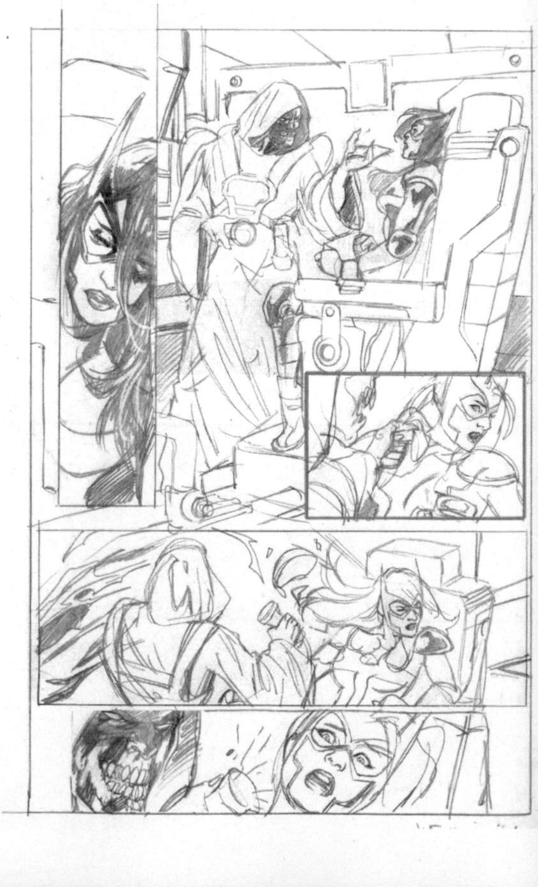

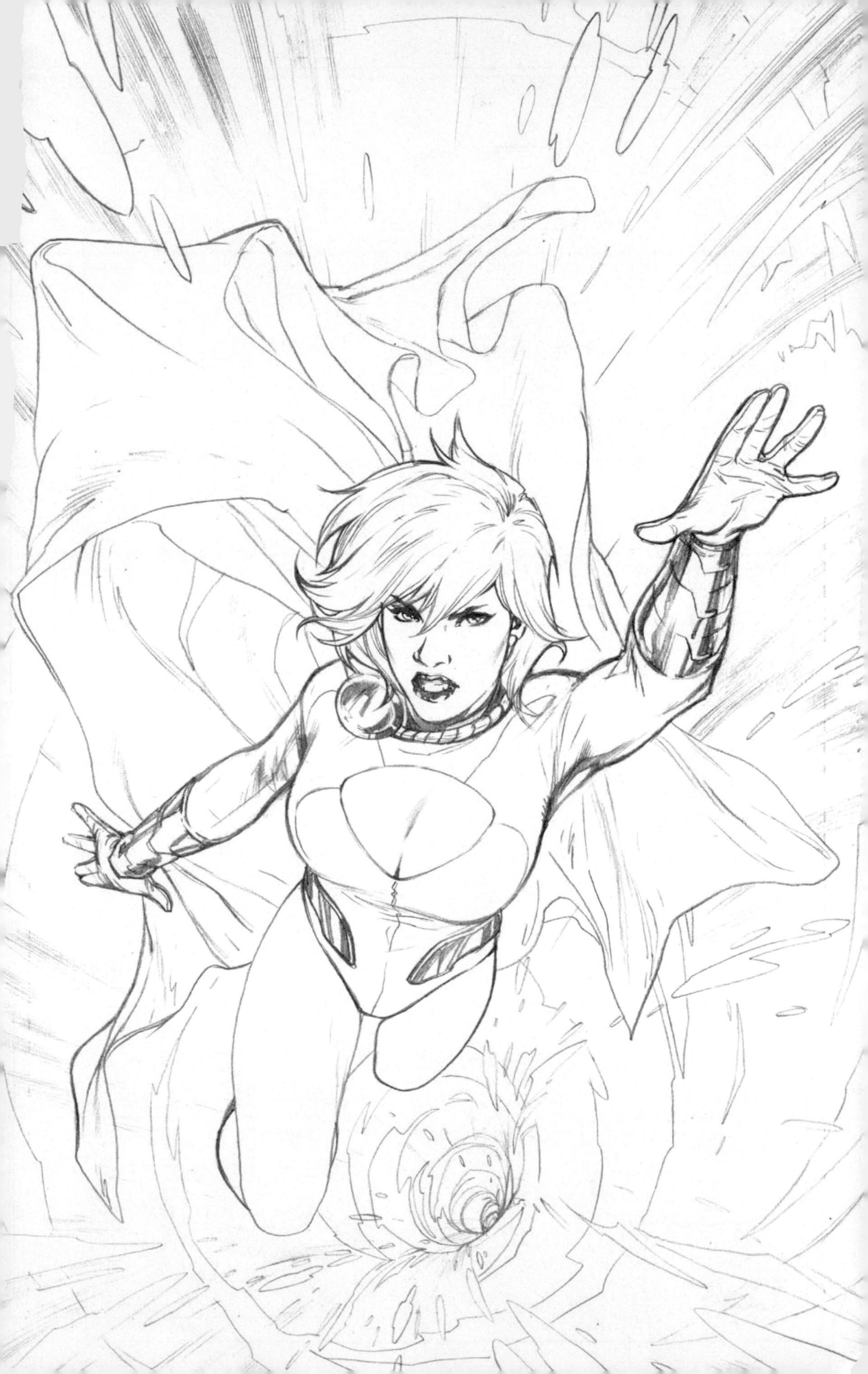

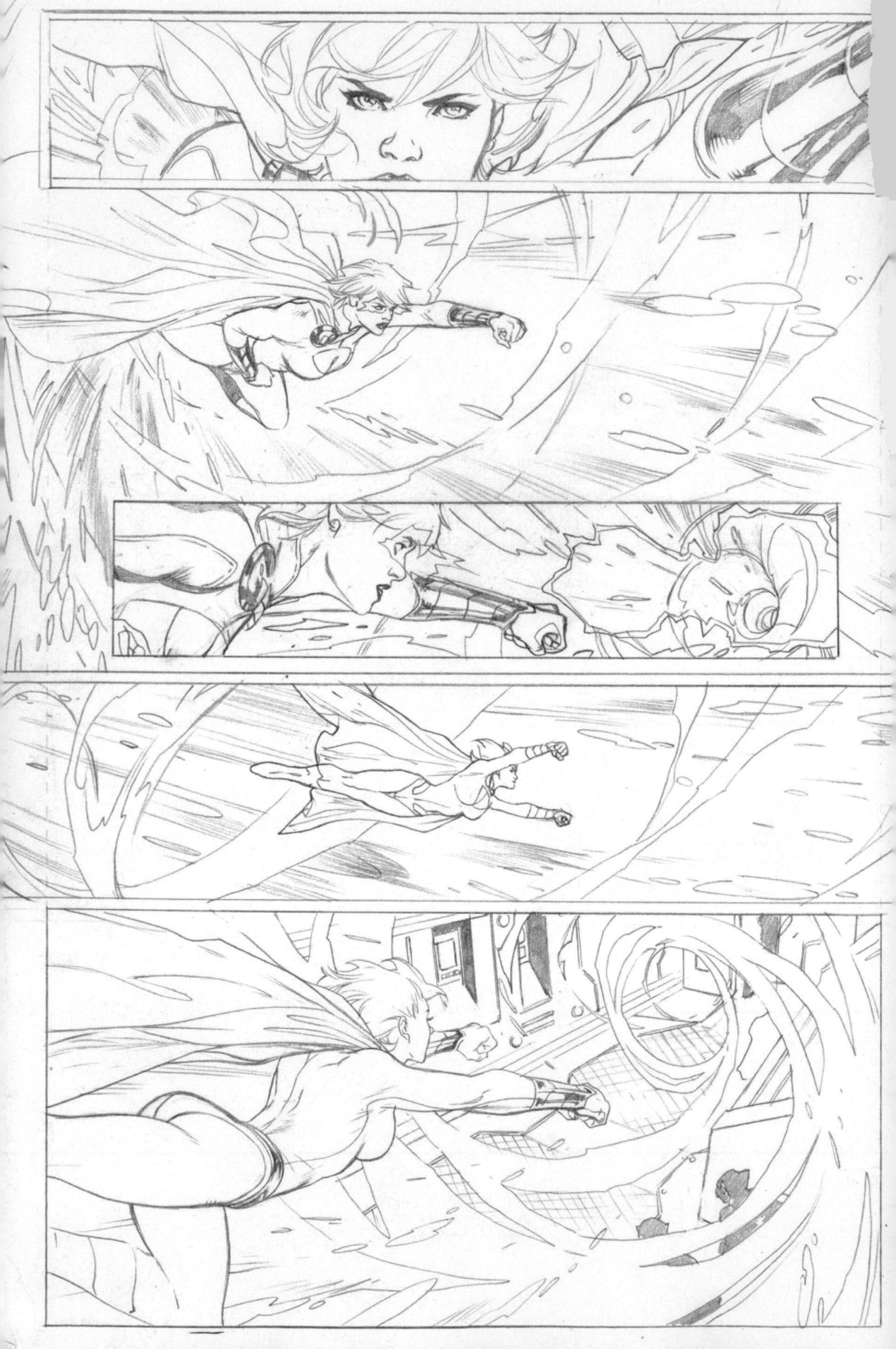

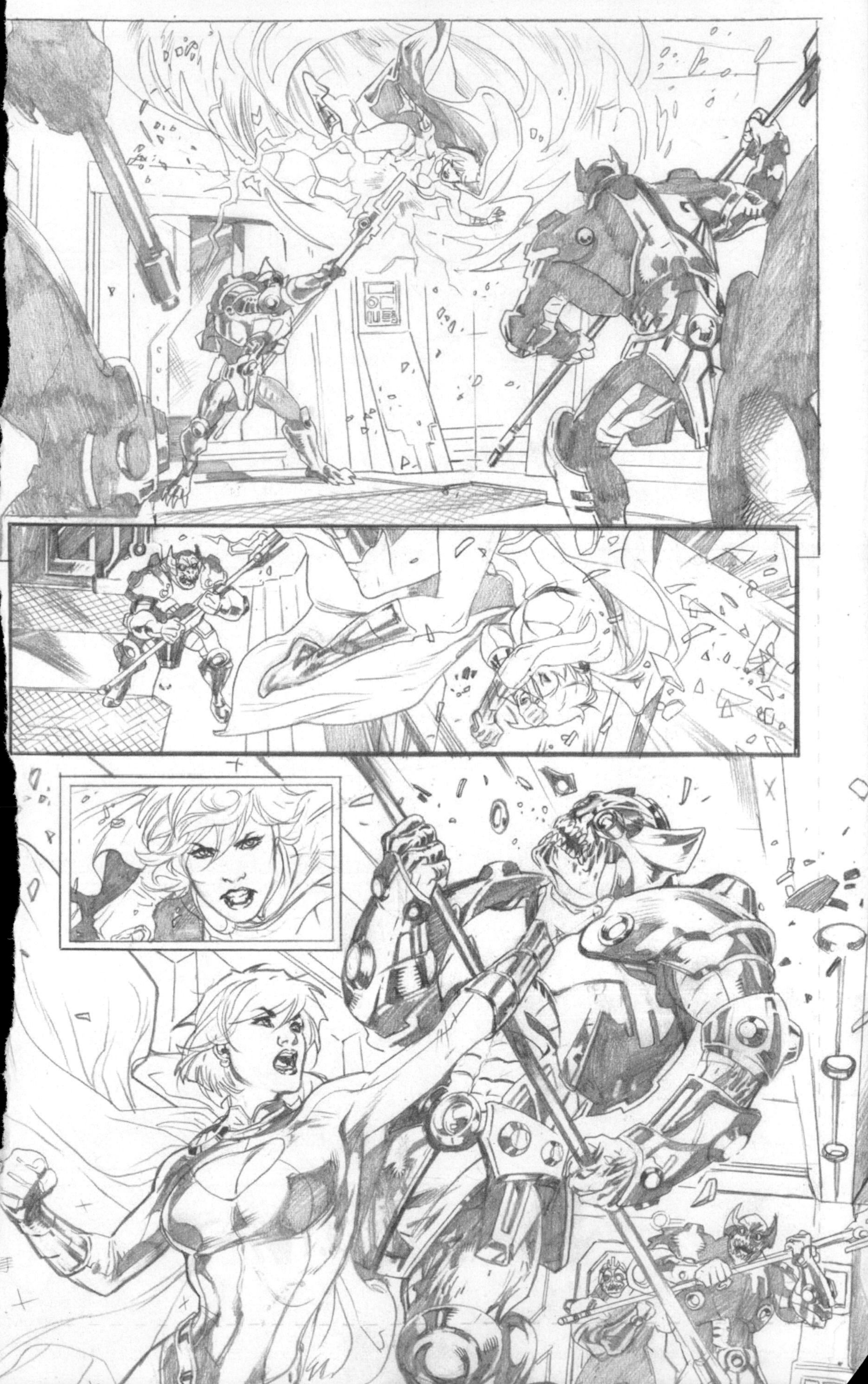

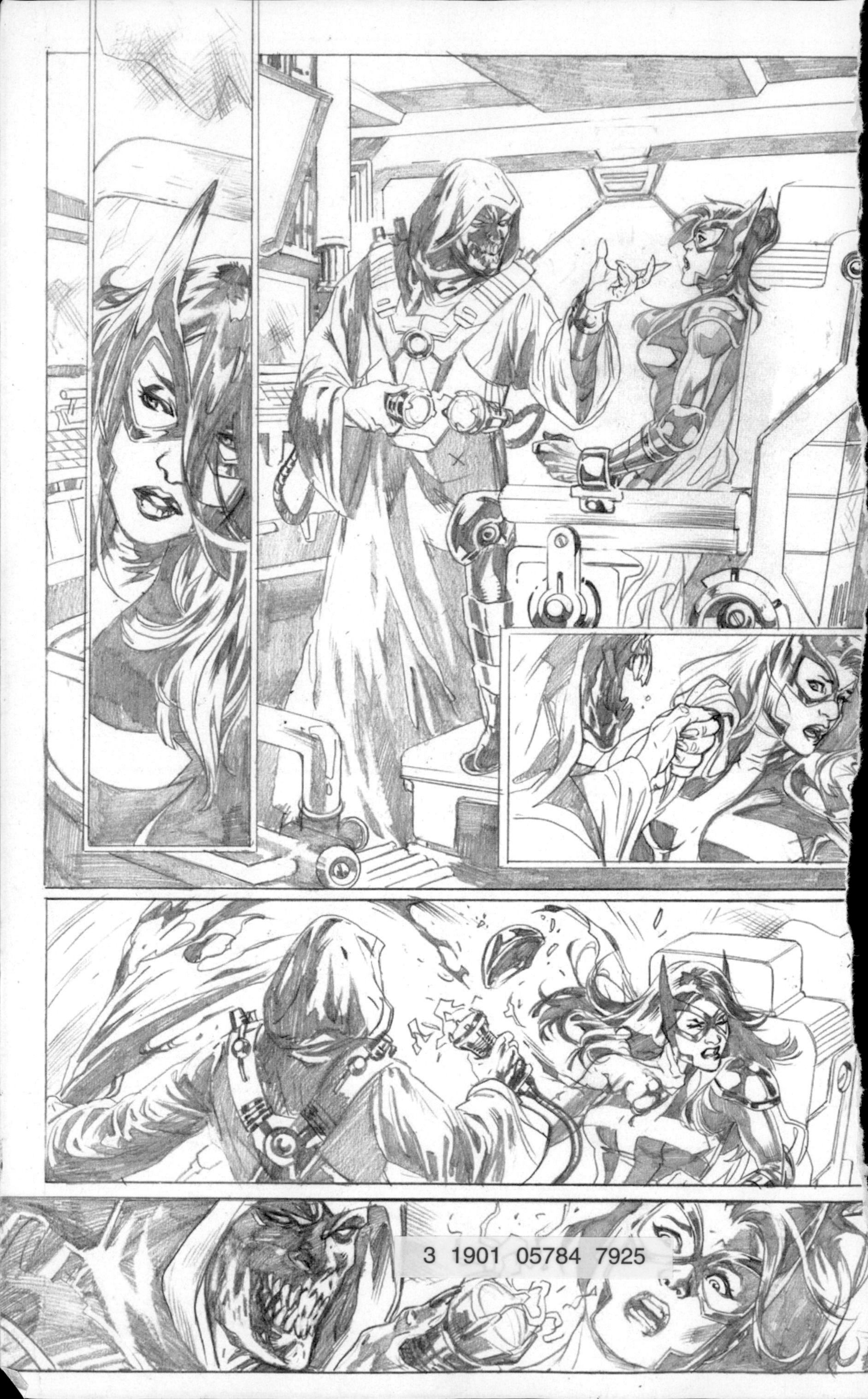